GUIDE TO

Photographic Collections

AT THE SMITHSONIAN INSTITUTION

GUIDE TO

Photographic Collections

AT THE SMITHSONIAN INSTITUTION

National Museum of Natural History
National Zoological Park
Smithsonian Astrophysical Observatory
Smithsonian Tropical Research Institute

VOLUME II

Diane Vogt O'Connor

Smithsonian Institution Press

Washington and London

Library of Congress Cataloging-in-Publication Data

Smithsonian Institution.
Guide to photographic collections at the Smithsonian Institution.

Includes indexes.
Contents: v. 1. National Museum of American History— v. 2. National Museum of Natural History; National Zoological Park; Smithsonian Astrophysical Observatory; Smithsonian Tropical Research Institute.
1. National Museum of American History (U.S.) Photograph collections. I. O'Connor, Diane Vogt. II. Title.
Q11.S79 1989 026'.779'074753 89-600116
ISBN 0-87474-927-1 (v. 1 : alk. paper)
ISBN 0-56098-033-8 (v. 2 : alk. paper)

British Library Cataloguing-in-Publication Data is available

Manufactured in the United States of America
98 97 96 95 94 93 92 91 5 4 3 2 1

∞The paper used in this publication meets the minimum requirements of the American National Standard for Permanence of Paper for Printed Library Materials Z39.48-1984.

Contents

Foreword

This second volume of a planned five-volume series of guides to Smithsonian photographs documents the collections of the Institution's four science bureaus, the National Museum of Natural History, the National Zoological Park, the Smithsonian Astrophysical Observatory, and the Smithsonian Tropical Research Institute. [See also *Guide to Photographic Collections at the Smithsonian Institution, Volume I: National Museum of American History.* Washington and London: Smithsonian Institution Press, 1989, 351pp.] The volume describes nearly two million images documenting the biological sciences, earth sciences, and astronomical and planetary sciences which serve the research, publication, exhibition, and education programs of the four Smithsonian museum and research bureaus.

Most of the images record natural phenomena for scientific research or document the actual research itself. Ranging from scanning electron micrographs of pollen granules to digital images of distant galaxies initially captured by radio telescopes, the photographs document animals, celestial bodies, culture groups, ecosystems, exploring expeditions, fieldwork sites, gems and minerals, geological formations, insects, plants, scientific research projects, scientists, and special topics such as endangered species and tropical deforestation.

The photographs were created to serve as a visual record supporting highly specialized research. They are less useful singly than as parts of a chain of documented evidence. A continuing relationship between the collections and ongoing research makes individual photographs less readily accessible for public reference than the more familiar collections in libraries and archives. When selected to illustrate publications, exhibits, or broadcast programs, a full grasp of the research context of images is essential to convey their significance.

Photographic collections of the National Anthropological Archives, although a part of the National Museum of Natural History, will appear in a later volume.

Acknowledgments

Many people helped with the production of this volume. First, the administrators, curators, and collections managers of the National Museum of Natural History, the National Zoological Park, the Smithsonian Astrophysical Observatory, and the Smithsonian Tropical Research Institute offered assistance to the project staff. Their cooperative spirit and informed assistance made this volume possible.

Particular thanks are due to Jessie Cohen at the National Zoological Park; James Cornell at the Smithsonian Astrophysical Observatory; and Elena Lombardo, Martin Moynihan, and Arcadio Rodaniche at the Smithsonian Tropical Research Institute in Panama. Tackling their complex institutions would have been much tougher without their generous assistance.

Second, the editors wish to thank Amy Pastan and Duke Johns of the Smithsonian Institution Press for production consultation, as well as Mary Stoughton and the staff of Editorial Experts for indexing, coding, and proofreading work. Their combined efforts have greatly facilitated the usefulness of this volume. As in previous years, the reference and interlibrary loan staff of the Smithsonian Institution libraries have been of great assistance.

At the Smithsonian Archives William Moss has acted as a sponsor for the project. Volunteers Nancy Kellman Maddox, Anne Rollins, and Margaret Thomson used their skills to research and help copy edit this volume. Volunteers Nathalie Morin and Sami Malouf offered computer consulting expertise. The project staff of the Photographic Survey Project including Deborah Kapper, Margaret Stevens, Donna DiMichele, Susi Barañano, Joan Redding, Pamela Whetstone, Laura Kreiss, Michael Frost, and B.H. Custer surveyed, wrote, and edited this volume. Their continuing efforts to discover, describe, and quantify the unknown deserve applause.

Finally, a special thanks to Joseph and Dorothy Vogt for offering an inspired introduction to science and to Hugh O'Connor for serving as a one-man support system.

Science Photography: The Captive Image and the Analytical Eye

Equipped with his five senses, man explores the universe around him and calls the adventure science.

—Edwin Powell Hubble, *The Nature of Science and Other Lectures.*

The sensitive photographic film is the true retina of the scientist . . . It faithfully preserves the images which depict themselves upon it and reproduces and multiplies them indefinitely on request; in the radiative spectrum it covers a range more than double that which the eye can perceive . . . and whereas our retina erases all impressions more than a tenth of a second old, the photographic retina preserves them and accumulates them over a practically limitless time.

—J.J.C. Janssen, Speech to the Société Française de la Photographie, 1880.

Heir to the technology of science and the aspirations of art, 19th century photography led to revolutionary changes in both disciplines. Following the introduction of photography, even the least gifted draftsman could create rapid and accurate photographic landscapes and portraits using natural light as a pencil. Scientists chose the camera for its ability to use optics and chemistry to stop time, freeze action, and reveal the hidden portions of the universe for analysis. Just as the microscope and telescope opened new worlds to science, so too did the camera.

Photography records the unseen from atomic particles to distant galaxies; reveals structures invisible under normal light from the bones under our skin to the corona of the sun; documents the typical and the unique from authoritative type specimens of a species to genetic mutations; and illustrates processes either too slow or too fast for human perception. Photography turns the distant, the tiny, the immense, the typical, the sequential, and the invisible into evidence ready for study and interpretation.

Cameras, as aids to vision, existed long before photography. Renaissance Italian artists used a pinhole viewing device, the camera lucida, to project views of natural scenes for tracing, which later became a popular Victorian activity. Long before the actual development of photography, chemists such as Sir Humphrey Davy investigated how to capture these camera images from nature on light-sensitive materials. Nineteenth century scientists and inventors, Joseph Nicéphore Niépce, William Henry Fox Talbot, and Louis Jacques Mandé Daguerre not only developed chemical processes for capturing the images, but also methods for fixing the images, to prevent their rapid destruction when exposed to light.

The photographers who came after them were often gifted chemists and camera designers who developed new processes in the search for faster and easier ways to develop captive images. The very language of photography refers back to the 19th century when scientists hired hunters and trappers to gather specimens. Sir John Herschel coined the word "snapshoot" in 1860, based upon hunting terminology. "Captive images," "shooting a picture," and "photo safaris" are but a few of the terms which describe photography as a way to entrap and possess a facsimile of reality.

Many of the earliest uses of photography were scientific. J.B. Reade of England made photographs on paper using a solar microscope as early as 1839, while A. Donne of France made photographs of bones and teeth in 1840. J.W. Draper of the United States took daguerreotypes of the moon and of invisible portions of the solar spectrum in 1840. As early as the 1840s scientific journals published plates from photographs and by the 1880s publishers produced illustrations directly from negatives, using newly discovered photomechanical processes. These improvements in visual communications enabled scientists worldwide to see each other's results, as well as read about them.

Photography's remarkable ability to convey detailed visual information led to its widespread use in the sciences, especially in astronomy, biology, geology, medicine, and physics: E.J. Mach's early photographic studies of bullets in flight revolutionized ballistics in the 1880s; in 1887 the Astrographic Congress of Paris called for the first systematic photographic map of the sky, completed in 1891; and in 1894 Wilhelm Roentgen discovered x-ray photographs, which later revolutionized medicine and astronomy. The collections of the Harvard College Observatory and the Smithsonian Astrophysical Observatory, described in this volume, contain many early astronomical images. Photography changed the ways scientists conduct research and record their results.

As photographic technology improved scientists used the new recording medium in innovative ways. Infrared photography came of age in the 1930s, later proving invaluable in aerial photography of the earth and in thermography for cancer and stroke diagnoses. While medical photographs were originally taken as early as the 1840s, it wasn't until 1942 that photographs documented the existence of viruses. In the 1950s x-rays first revealed the spiral helix shape of DNA and underwater flash cameras revealed deep-sea fish on the floor of the Mediterranean Sea. By the 1960s the first photographic portraits of the atom were being produced, while *Mariner 9* was sending back detailed images of the surface of Mars. Scientists facing the second millenium have an unprecedented array of new photographic technologies at their command including digital images; high-speed and time-lapse photography; infrared, ultraviolet, and x-ray photography; and sophisticated cameras for interstellar and deep underwater use.

Photography extended the perceptive powers of science by capturing previously unavailable visual data from which scientists could draw hypotheses. What the human mind could conceive of, or the telescopically or microscopically enhanced human eye could see, could now be confirmed and studied via photography. In a sense these photographs are the equivalents of field notebooks, functioning as a way of possessing visual experience in a tangible, permanent form.

Yet despite their value as evidence, photographs are not surrogates for reality. Photographs differ from the external world, as they are selective two-dimensional images of a particular detail at one specific moment composed by a guiding human intelligence. In attempting to record reality, the photographer creates a new object, the photograph, which has a reality of its own apart from its intended subject, and which can stand on its own as an object of study.

While often beautiful or visually startling, the scientific value of these images is due to their existence within a large well-documented body of similar images which provide an overview of the subject over time and under variant conditions. No matter how visually compelling a single photograph is, it is apt to be misinterpreted when removed from its larger descriptive context. Visual databases are often painstakingly documented (as to time, place, and conditions of creation; subject matter; and photographic process and format) in captions, finding aids, and guides. Contextual information offers insight into the purpose, function, and history of the photographs—a glimpse into the tool chest of science.

The photographs described in this volume represent a legacy of visual information captured by hundreds of Smithsonian scientists over almost one-and-a-half centuries of expeditions, fieldwork, and laboratory research. The photographic collections are a heritage of imagery, invaluable as a record of change in our world and the larger universe and as a precise record of the unchanged components of the physical world, documenting the processes of life at the molecular level and the structures of the universe.

Diane Vogt O'Connor, Audiovisual Archivist

Introduction

The *Guide to Photographic Collections at the Smithsonian Institution: National Museum of Natural History, National Zoological Park, Smithsonian Astrophysical Observatory, and Smithsonian Tropical Research Institute* is the second volume of a five-volume series documenting the Smithsonian Institution's vast holdings of photographs. This volume provides a comprehensive overview of 153 collections containing almost two million photographs housed at four major science museums and research bureaus of the Smithsonian. The existence of many of the collections was previously unknown outside their own divisions.

Photographic collections serve many purposes. They document day-to-day management of collections, expeditionary discoveries, exhibitions, fieldwork, in-house analysis and research, and staff in the fields of anthropology, astronomy, biology, and earth sciences—from the arctic to the tropics. The collections illustrate the lives of American scientists and the process of discovery, exploration, analysis, and description worldwide during the 19th and 20th centuries. The photographs represent the work of both professional and amateur photographers in a wide range of photographic processes and formats.

These diverse photographic collections were surveyed at the collection level by the project staff of the Smithsonian Institution Archives. Both organic and assembled collections are represented. Organic collections include photographs from a single photographer or studio, or photographs created to further the work of a particular corporate entity. Assembled or artificial collections are photographs gathered from disparate sources around a central purpose or theme. This volume serves as an introduction, not as an inventory, to photographs within the personal papers of working scientists, scientific laboratories, and educational or public relations offices, as well as non-active personal papers on their way to becoming historical collections.

Researchers use the photographic collections for diverse purposes. Some are interested only in the images' subject content; others in the photographer's relationship to his work; while still others study photographs as physical artifacts. The *Guide* is inclusive in its descriptions, offering indexes which provide access by subject, by collection origins (including photographer), and by process and format in order to serve the broadest audience of researchers.

Scope of the *Guide*

This *Guide* focuses on still photographs, defined here as images captured by the action of radiation (usually light) on a photosensitive surface, often by means of a camera, lens, mirror, or other optical device. Photography thus includes photonegatives, photoprints, phototransparencies, and direct positive processes. Architectural plans, audio recordings, drawings, graphic prints, manuscripts, motion-picture film footage, photomechanical prints, videotapes, and xerographic copies are not described, although they are listed when they are found in collections which also contain photographs.

Preparation of the *Guide*

To describe the photographic collections included in this volume, the project staff visited each science bureau office. With the assistance of the scientific staff, they identified, located, and examined all collections which contain photographs. Using a survey form based on the MARC-VM (Machine-Readable Cataloging Visual Materials) format, the project staff gathered data on access policies, copyright, creators, dates, location, ownership, physical characteristics, subject contents, and other pertinent data for each collection.

Descriptive subject terms are taken directly from collection captions and finding aids, from science bureau style guides and reference sources (see the subject index for a listing), or from the *L.C. Thesaurus for Graphic Materials: Topical Terms for Subject Access* of the Library of Congress Prints and Photographs Division. Photographers' and other creators' names were checked in a variety of name authority files listed in the introduction to the Forms and Processes Index.

During the preparation of this guide, a hierarchical authority file of photographic process and format terminology was created to facilitate consistent image identification and description. This authority file forms the basis for the Forms and Processes Index found at the end of the guide.

From the completed survey forms, a report was drafted for each collection. Following review by the division curators and custodians, these reports were edited for use in this volume.

Organization and Use of the *Guide*

This volume describes the photographic holdings of four science bureaus at the Smithsonian: the National Museum of Natural History (NMNH), the National Zoological Park (NZP), the Smithsonian Astrophysical Observatory (SAO), and the Smithsonian Tropical Research Institute (STRI). Each bureau is introduced by an overview of its collecting interests and history. Following the bureau introduction, each department, division, or office is introduced and described in alphabetical order.

The introduction to each department, division, or support office describes its research objectives, collecting policies, and access and usage policies. The description of access and usage policies usually includes restrictions, and access procedures including the address, telephone number, contact person's name or title, and hours of operation. The introduction also includes the number of collections, total number of images, major subjects documented in the holdings, photographic processes represented, and non-photographic materials included such as manuscripts and objects.

The heart of the *Guide* consists of a detailed description or "entry" for each collection found within the curatorial divisions or support offices. Each collection is identified by a collection title and by an alphanumeric code assigned by the writers of the *Guide*. The code consists of a two-letter abbreviation for the bureau to which the collection belongs: NH stands for the National Museum of Natural History, ZP stands for the National Zoological Park, SA stands for the Smithsonian Astrophysical Observatory, and ST stands for the Smithsonian Tropical Research Institute. The number following the two-letter code indicates the sequence of that collection within the bureau. The table of contents outlines the arrangement of divisions/offices and collections and lists collections by their alphanumeric codes and page numbers.

The *Guide* is extensively indexed, providing precise access to specific photographic collections. There are three separate indexes: a Creators Index, a Forms and Processes Index, and a Subject Index. The indexer used the Library of Congress Prints and Photographs Division's *L.C. Thesaurus for Graphic Materials: Topical Terms for Subject Access* and several scientific reference books as the authority files for the subject terms; the Photo Survey Project's "Draft Photographic Thesaurus" for the form and process terms; and the International Museum of Photography's *Photographers Name Authority File* and other publications for creator names. The alphabetical index terms are keyed to the collection codes. Further information on index search strategies and other authority files used in indexing may be found at the beginning of each index.

Collection-Level Descriptions

The collection descriptions vary in length, reflecting the size, coherence, and complexity of the collections described. More diverse and eclectic collections demand longer descriptions to provide equivalent descriptive detail. Each collection-level description is itself a complex arrangement of information organized as follows:

Collection Code. The unique alphanumeric code assigned to this collection. For more information on this, see "Abbreviations."

Collection Name. The full title by which the collection is known in the museum. The phrase *"A.K.A."* (meaning "also known as") following a collection name indicates an alternate title or name by which staff may refer to the collection.

Dates of Photographs. The dates used are inclusive, describing the period during which the images in the collection were produced. These dates do not describe the period during which the non-photographic materials were produced, nor do they describe the dates of other generations of images which may exist in other repositories, for example, original photonegatives in other museums. Dates of original negatives which were used to create copy images in Smithsonian collections are listed in the subject description.

Collection Origins. This section gives the name, dates, and a capsule biography of the collection creator or assembler. It explains by whom, when, and why the collection was created. If a single photographer, studio, or other corporate creator produced these materials as an organic collection, he, she, or it will be identified as the collection creator. If the collection is assembled or artificial, the collection origins field will list names of specific photographers, studios, or other creators, such as correspondents or authors, whose work is included in the collection. When the field states "Unknown," no information exists on the collection origins, either within the division's records or as clear internal evidence within the collection itself.

Physical Description. The total number of photographs in the collection is given first. This number may change over time as collections continue to grow. Next, all photographic processes and formats are listed. Unusual sizes and support materials are noted, as are albums, scrapbooks, and notebooks. Other mediums found with the photographs, such as archival document types or specimens, are also listed.

Subjects. This field opens with a sentence summarizing the range of subject dates, geographic areas, and major subject emphases in the collection. This summary statement may be followed by more specific descriptions of culture groups; occupations or disciplines; genres such as landscapes and portraits; geographic locales; individuals; and topical information such as activities, animals, events, objects, and themes represented in the collection. Related subject information is listed alphabetically in a single paragraph, for example, "Animals illustrated include cats, dogs, and hogs."

Arrangement. This section identifies the collection's major series, which are the natural and coherent sections within a collection. If the series are few, they will be listed by name, for example, "In three series. 1) Cats. 2) Dogs. 3) Hogs." If the series are many, their number and organizing principle will be identified, for example, "In 25 series by year of creation." Organization within the series may be noted if it aids in locating photographs, for example, "Series 2, photographic portraits, arranged chronologically by subjects' dates of birth." When a collection consists mainly of nonphotographic materials, all series containing photographs will be indicated.

Captions. All information accompanying photographs will be described in this field, including cutlines and album labels. When similar data elements are used in most captions, the information provided will be noted, for example, "With location, date, and culture group name."

Finding Aids. This section includes descriptions of the registers, indexes, and other guides used by the division staff to search the collection. When a finding aid has a title, a full citation is given. When a finding aid uses standard categories of data to describe photographs, those data elements and any cross-referencing will be noted, for example, "A card catalog which lists subject, negative number, and on occasion, the source of the image." When they are consistent, the filing rules for card catalogs are noted, for example, "The cards are filed by 1) last name of subject, 2) negative number, and 3) object name." If several finding aids exist to a collection, they are described in sequence, for example, "1) Card catalog. 2) Index." Where another form of document such as an object inventory sheet may serve as a finding aid, it will be described here.

Some major forms of finding aids and their definitions as used in this *Guide* include the following:

Authority file: A list of approved names and terms to be used in describing a collection.

Card catalog: An item-level index on cards which may include cross-references and broader and narrower terms.

Container list: A box-by-box or drawer-by-drawer list of materials to be found in each container, often further divided into folder-by-folder listings.

Guide entry: A brief summary description of a collection as it would appear in a published guide to a repository's holdings or a database.

Index: An alphabetical list of terms used to identify and locate all items relating to that term. An index is often in card form, with one term used per card.

Inventory: A list by document types (forms of material) or occasionally by subject or creator.

List: An item-level enumeration in sequential order.

Log book: An item-level list of photographs created by a photographer as he or she works, sometimes called a "shot log." It can include an image number; date; technical information, such as light conditions, filters used, camera settings, and film used; a brief summary of the subject in the photographer's own terms; and the purpose of the shot.

Register: An inventory of all collection document types, usually in a book or ledger format.

Restrictions. The last section of the collection-level entry explains any special restrictions that limit access to or use of the collections. The actual effect of the restrictions on the user will be noted in the restrictions field, for example, "For reference only. No copying allowed." Restrictions information may also appear in the "Collection Origins" field if the creator, in the process of creating the images, caused the restrictions, for example, "This copyrighted collection was created for a planned publication." Restrictions may be due to copyright status, donor wishes, on-going research demands, preservation issues, privacy legislation concerns, patent or trademark status of the subject matter, or security concerns, for example, insurance photographs of high value items.

Abbreviations

Each of the four bureaus was assigned an abbreviation, and each photograph collection is assigned a number. For example, the National Zoological Park is ZP; the Zoo's Office of Design and Exhibit Planning Historical Photograph Collection is ZP7. These alphanumeric codes are used throughout the book indexes. A full list of bureau abbreviations is available in the table of contents and under "Organization and Use of the *Guide.*" The text of the *Guide* is divided into sections first by bureau, and then by curatorial department, division, or administrative support office. The curatorial divisions or departments appear first in alphabetical order, followed by the support offices, also in alphabetical order. Abbreviations used throughout the book are as follows:

A&I	Arts and Industries Building.
A.K.A.	Also Known As. This phrase is used to indicate alternate titles of collections or pseudonyms of photographers.
ANON.	Anonymous. The creator of these images is unknown.
BAE	Bureau of American Ethnology.
DOP	Developing-Out-Paper photoprints.
ND	No Date. The date of these images is unknown.
NMAH	National Museum of American History.
NMNH	National Museum of Natural History.
NZP	National Zoological Park.
OPPS	Office of Printing and Photographic Services, the central Smithsonian photographic duplication laboratory.
POP	Printing-Out-Paper photoprints.
SAO	Smithsonian Astrophysical Observatory.
SEM	Scanning Electron Microscope images.
SI	Smithsonian Institution.
STRI	Smithsonian Tropical Research Institute.
TEM	Transmitting Electron Microscope images.
USBS	United States Biological Survey.
USNM	United States National Museum.

Public Access

Appointments are required for any collection not on public exhibition. Collections and divisions described in the *Guide* will be added to, weeded, and physically relocated over time. Researchers should call ahead to confirm collection availability and location. Since no department, division, or office has a full-time reference staff, researchers should allow ample time for scheduling appointments, locating collections, and creating copy images.

Recommended times for research appointments are stated in the division introductions, as are appropriate addresses and phone numbers. Written requests for appointments should explain the purpose and scope of the research project and any publication or exhibition plans. Most Smithsonian offices are open to the public from 10 a.m. to 5 p.m., Monday through Friday (except federal holidays).

Handling Photographs

Researchers must respect the requests of staff members to ensure preservation of Smithsonian photographic collections. Gloves may be required while working with these collections, and only pencil should be used for note-taking near photographs. Researchers must not bend or touch photographic emulsions or eat, drink, or smoke while working near photographs. Following completion of research, individual photographs must be returned to their original position in the collection. Future availability of these collections depends upon the care with which they are treated today.

Photoduplication Service

Unless restricted, xerographic or photographic copies of images in Smithsonian collections (including images from the Harvard College Observatory, Fred Whipple Observatory, Multiple Mirror Telescope Observatory, and other related units) are available to researchers once written permission has been obtained from the appropriate administrative unit (department, division, office, or the individual scientist). Most administrative units have a single contact person listed in their introductions. In several cases, however, an additional contact person is listed for a specific collection in the restrictions field. In general, these specific collection contacts have more detailed knowledge of the collection. Restricted materials require additional clearance. If the copyright is held outside the Smithsonian, the researcher is responsible for obtaining the necessary permissions.

Researchers requesting photographs for publications, exhibitions, or other commercial use must complete a permission request form which must be approved by the Institution before copying can take place. These photographs may not be used to show or imply Smithsonian endorsement of any commercial product or enterprise, or to indicate that the Smithsonian concurs with opinions expressed in, or confirms the accuracy of, any text used with these photographs.

Photo order forms, photographic policies and charges explanation sheets, and permission request forms are available from each bureau's photographic laboratory. The Services Branch of the Smithsonian Institution Office of Printing and Photographic Services (OPPS) is the laboratory for the Natural Museum of Natural History (NMNH). The National Zoological Park (NZP), the Smithsonian Astrophysical Observatory (SAO), and the Smithsonian Tropical Research Institute (STRI) each have their own photographic laboratories, whose policies are very similar to those of OPPS. Addresses and contact persons for the Smithsonian bureaus included in this volume are as follows: 1) For NMNH, Nicholas Parrella, OPPS, CB054, 14th and Constitution Ave., NW, Washington, D.C. 20560. Telephone: (202) 357-1933. 2) For NZP, Jessie Cohen, Office of Design and Exhibit Planning, National Zoological Park, Washington, D.C. 20008. Telephone: (202) 637-4863. 3) For SAO, James C. Cornell, Jr., 60 Garden St., Cambridge, Massachusetts 02138. Telephone: (617) 495-7461. 4) For STRI, Carl Hansen, P.O. Box 2072, Balboa, Republic of Panama. Telephone: (011-507) 62-3227.

Photo order forms must be completely filled out with the negative numbers corresponding to the images to be copied. Negative numbers must be obtained from the image's custodial division, since there is no master index to the twelve million images at the Smithsonian. The division introductions provide the name and address of the contact person who can provide further instructions on how to proceed. The photo order form must be submitted with a check or money order. Reproduction costs are determined by each Smithsonian bureau's photographic laboratory. In general, processing a photo order takes at least four weeks from the time the completed order and advance payment arrive at the bureau. Larger orders and orders that require original photographic work or research will take longer. All orders are shipped via U.S. mail. Researchers must follow the specific policies of each department or division regarding captions, publication, credit lines, and exhibitions. This information is listed in division introductions. Some bureaus request the return of photographic materials after use and appreciate copies of any publications resulting from this use.

Other Related Publications

This volume is one of several guides to the relatively unknown visual research resources of the Smithsonian Institution. These guides include one photographic guide, the *Guide to Photographic Collections at the Smithsonian Institution: National Museum of American History* (1989), and two nonphotographic guides, the *Finders' Guide to Prints and Drawings in the Smithsonian Institution* (1981) and the *Finders' Guide to Decorative Arts in the Smithsonian Institution* (1985). All are available from the Smithsonian Institution Press at Department 900, Blue Ridge Summit, Pennsylvania 17294-0900, (717) 794-2148.

Subsequent volumes in the series will cover photographic collections in other Smithsonian museums, research bureaus, public service bureaus, and administrative offices. The third photographic guide volume will be the *Guide to Photographic Collections at the Smithsonian Institution: The Cooper-Hewitt Museum, the Freer Gallery of Art and Arthur M. Sackler Gallery, the Hirshhorn Museum and Sculpture Garden, the National Museum of African Art, the National Museum of American Art, the National Portrait Gallery and the Office of Horticulture.* These 250 collections contain almost three-and-a-half million photographs, primarily in the fine arts. Subsequent voumes will cover the National Air and Space Museum and Smithsonian Institution archives and manuscript collections.

NH

THE NATIONAL MUSEUM OF NATURAL HISTORY

Frank H. Talbot, Director

The National Museum of Natural History (NMNH) is the world's largest research museum, containing over 100 million scientific specimens including animals, cultural artifacts, fossils, plants, and rocks and minerals representing the natural history of our planet. Many accessions are type specimens, used as the basis of naming and describing a taxonomic species or variety of plant or animal. Museum holdings are used by NMNH research associates, staff, U.S. government scientists, students, and visiting scholars, primarily to study systematics and evolutionary biology, as well as in outreach programs.

NMNH's earliest artifact and specimen collections were gathered by Spencer F. Baird, assistant to first Smithsonian Secretary Joseph Henry. Additional collections were received from the U.S. Exploring Expedition (1838–1842) and the U.S. Geological Survey of the Territories (1872–1874). Early NMNH specimen collections originally formed part of the U.S. National Museum (USNM) and were exhibited in the Smithsonian Institution Building from around 1846 to 1881, in the Arts and Industries Building from 1881 to 1909, and since August 1909 in the Natural History Building. On March 24, 1969, the bureau was officially named the National Museum of Natural History. Since 1984 a newly created Museum Support Center has housed a significant portion of NMNH collections.

The museum's 135 doctoral-level scientists are grouped into seven departments: 1) Anthropology, 2) Botany, 3) Entomology, 4) Invertebrate Zoology, 5) Mineral Sciences, 6) Paleobiology, and 7) Vertebrate Zoology. A Laboratory of Molecular Systematics and a Scanning Electron Microscope Laboratory, as well as an Oceanographic Sorting Center and a Marine Station at Link Port, Florida, supplement these departments. In addition, the Anthropology Processing Laboratory, the Human Studies Film Archives, and the National Anthropological Archives provide resources in anthropology. NMNH staff conduct on-going research both in the field and at the museum. Their work results in specialized scientific publications and popular exhibits attended by more than 7 million visitors each year.

NMNH's 833,500 photographs are contained in 110 photographic collections which document the subject matter of the sciences from the natural universe to man's place in it, as well as illustrating the research and outreach methods of NMNH scientists. The photographic collections include documentary images of culture groups worldwide, expeditions, fieldwork, geographical and geological landscapes, natural phenomena, special projects, scientists, specimens, and Smithsonian buildings, events, exhibits, and staff. In addition to the holdings of specimens and photographs, NMNH's resources are supplemented by specialized libraries, online databases, and information systems.

NH

Department of Anthropology

Department of Anthropology
National Museum of Natural History
Smithsonian Institution
Washington, D.C. 20560
Candace Greene, Collection Manager
(202) 357-2483
Hours: By appointment.

Scope of the Collections

There are seven photographic collections with approximately 100,300 images.

Focus of the Collections

The photographs document conservation techniques; the department's archeological, ethnographic, and physical anthropological objects; field research; museum exhibits and models; and portraits of anthropologists and NMNH staff members. Photographs of culture groups and material culture emphasize Arctic Eskimo and Inuit peoples, Canela (also Canala or Canella) Indians of Brazil, and North American Indians.

The department also conducts research in the cultures, development, and origins of man. The department runs several programs, including the American Indian Program and the Center for Arctic Studies. Special departmental research facilities include the Conservation Laboratory, the Human Studies Film Archives, the National Anthropological Archives (NAA), and the Processing Laboratory. There are also divisions of Archeology, Ethnology, and Physical Anthropology. Note: While all other Anthropology Department collections are described here, the NAA will be included in the *Guide* series' final volume, with other manuscript repositories.

In 1965, when the Bureau of American Ethnology (BAE) merged with the Department of Anthropology, the Smithsonian Office of Anthropology (SOA) was created. To serve this new office and to manage and process the archeology and ethnology object collections, the Anthropology Processing Laboratory was also established in 1965. In 1968 SOA was renamed the Department of Anthropology, and the Processing Laboratory was expanded to include the physical anthropology collections, housed after 1986 in the Processing Laboratory Physical Anthropology Annex. The Human Studies Film Archives (HSFA) was established in 1981 in the Department of Anthropology to locate, collect, preserve, and make available ethnographic motion-picture film footage.

Departmental publication projects include the following series: 1) William C. Sturtevant, ed., *Handbook of North American Indians*. Washington, D.C.: Smithsonian Institution Press, 1978– . 2) *Smithsonian Contributions to Anthropology*. Washington, D.C.: Smithsonian Institution Press, 1965– . 3) *Smithsonian Series in Archaeological Inquiry*. Washington, D.C.: Smithsonian Institution Press, 1987– . 4) *Smithsonian Series in Ethnographic Inquiry*. Washington, D.C.: Smithsonian Institution Press, 1985– .

Photographic Processes and Formats Represented

There are color dye coupler photonegatives, photoprints, and slides; cyanotypes; dye diffusion transfer photoprints; platinum photoprints; and silver gelatin photonegatives (some radiographs), photoprints, and slides.

Other Materials Represented

The department also contains artifacts, audiotapes, birth certificates, census records, diaries, field notes, manuscripts, motion-picture film footage, notes, photomechanicals, scripts, specimens, translations, and xerographic copies.

Access and Usage Policies

The photograph collections are open to scholarly researchers by appointment. Interested researchers should write to the department and describe their research topic, the type of material that interests them, and their research aim.

Publication Policies

Researchers must obtain permission from the Smithsonian Institution to reproduce a photograph and may also have to obtain permission from the copyright holder, which is not necessarily the Smithsonian Institution. The preferred credit line is "Courtesy of the Department of Anthropology, National Museum of Natural History, Smithsonian Institution."

NH·1

Anthropology Conservation Laboratory Photograph Collection

Dates of Photographs: 1966–Present

Collection Origins

The Conservation Laboratory staff created the collection to document their work preserving and restoring departmental specimens. The Anthropology Processing Laboratory was established in 1965 to process and manage archeological and ethnological object collections through preventative care, research, and treatment. In 1968 it was expanded to include the physical anthropology collections. The laboratory was organized to serve the newly created Smithsonian Office of Anthropology (SOA), the result of merging the Department of Anthropology and the Bureau of American Ethnology (BAE). In 1968 the SOA was renamed the Department of Anthropology and the Processing Laboratory Physical Anthropology Annex was created. Photographs record the condition of objects before, during, and after conservation treatment, as well as the object before and after samples are removed for testing.

Physical Description

There are 9,680 photographs including color dye coupler photonegatives and slides and silver gelatin radiographs. Some photographs were taken in infrared and ultraviolet light and under x-rays.

Subjects

The photographs document the condition of archeological, ethnographic, and physical anthropology specimens before, during, and after conservation analysis or treatment. Treatments illustrated include cleaning, mending, restoring, and stabilizing. Specimen analysis and sampling are also illustrated. While some photographs document preservation and restoration research, the earliest photographs record only treatment results.

Arranged: In three series by type of material. 1) Slides, then numerically by catalog number into two subseries: a) archeology and b) ethnography. 2) Photonegatives, then chronologically. 3) Radiographs, then numerically by specimen catalog number.

Captioned: Photonegatives with a numerical code that cross-references them to specimen treatment reports. Slides with subseries, catalog number, and whether the slide was taken before or after treatment. Many slides also with subject or temporary conservation numbers.

Finding Aid: 1) A photonegative series list giving the frame number, object catalog number, page number, roll number, and year. The list is also cross-referenced to specimen treatment reports. 2) A list titled "Computer Indexing System for Anthropology Conservation Laboratory Reports" explains the catalog and serial numbers, and the contents, lines, and numerical categories of the series list.

Restrictions: No. Contact Carolyn Rose, Conservation Program Analyst, Department of Anthropology, NMNH, Room 368-A, MRC NHB 112, Smithsonian Institution, Washington, D.C. 20560. (202) 357-2016.

NH·2

Anthropology Processing Laboratory Photograph Collection

Dates of Photographs: 1890s–Present

Collection Origins

The staff of the Anthropology Processing Laboratory assembled the collection to document the department's artifact holdings as well as exhibits in the U.S. National Museum (USNM) and the NMNH. The history of the laboratory is described in the *Collection Origins* field of *NH·1*.

OPPS created and houses most of the original images. Other photographers and studios represented include the American Museum of Natural History, New York City; Peter A. Juley, New York City; and the Royal Ontario Museum, Toronto, Canada.

Physical Description

There are 38,000 photographs including color dye coupler phototransparencies and slides, cyanotypes, platinum photoprints, and silver gelatin photoprints. Most of the photographs are copies or duplicates.

Subjects

Most of the photographs document North American Indian material culture. Culture groups in Africa, Asia, Central America, the Middle East, Oceania, and South America are also shown. Approximately five percent of the artifacts in the Department of Anthropology holdings are photographically reproduced here.

American Indian culture groups photographed include Aleut, Apache, Arapaho, Assiniboin, Blackfoot, Cahuilla, Cherokee, Cheyenne, Choctaw, Cochiti, Cocopa, Comanche, Cree, Creek, Crow, Delaware, Eskimo, Haida, Hopi, Hupa, Iroquois, Isleta, Karok, Kiowa, Kwakiutl, Laguna, Luiseño, Makah, Mandan, Mohave, Navajo, Nez Perce, Ojibwa, Omaha, Paiute, Papago, Pima, Pomo, Ponca, San Ildefonso, Santa Clara, Seminole, Sioux, Taos, Tlingit, Tsimshian, Ute, Yurok, and Zuñi.

Material culture illustrated includes baskets; beadwork; boats; body ornaments (including belts, bracelets, headbands, necklaces, and other jewelry); ceremonial and sacred objects (including fetishes, kachinas, masks, sand paintings, and totem poles); cooking and food preparation utensils (including cooking pouches, metates, mortars, and pestles); feather headdresses; leather work; pottery (including bowls, jars, pots, and potshards); quillwork; shelter (including tipis); textiles (including clothing and rugs); tools (including bone, stone, and wood); transportation (including travois and sleds); and weapons (including atlatls, blowguns, bows, obsidian knives, projectile points, and shields). There are also many original photoprints of NMNH and USNM exhibit cases.

Arranged: In three series by type of material. 1) Photoprints, then in three subseries: a) archeology, b) ethnology, and c) exhibition photoprints. 2) Phototransparencies, then by state or region and OPPS number. 3) Slides, then in two subseries: a) archeology and b) ethnology.

Subseries 1a, ethnological photoprints, is filed first by continent or other major world division and then alphabetically by ethnic group, country, or region, in accordance with the following publication: George Peter Murdock. *The Outline of World Cultures*. 5th edition. New Haven, Connecticut: Human Relations Area Files, 1975. Subseries 1b, archeological photoprints, is filed alphabetically by state or foreign country. Subseries 1c, exhibit photoprints, is arranged by exhibit hall and by whether the exhibits are permanent or temporary. Subseries 3a, ethnological slides, is arranged by country or culture group. Subseries 3b, archeological slides, is arranged by state.

Captioned: Most photoprints with catalog number, culture group, object description, and OPPS number. Photoprint envelopes with subject and sometimes catalog number and OPPS number. Phototransparencies with culture group, object description, and OPPS number. Slides with catalog number, culture group, object description, and OPPS number.

Finding Aid: Five item-level indexes. 1) Specimen card catalog giving OPPS and specimen numbers. 2) OPPS negative number file cross-indexed to catalog numbers, object names, and print storage locations. 3) Subject index of ethnological objects organized by continent or major world area listing catalog numbers, OPPS numbers, and print locations for objects photographed by OPPS. Because object names used are arbitrary, searching by synonyms is necessary. 4) Color phototransparency index. 5) Color slide index. The color transparency and slide indexes are divided into archeological and ethnological segments, then organized by continent or cultural area.

Restrictions: No. Contact Felicia G. Pickering, Museum Technician, Department of Anthropology, NMNH, Room 311, MRC NHB 112, Smithsonian Institution, Washington, D.C. 20560. (202) 357-2483.

NH·3

Anthropology Processing Laboratory Physical Anthropology Annex Collection

Dates of Photographs: 1940s–Present

Collection Origins

The staff of the Anthropology Processing Laboratory assembled the collection to document the department's holdings of skeletal remains and plaster casts. The history of the laboratory is described in the *Collection Origins* field of *NH·1*.

OPPS created most of these copy and duplicate photographs and retains the original photonegatives, phototransparencies, and slides. Other photographers and studios represented include the American Museum of Natural History, the Bureau of American Ethnology (BAE) and De Lancey Gill.

Physical Description

There are 500 copy or duplicate photographs including color dye coupler slides and silver gelatin photonegatives and photoprints. Other materials include photomechanicals.

Subjects

The photographs document the Department of Anthropology's holdings of burial remains, modern human skeletal remains, pathology findings, and plaster casts of burial and skeletal remains. Some photographs also document anthropological equipment, exhibits, facilities, and instruments.

Arranged: In three series by type of material. 1) Slides. 2) Photoprints. 3) Photonegatives.

Captioned: Slides with the museum catalog number and subject. Photonegatives and photoprints with subject.

Finding Aid: A card catalog titled "Index to File Prints," divided into two sections: 1) organized by specimen catalog number from 1 to 350,000, and 2) organized by skeletal parts. Subdivisions include burials, charts, dwarfs, early man, and racial types.

Restrictions: Some materials are restricted because of copyright status. Contact David Hunt, Department of Anthropology, NMNH, Room 342, MRC NHB 112, Smithsonian Institution, Washington, D.C. 20560. (202) 786-2501.

NH·4

Arctic Archeology Division Inua File *A.K.A.* Edward W. Nelson Collection

Dates of Photographs: 1982–1984

Collection Origins

Curator of Arctic Archeology William W. Fitzhugh (1943–) created the collection for the 1982 exhibit "Inua: Spirit World of the Bering Sea Eskimo" and for related lectures and publications. Fitzhugh joined the NMNH staff in 1968 and earned a Ph.D. from Harvard in 1970. He specializes in the prehistory of eastern Canada and the northeastern United States, as well as in Arctic material culture and circumpolar archeology and ethnology. Fitzhugh also worked on a related 1989 exhibit, "Crossroads of Continents: Cultures of Siberia and Alaska."

Most of the Bering Sea Eskimo artifacts used in the "Inua" exhibit were donated to NMNH by Edward W. Nelson (1855–1934), who went to Alaska as a weather observer in 1877 and stayed until 1881. Nelson observed Eskimos and Indians and collected their material culture. Note: This collection was not available for viewing. The information was provided by the collection curator.

Physical Description

There are 1,000 color dye coupler slides.

Subjects

The photographs document Bering Sea Eskimo material culture, primarily objects from the Edward W. Nelson Collection.

Arranged: No.

Captioned: No.

Finding Aid: No.

Restrictions: Access only by special permission of the curator. Contact William W. Fitzhugh, Curator, Department of Anthropology, NMNH, Room 307, MRC NHB 112, Smithsonian Institution, Washington, D.C. 20560. (202) 357-2682.

NH·5

Arctic Archeology Division Labrador Field Photographs Collection *A.K.A.* William W. Fitzhugh Collection

Dates of Photographs: 1968–Present

Collection Origins

William W. Fitzhugh created the collection for exhibitions, publications, and research purposes. For a biography of Fitzhugh see the *Collection Origins* field of *NH·4*. Photographers represented include various researchers who collaborated with Fitzhugh on archeological and environmental research in Labrador, Canada. Note: This collection was not available for surveying. The information was provided by the collection curator.

Physical Description

There are 20,000 photographs including color dye coupler slides and silver gelatin photonegatives.

Subjects

The photographs document archeological and environmental research in Labrador, Canada, as well as its culture, geography, and local inhabitants in still lifes, portraits, and landscapes.

Arranged: Chronologically.

Captioned: With subject.

Finding Aid: No.

Restrictions: Access only by permission of the curator. Contact William W. Fitzhugh, Curator, Department of Anthropology, NMNH, Room 307, MRC NHB 112, Smithsonian Institution, Washington, D.C. 20560. (202) 357-2682.

NH·6

Human Studies Film Archives Supplementary Materials Collection

Dates of Photographs: 1925–1980s

Collection Origins

The Human Studies Film Archives (HSFA) staff assembled the collection to document and supplement their more than three million feet of motion-picture film footage. Established in 1981 as part of the NMNH Department of Anthropology, HSFA locates, collects, preserves, and makes available films that contain ethnographic information. Created by anthropologists and other social scientists, documentary filmmakers, early explorers, missionaries, and travelers, the films include both amateur and professional, black-and-white and color, contemporary and historical, edited and unedited, and silent and sound moving-image footage on both film and videotape. The photographs described here supplement approximately 25 percent of the moving-image collections. Photographers represented include Cynthia Cort, Diane Gardsbane, Allison and Marek Jablonko, and Paul Sully.

Physical Description

There are 3,100 photographs including color dye coupler photonegatives, photoprints, and slides and silver gelatin photonegatives and photoprints. Other materials include manuscripts, motion-picture film footage, notes, scripts, translations, videotapes, and xerographic copies. HSFA contains more than three million feet of motion-picture film footage and videotape.

Subjects

Most of the photographs are stills from motion-picture film footage, primarily informal portraits, cityscapes, and landscapes worldwide. Areas documented include Afghanistan, Africa, Brazil, the Cook Islands, India, Mexico, Micronesia, Nepal, Papua New Guinea, the New Hebrides, and western Tibet.

African scenes shown include an Austrian motorcycle expedition traveling from Capetown to Cairo;

Cairo's pyramids; a Malawian man in Swaziland; and Tangoma initiation ceremonies in Swaziland. Scenes of India represented include an informal portrait of a weaver in the village of Patan in Gujarat. Photographs of Papua New Guinea show the Kasapu people in the Laigaipu Valley and the Maring tribe of the Highlands.

Arranged: By project, keyed to motion-picture film footage, then by type of material.

Captioned: Some with date, photographer, project name, and subject.

Finding Aid: 1) "Human Studies Film Archives—Guide to the Collection," includes a history of the Archives, a list of the moving-image collections, and directions for using the collection list. It is arranged by geographical region, then alphabetically by each collection's subject or title. 2) An item-level list to the Swaziland Project, by Paul Sully and Diane Gardsbane, keyed to the photographs by an assigned number.

Restrictions: No. Contact Wendy Shay, Director, Human Studies Film Archives, Department of Anthropology, NMNH, Room E-307, Smithsonian Institution, Washington, D.C. 20560. (202) 357-3349.

NH·7

South American Ethnology Division Canela Indians Photograph Collection *A.K.A.* William H. Crocker Photograph Collection

Dates of Photographs: 1957–Present

Collection Origins

NMNH Curator William H. Crocker (1924–) created the collection to document his research. Crocker received a Ph.D. in anthropology from the University of Wisconsin in 1962 and joined NMNH the same year. Since 1957 Crocker has worked among the Canela (also Canala or Canella) Indians, a hunting, gathering, and horticultural society located in the dry savannah of central Brazil. The Canela are divided into two groups, Ramkokamekra and Apanyekera, both of which belong to the Ge language family.

Photographers represented include Raymond Roberts-Brown. Several of the photographs appeared in the following publication: National Museum of Natural History. *The Magnificent Foragers.* Washington, D.C.: NMNH, Smithsonian Institution, 1978.

Physical Description

There are 28,000 photographs including color dye coupler photonegatives, photoprints, and slides; dye diffusion transfer photoprints; and silver gelatin photonegatives and photoprints. About 18,000 photographs are duplicates and about 10,000 are originals. Other materials include audiotapes, birth certificates, census records, diaries, field notes, and motion-picture film footage.

Subjects

The photographs record daily life among the Canela (also Canala or Canella) Indians of Brazil from 1957 to the present including body ornamentation, ceremonies, dancing, eating, festivals, food preparation, games, and other village activities. There are group and individual portraits as well as some landscape scenes of surrounding areas in Brazil.

Arranged: By type of material, then chronologically.

Captioned: A few with subject. Most slides with date, field trip number, and/or negative number. Note: Each field trip has its own coded numbering sequence. Boxes and albums are dated.

Finding Aid: A computer-generated chart listing broad subject categories (e.g., body decoration, cooking, festivals, games) is an index to some of the slides. The entire collection will be entered into this system in the future.

Restrictions: No. Contact William H. Crocker, Curator, Department of Anthropology, NMNH, Room 333, MRC NHB 112, Smithsonian Institution, Washington, D.C. 20560. (202) 357-4731.

NH

Department of Botany

Department of Botany
National Museum of Natural History
Smithsonian Institution
Washington, D.C. 20560
(202) 357-2534
Hours: Monday–Friday, 10 a.m.–4 p.m.

Scope of the Collections

There are 18 photographic collections with approximately 116,400 images.

Focus of the Collections

The Department of Botany's five divisions (Cryptogams, Ferns, Grasses, Palynology, and Phanerogams) conduct research on the destruction of the tropical rain forest, endangered flora, the environment, and on the use of plants for food and drugs. The photographic collections document structural and taxonomical information on bamboo, New and Old World ferns, flowering neotropical and tropical plants, grasses, lichen, marine algae, and pollen; plant habitat locations; plant species; and plant type specimens—individual specimens selected by taxonomists as the basis for describing or naming a species. Images of arboretums, botanical gardens, botanists, fauna, field study sites, international herbaria including the U.S. National Herbarium, and parks, as well as portraits of staff members also appear in the collections.

Photographic Processes and Formats Represented

There are color dye coupler photoprints and slides, silver gelatin dry plate lantern slides, and silver gelatin photonegatives on nitrate and safety film and photoprints. Some of the photoprints are scanning electron microscope (SEM) images.

Other Materials Represented

The department also contains charts, correspondence, drawings, maps, newsletters, notebooks, notes, photostats, reprints, research observations and reports, seed samples, specimens, and xerographic copies.

Access and Usage Policies

The collections are open to scholarly researchers by appointment. Interested researchers should write to the department and describe their research topic, the type of material that interests them, and their research aim.

Publication Policies

Researchers must obtain permission from the Smithsonian Institution to reproduce a photograph and may also have to obtain permission from the copyright holder, which is not necessarily the Smithsonian Institution. The preferred credit line is "Courtesy of the Department of Botany, National Museum of Natural History, Smithsonian Institution."

NH·8

Botany Department Library Botanists' Portrait Collection

Dates of Photographs: 19th Century–Present

Collection Origins

The Department of Botany Library staff assembled the collection as a reference file in the early 1960s. The portraits were sent to the Hunt Institute for Botanical Documentation at Pittsburgh's Carnegie-Mellon University for copying, cataloging, and rehousing. They were then sent to the Smithsonian Institution Archives, which returned them to the Department of Botany. Photographers and studios represented include the Hessler Studio, Washington, D.C.; OPPS; and William Trelease, Paraje Nuevo, Mexico.

Physical Description

There are 265 photographs including color dye coupler photoprints and silver gelatin photoprints. All but six are copy photoprints.

Subjects

The photographs portray primarily North and South American botanists from the 18th through the 20th centuries. Most are formal portraits, although there are some informal portraits at fieldwork and research sites. Several images are photographic reproductions of engravings.

Botanists portrayed include Harley H. Bartlett, John M. Coulter, Charles Darwin, Walter Deane, Henry W. Elliott, George Engelmann, Asa Gray, Benjamin D. Greene, Edward L. Greene, William Griffith, David Griffiths, Albert S. Hitchcock, Sir Joseph D. Hooker, Friedrich H.A. von Humboldt, Ellsworth P. Killip, Frank H. Knowlton, Jean-Baptiste de Lamarck, Carl A. Magnus Lindeman, Carolus Linnaeus, John Macoun, William R. Maxon, Elmer D. Merrill, Charles F. Millspaugh, Charles T. Mohr, Conrad V. Morton, Charles V. Piper, Charles L. Pollard, Constantine S. Rafinesque-Schmaltz, Albert Charles Smith, John D. Smith, Paul C. Standley, John Torrey, George Vasey, Addison E. Verrill, Lester F. Ward, Sereno Watson, and Thomas Wilson. Other subjects illustrated include the Division of Plant Exploration and Introduction garden and Kew Gardens, London, England.

Arranged: Alphabetically by last name.

Captioned: Some with name and date.

Finding Aid: An index titled "Photographs of Botanists" by the Hunt Institute for Botanical Documentation at Carnegie-Mellon, Pittsburgh, 1965. Includes department, negative number, office, and subject names.

Restrictions: No.

NH·9

Cryptogams Division Air Pollution Studies Collection

Dates of Photographs: 1978–1981

Collection Origins

The U.S. Forest Service created the collection while conducting research on lichens as indicators of air pollution in the Flat Tops Wilderness Area of Colorado from 1978 to 1981. Mason E. Hale, Jr. (1928–1990), who received a Ph.D. in botany in 1953 from the University of Wisconsin, was the project's contributing research scientist and lichen specialist. Hale was Curator of Lichens in the NMNH Department of Botany's Division of Cryptogams from 1961 until his death.

Photographers represented include Harriet Lee of Turlock, California, and Frank P. McWhorter of Carmel, California. The collection has been used in research reports, such as the following: Mason E. Hale, Jr. "Lichens as Bioindicators and Monitors of Air Pollution in the Flat Tops Wilderness Area, Colorado." Final report, Forest Service Contract no. OM RFD R2-81-SP35, November 22, 1982.

Physical Description

There are 370 photographs including color dye coupler photoprints and slides and silver gelatin photonegatives and photoprints (some SEM). Other materials include correspondence, drawings, maps of southern California and the White River area of Colorado, and photostats.

Subjects

The photographs document a study of lichens at the Flat Tops Wilderness Area, Colorado, and at Merced Falls, California.

Arranged: No.

Captioned: Slides with plate numbers. Some photoprints with specimen name.

Finding Aid: No.

Restrictions: No.

NH·10

Cryptogams Division Antarctic Research Program Collection

Dates of Photographs: 1980–1985

Collection Origins

Mason E. Hale, Jr., created the collection to record taxonomic research on lichens in McMurdo Sound, Antarctica. For a biography of Hale see the *Collection Origins* field of *NH·9*.

Physical Description

There are 380 photographs including color dye coupler photoprints and slides and silver gelatin photonegatives and photoprints (some SEMs). Other materials include correspondence, newsletters, notes, reprints, and xerographic copies.

Subjects

The photographs record lichen species and exfoliating rocks at McMurdo Sound, Antarctica. There are also some landscapes of fieldwork research sites at Big Sandy Lake and Lake Vera, in Antarctica.

Arranged: No.

Captioned: Some with taxonomic name or date, location, and specimen number.

Finding Aid: No.

Restrictions: No.

NH·11

Cryptogams Division Lichen Habitat Slide Collection

Dates of Photographs: 1967–Present

Collection Origins

Mason E. Hale, Jr., created the collection to document the habitats and locales of lichen species. For a biography of Hale see the *Collection Origins* field of *NH·9*.

Physical Description

There are 4,400 color dye coupler slides (Anscochrome, Ektachrome, and Kodachrome).

Subjects

The photographs document lichen in natural settings, primarily in the United States. Locales shown include Point Lobos, Point Reyes, and Yosemite National Park, California; Kona, Hawaii; Upper Copper Falls, Idaho; Glacier National Park, Montana; Black Hills, North Dakota; Bryce National Park and Zion National Park, Utah; the Mississippi River, Wisconsin; and Grand Teton National Park, Wyoming. Other parks shown include Bako National Park in Sarawak, Borneo, and Banff National Park in Alberta, Canada. There are also images of charts, lichen species, and SEMs of lichen.

Arranged: By geographical region.

Captioned: With date, location, and species name.

Finding Aid: No.

Restrictions: No.

NH·12

Cryptogams Division Lichen Photograph Collection

Dates of Photographs: 1965–Present

Collection Origins

Mason E. Hale, Jr., created the collection as a general information file on lichens. For a biography of Hale see the *Collection Origins* field of *NH·9*.

Physical Description

There are 2,500 photographs including silver gelatin photonegatives and photoprints.

Subjects

The photographs document lichen specimens from Africa; New South Wales in Australia; the Hawaiian Islands; the states of Karnataka, Kerala, Maharashtra, and Tamil Nader in India; western India; Japan; Sabah in Malaysia; eastern Nepal; and the Himalayas in Nepal. Some of the lichen specimens shown are type specimens used by taxonomists as the basis for naming and describing a species. The images also include some landscapes of research sites and lichen habitats.

Arranged: Alphabetically by genus and species.

Captioned: Photoprints with specimen identification labels from the U.S. National Herbarium. Labels include genus and species, museum code, photograph distribution number, specimen accession number, specimen discovery site location, and whether the specimen is a holotype.

Finding Aid: No.

Restrictions: No.

NH·13

Cryptogams Division Mayan Ruins Project Collection

Dates of Photographs: 1975–1980

Collection Origins

Mason E. Hale, Jr., created the collection to document a lichen-removal project funded by a research grant from the National Geographic Society. For a biography of Hale see the *Collection Origins* field of *NH·9*. The Mayan Ruins Project staff removed lichens and other biological growth from stone monuments in Guatemala and Honduras between 1975 and 1980. The collection documents the monuments before, during, and after cleaning with a chemical spray, as well as the process of measuring the lichens' growth.

Photographers represented include Julia Gould and John M. Keshishian of Washington, D.C. Photographs and research documentation from the collection were published in a National Geographic Society Research and Exploration report by Mason E. Hale titled "Control of Biological Growths on Mayan Archeological Ruins in Guatemala and Honduras: Final Report." Washington, D.C.: National Geographic Society, 1978.

Physical Description

There are 4,000 photographs including color dye coupler photoprints and slides (Agfachrome, Ektachrome, and Kodachrome) and silver gelatin photonegatives and photoprints. Other materials include articles on stone conservation, correspondence, notes, research observations and reports, and travel information.

Subjects

The photographs document the historic preservation of Mayan architectural ruins at Quirigua and Tikal, Guatemala, and Copàn, Honduras. Images show the ruins during various stages of deterioration and conservation treatment. Many images reproduce details of large sections of bas reliefs or structures such as sculpture at the North Acropolis and the Steles at Copàn. Specific archeological sites at Copàn illustrated include Altars C-1, M, and N; the Ball Court; Stairway Str. 11; and the Wall at I. Quirigua sites shown include Altar P, Monument 14, and Steles A, C, and I.

Arranged: By site location and sequence and purpose of photograph.

Captioned: Some with site and subject.

Finding Aid: No.

Restrictions: No.

NH·14

Cryptogams Division SEM Lichen Collection

Dates of Photographs: 1960s–1970s

Collection Origins

Mason E. Hale, Jr. created the research collection of SEM photographs of lichen. For a biography of Hale see the *Collection Origins* field of *NH·9*.

Physical Description

There are 4,900 silver gelatin photonegatives and photoprints (SEMs).

Subjects

The images are scanning electron microscope (SEM) cross-sections and long-sections of lichen from Florida, Georgia, Kentucky, Maine, and Washington, D.C., in the United States; and from Borneo; Canada; the Dominican Republic; France; Guyana; Mexico; the Philippines; Sweden; and Venezuela.

Arranged: 1) Photoprints by lichen genus and species. 2) Photonegatives by negative number.

Captioned: 1) Some photoprints with collection, country, date, family, herbarium, magnification, number, species, and subgroup. 2) Photonegatives with negative number.

Finding Aid: No.

Restrictions: No.

NH·15

Ferns Division Fern Type Collection *A.K.A.* Conrad Morton Collection

Dates of Photographs: 1954–1971

Collection Origins

Conrad V. Morton (1905–1972) created the collection for his research on the systematics of ferns in North and South America. Morton, who received a bachelor's degree from the University of California at Berkeley in 1928, joined the U.S. National Museum the same year as an aide in the plant division. He was a Curator at the NMNH Department of Botany's Division of Ferns from 1948 to 1972.

Physical Description

There are 33,200 photographs including silver gelatin photonegatives and photoprints. Many of the photoprints have duplicates that are either kept in the files or distributed to other herbaria.

Subjects

Images illustrate New World fern herbarium specimens. Most of the specimens shown are types—that is, specimens selected by taxonomists as the basis for describing or naming a species.

Arranged: Alphabetically by genus name.

Captioned: Photoprints with citation, collector, date, habitat, location, Morton's negative number, museum, name to be filed under, number, remarks, specimen name, status, and synonymy.

Finding Aid: 1) Conrad Morton's notebooks, written in abbreviated form with a list of negative numbers. 2) A photographic label file (housed separately from the collection), of photoprints that have been distributed to other herbaria.

Restrictions: Available only to Smithsonian Institution staff.

NH·16

Ferns Division Research File *A.K.A.* William R. Maxon Research Collection

Dates of Photographs: 1928–1930

Collection Origins

William Ralph Maxon (1877–1948) created the collection for his research on ferns and flowering plants. Maxon, who received an honorary Sc.D. in 1922 from Syracuse University, worked for the USNM from 1898 until his retirement in 1946. He served as Curator of Pteridophyta from 1905 to 1946. Maxon made nine field trips to the American tropics between 1903 and 1926, visiting Jamaica (repeatedly), Cuba, and various places in Central America to collect ferns and flowering plants. In 1928 and 1930 Maxon worked in European herbaria, including those in Berlin, Copenhagen, and London.

These and other photographs have been added to the National Herbarium and shared with other institutions. Maxon used them in his regular series of articles: 1) "New Tropical American Ferns," *American Fern Journal,* Burlington, Vermont, and 2) "Notes on North American Ferns," *Fern Bulletin,* Binghamton, New York: Willard N. Clute.

Physical Description

There are 760 photographs including silver gelatin photonegatives on nitrate and photoprints.

Subjects

The photographs document New World tropical fern specimens from British Guiana (now Guyana), the Caribbean, Colombia, Ecuador, Grenada, Jamaica, and Trinidad. Most images are of type specimens, which are specimens chosen by taxonomists as the basis of naming and describing a new species.

Arranged: Photonegatives by negative numbers.

Captioned: Photoprints with genus, species, location, and negative number. Photonegatives with negative number.

Finding Aid: An index listing the negative number, subject, and whether a photoprint is in the U.S. Herbarium.

Restrictions: No.

NH·17

Grasses Division Bamboo Research Collection

Dates of Photographs: 1943–Present

Collection Origins

The staff of the Division of Grasses created this collection as a working file to document field research, specimens, and staff members. Photographers represented include Cleofe E. Calderon, Victor Krantz, Thomas R. Soderstrom, and Steve M. Young. Studios represented include OPPS, the U.S. Bureau of Standards Photo Laboratory, and the U.S. Department of Agriculture Plant Introduction Section.

Physical Description

There are 15,200 photographs including color dye coupler photoprints and slides and silver gelatin photonegatives and photoprints (many are contact prints). Other materials include correspondence, notes, and seed samples.

Subjects

The photographs show bamboo, field research locations for studying bamboo, scientists, and specimens. Specific locations include Belem and Mato Grosso, Brazil; Burma (now Myanmar); Ceylon (now Sri Lanka); Colombia; Costa Rica; Ecuador; Kew (London), England; Paris, France; Calcutta, India; Indonesia; Mexico; Panama; Surinam; and Puerto Rico, U.S.

Scientists shown include Cleofe E. Calderon, Lynn Clark, Dave Edelman, Floyd A. McClure, Mary S. Sangrey, Thomas R. Soderstrom, and Steve M. Young. Botanical subjects illustrated include arboretums, bamboo (microphotography), bamboo seed germination, bamboo starch studies, and herbaria. Some of the bamboo specimens shown are type specimens from the Lingnan University Collections in Canton (now Guangzhou), China. A type specimen is one chosen by taxonomists as the basis of naming and describing a new species.

Arranged: Chronologically by date of field research.

Captioned: Folders with date of research trip, location, and scientist's name.

Finding Aid: Folder lists with frame numbers, photographer, roll number, subject, and year.

Restrictions: No.

NH·18

Grasses Division Bamboo Slide Collection

Dates of Photographs: 1948–Present

Collection Origins

Thomas R. Soderstrom (1936–1987) and his assistant Steve Carr organized the collection in 1970 as a Department of Botany working file used for lectures, publications, and research. Soderstrom, who received a Ph.D. from Yale University in 1961, specialized in taxonomy and morphology of tropical grasses, especially bamboos.

Photographers represented include Cleofe E. Calderon, Lynn Clark, Dave Edelman, Victor Krantz, Ximena Londono, Floyd A. McClure, Mary S. Sangrey, Thomas R. Soderstrom, Mario Vazquez, and Steve M. Young. Smithsonian Institution bureaus which contributed photographs include the Freer Gallery of Art, the National Gallery of Art, and OPPS.

Physical Description

There are 13,800 color dye coupler slides.

Subjects

The photographs document bamboo field research worldwide, bamboo specimens in the department's collection, botanists, and other departmental staff members. Research sites illustrated include Brazil; the Botanical Gardens and Kaieteur Falls, Georgetown, British Guiana (now Guyana); Burma (now Myanmar); China; El Salvador; Guatemala; Honduras; India; Java, Indonesia; Japan; Tunisia; Puerto Rico, U.S.; and Leningrad, USSR.

People portrayed include Johann Bauhin, Cleofe E. Calderon, Gerald Deitzer, Nees V. Esenbeck, Helen Kennedy, C.S. Kunth, Floyd A. McClure, A.J. Retzius, Joe Shenker, Thomas R. Soderstrom, and Paul Warner. Other subjects illustrated include charts and maps, dung mounds, landscapes, lichens on a mora tree, sugar processing, and uses of bamboo and bamboo products. There are also images of the Forest Research Institute.

Arranged: In two series. 1) Field slides by assigned number. 2) All other slides by letter code.

Captioned: Most slides with creator, date, location, number, and subject.

Finding Aid: 1) Card catalog. 2) A planned computer inventory will include habitat, photographer, slide number, and subject description.

Restrictions: Restricted to scholarly researchers.

NH·19

Grasses Division Illustration Lantern Slide Collection

Dates of Photographs: ND

Collection Origins

Albert Spear Hitchcock (1865–1935) and Mary Agnes Chase (1869–1963) created the collection for research and lecture purposes. Hitchcock, an agrostologist, received a D.S. from Iowa Agricultural College in 1920. He worked for the U.S. Department of Agriculture from 1901 through 1935. In 1905 he took charge of the grass herbarium, and when it was transferred to the Smithsonian U.S. National Museum Division of Plants in 1912, he became Custodian of Grasses until 1935. From 1924 until his death Hitchcock held the title of Principal Biologist in charge of Systematic Agrostology.

Chase joined the U.S. Department of Agriculture in 1903 as a botanical illustrator and worked there with Hitchock for almost 30 years, serving as agrostologist (1907) and botanist (1923–1935). Upon Hitchcock's death in 1935, she became Principal Botanist at the Department of Agriculture and Custodian of Grasses at the Smithsonian USNM. Chase retired from the Department of Agriculture in 1939 but remained Custodian of Grasses at the Smithsonian. When the Smithsonian's Department of Botany was formed in 1947, Chase was made a Research Associate. She received an honorary Sc.D. from the University of Illinois, bestowed when she was 89. Chase served as Custodian of Grasses until her death.

The images in this collection appear in the following book: Albert Spear Hitchcock. *Manual of Grasses in the United States*, miscellaneous publication no. 200. U.S. Department of Agriculture. Washington, D.C.: U.S. Government Printing Office, 1935. 2nd edition revised in 1951 by Agnes Chase. (Reprint: Albert Spear Hitchcock and Agnes Chase. *Manual of the Grasses of the United States*. New York: Dover Publications, 1971.)

Physical Description

There are 50 silver gelatin dry plate lantern slides.

Subjects

The photographs are of native North American grasses such as buffalo grass and burro grass. Also included are photographic reproductions of drawings of plants and maps of North American grass species concentration.

Arranged: No.

Captioned: Most images are numbered (possibly with book illustration plate numbers). Illustrations are also captioned with the specimen's genus and species.

Finding Aid: No.

Restrictions: No.

NH·20

Grasses Division Photograph Collection *A.K.A.* Floyd A. McClure Photograph Collection

Dates of Photographs: 1925–1970

Collection Origins

Floyd A. McClure (1897–1970) began the collection in 1925 to document the bamboo plant. McClure, who received a Ph.D. from Ohio State University in 1935, taught for 24 years at Lingnan University in Canton (now Guangzhou), China, and worked for the Smithsonian Institution, the U.S. Department of Agriculture, and the U.S. National Research Council. In 1943 he was appointed an honorary research associate for the Smithsonian Institution Department of Botany. McClure took most of the photographs. He published a compendium of his research in the following book: Floyd A. McClure. *The Bamboos: A Fresh Perspective*. Cambridge, Massachusetts: Harvard University Press, 1966.

Physical Description

There are 10,250 photographs including silver gelatin photonegatives and photoprints. Ninety-five percent of the photonegatives are nitrate.

Subjects

This collection documents bamboo species and habitats in Ceylon (now Sri Lanka), China, Colombia, Cuba, Ecuador, El Salvador, Guatemala, Honduras, India, Jamaica, Nicaragua, east Pakistan, the Panama Canal Zone, the Philippines, and in Florida, Georgia, Maryland, Puerto Rico, and Texas in the United States. Botanists portrayed include Albert W. Close, Norman Kearns, Walter R. Lindsay, Lewis Long, Ernesto Molestina, John Popeno, Juvenal Valerio Rodriquez, and R.A. Young.

Arranged: By year, then alphabetically by collecting trip.

Captioned: With assigned number. Envelopes with assigned number, growth patterns, indigenous location, narrative description of the specimen, size, taxonomic order, and use by humans.

Finding Aid: Card catalog titled "Index for Photographs" with assigned number, date, and location.

Restrictions: Available only to Smithsonian Institution staff.

NH·21

Palynology Division Pollen SEM Collection

Dates of Photographs: 1972–Present

Collection Origins

Joan W. Nowicke created the collection as part of her ongoing research in palynology (pollen analysis). Nowicke, who received a Ph.D. in biosystematics from Washington University in St. Louis, Missouri, in 1968, has been a curator in NMNH's Department of Botany since 1972. Photographers represented include NMNH SEM technicians.

Many of the SEMs have appeared in the following journals: 1) *American Journal of Botany.* Oxford, Ohio: Botanical Society of America. 2) *Brittonia.* Bronx, New York: New York Botanical Garden. 3) *Grana.* Stockholm, Sweden: Almquist and Wiksell. 4) *National Geographic.* Washington, D.C.: National Geographic Society. 5) *Nature.* London: Macmillan. 6) *Scientific American.* New York: Scientific American. 7) *Smithsonian Contributions to Botany.* Washington, D.C.: Smithsonian Press. 8) *Taxon.* Utrecht, Netherlands: International Bureau for Plant Taxonomy and Nomenclature. 9) *World Pollen and Spore Flora.* Stockholm, Sweden: Almquist and Wilksell.

Physical Description

There are 10,000 photographs including silver gelatin photonegatives and photoprints in SEM format.

Subjects

There are SEM images of pollen grain specimens from Angiosperms. Angiosperms are plants—frequently herbs, shrubs, or trees—which produce seeds within a flower or fruit, such as bellflowers, cockscomb, dianthus, spinach, and sugar beets.

Arranged: Taxonomically.

Captioned: With magnification and specimen number.

Finding Aid: *A Pollen Primer*, by Joan W. Nowicke, is a six-page publication for non-botanists, with general descriptions of the function, identification, and morphology of pollen grains.

Restrictions: Available only for Smithsonian staff use.

NH·22

Phanerogams Division Gesneriaceae Species File Collection

Dates of Photographs: 1950–Present

Collection Origins

Laurence E. Skog (1943–), Curator in the NMNH Department of Botany, created the collection to document his research. Skog, who received a Ph.D. from Cornell University in 1972, has been with the Smithsonian Institution since 1973. These photographs, which are used by researchers and botanical artists within the Smithsonian Institution, rotate to other herbaria on an ongoing basis. Photographers and institutions represented include Andrews, Sarawak; Liberty Hyde Bailey Hortorium, Cornell University; Frances Batchelor; H. Butcher; R.E. Dengler; Jonathan Ertent; James P. Folsom; Robin Foster; Kartuz Greenhouses, Wilmington, Delaware; L.P. Kvist; J. Reark; Royal Botanic Garden, Edinburgh, Scotland; Thomas R. Soderstrom; Margaret H. Stone; Tinari Greenhouses; and Jerry Williams.

Physical Description

There are 2,900 color dye coupler slides.

Subjects

The images document live specimens of tropical Gesneriaceae, primarily from the Western Hemisphere. The Gesneriaceae family of flowering herbs and shrubs includes such ornamentals as African violets, gloxinia, goldfish plants, lipstick plants, and primroses. The specimens are from Argentina, Bolivia, Colombia, Costa Rica, Ecuador, Java, New Guinea, Peru, and Thailand. A Gesneriaceae specimen is reproduced in this volume's illustrations.

Arranged: Alphabetically by genus and species.

Captioned: Half of the slides with genus and species, collector, species number, and country.

Finding Aid: No.

Restrictions: No.

NH·23

Phanerogams Division Gesneriaceae Type Specimen File

Dates of Photographs: 1968–Present

Collection Origins

Laurence E. Skog created this collection for his personal research. For a biography of Skog see the *Collection Origins* field of *NH·22*.

Physical Description

There are 7,250 photographs including color dye coupler slides and silver gelatin photonegatives and photoprints. Some of the photoprints are SEMs magnified 50, 200, or 500 times.

Subjects

This collection documents Gesneriaceae specimens in European herbaria. The Gesneriaceae family of flowering tropical herbs and shrubs includes such ornamentals as African violets, gloxinia, goldfish plants, lipstick plants, and primroses. Some images are of tropical Gesneriaceae specimens found in European herbaria or of type specimens in the Department of Botany's herbarium. A type specimen is one chosen by taxonomists as the basis for naming and describing a new species.

Arranged: In three series by type of material. 1) Slides. 2) Silver gelatin contact photoprints and photonegatives. 3) SEM photoprints and photonegatives. Each series in numerical order (starting with 18,000).

Captioned: With a number.

Finding Aid: A list of the slides with collector's name, collection number, holotype museum code (museum or herbarium location), slide number, specimen name (genus and species), and status of the specimen (holotype, isotype, lectotype, or paratype).

Restrictions: No.

NH·24

Phanerogams Division Neotropical Vegetation Slide File

Dates of Photographs: 1978–Present

Collection Origins

Vicki A. Funk (1947–   ), NMNH Associate Curator of Botany, assembled this collection in 1978 for presentations, publications, and personal research purposes. Since receiving a Ph.D. from Ohio State University in 1980, Funk has conducted research on systematics and theoretical cladistics (special taxonomic system applied to the study of evolutionary relationships) of Compositae. Photographers represented include Deborah Bell, Jonathan Coddington, Vicki A. Funk, Brian Kahn, Jerry A. Louton, Roy W. McDiarmid, Janice Sacco, Linda L. Sims, M.H. Stone, and George R. Zug.

Physical Description

There are 6,000 color dye coupler slides (Agfachrome, Ektachrome, and Kodachrome).

Subjects

The photographs document taxonomic research on the New World neotropical Compositae, a large family of plants with flower heads that have both rays and disks (such as the daisy), disks only (such as wormwood), or rays only (such as the dandelion).

Specimen habitat locations shown are Belize; Rio Negro, Brazil; Bogotá, Zipaquirá, Colombia; the Galápagos Islands, Ecuador; Suffolk County, England; Paris and Versailles, France; Jalisco, Mexico; Chhomrong, Ghorapani, Hinko Cave, Kathmandu, Rhedo Forest, and Vari, Nepal; Cuzco, Lake Titicaca, Machu Picchu, Nazca, Pasco, Rio Tambopata, and Rio Urubamba Valley, Peru; and Jekyll Island, Georgia, United States. Landscapes shown include Lake Arenal; Belize; windmills at Bogotá, Colombia; a waterlily pond at Zamorano, Honduras; and a lavafield at Jalisco, Mexico. Cityscapes shown include the Montreal Botanical Garden; Botanical Gardens, Eiffel Tower, and the Left Bank in Paris; Mexico City; the Chicago Art Fair; and the Smithsonian Institution museums in Washington, D.C.

Other images include photographic reproductions of charts, diagrams, and graphs of habitat construction, hybridization, and specimens' general structure; and photographs of unidentified greenhouses. Animals shown include flamingos, llamas, pelicans, and pygmy anteaters. Scientists pictured include George Ball, Judy Canne, Vicki A. Funk, Roy W. McDiarmid, Scott Ransom, and Denise Schriner. There are images of unidentified workers and specimens at field sites. A photograph from this collection is reproduced in this volume's illustrations.

Arranged: Chronologically by field trip.

Captioned: With date, photographer, roll number, shot number, and subject.

Finding Aid: No.

Restrictions: No.

NH·25

Phanerogams Division Peruvian Plants Color Photoprint Collection

Dates of Photographs: 1982–Present

Collection Origins

Vicki A. Funk started the collection in 1982 to document her research on the taxonomy and cladistics of Peruvian plants. For a biography of Funk see the *Collection Origins* field of *NH·24*. One copy of the collection is housed in Peru and the other at the National Museum of Natural History. Photographers represented include Vicki A. Funk, Brian Kahn, Janice Sacco, and Linda L. Sims.

Physical Description

There are 140 color dye coupler photoprints.

Subjects

This collection shows the taxonomy and cladistics of Compositae plants in Peru. The Compositae is a large family of plants with flower heads that have both rays and disks (daisy), disks only (wormwood), or rays only (dandelion).

Arranged: No.

Captioned: With common plant name, date, location, and photographer.

Finding Aid: Card catalog with location and plant name.

Restrictions: No.

Selected Photographs from the Collections at the National Museum of Natural History, the National Zoological Park, the Smithsonian Astrophysical Observatory, and the Smithsonian Tropical Research Institute

Note: Captions in quotations were provided by Smithsonian Institution scientists, staff, or collection custodians.

Robin Foster. "Gesneriaceae Besleria; from Tono, Peru, Manu." December 1985. Silver gelatin photoprint from color dye coupler slide. Phanerogams Division Gesneriaceae Species File Collection (NH·22). OPPS Negative #89-19843.

M.H. Stone. "Episcia x variabilis, type specimen; 'Noel,' G-453." N.D. Silver gelatin photoprint from color dye coupler slide. Phanerogams Division Neotropical Vegetation Slide File (NH·24). OPPS Negative #89-19842.

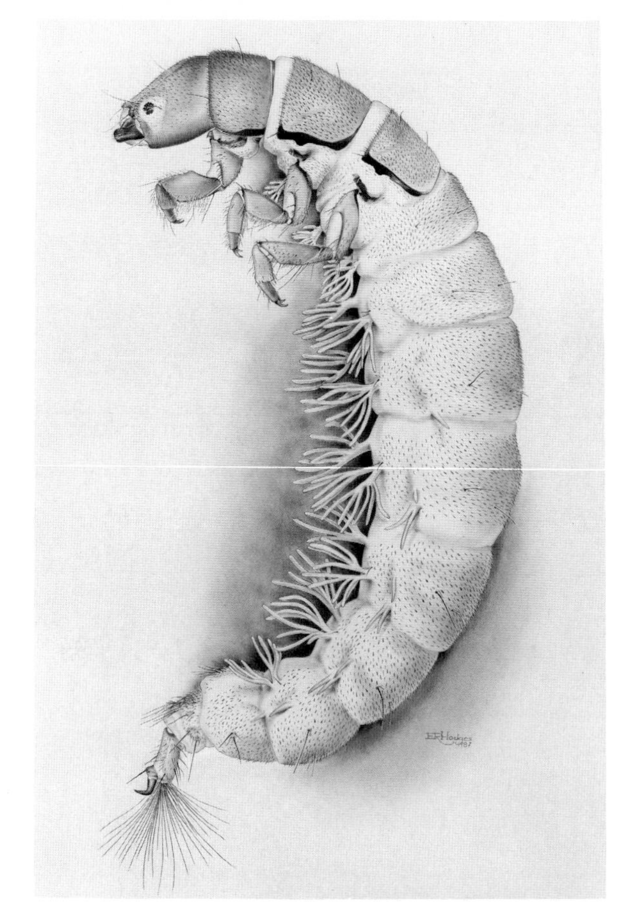

Elaine R.S. Hodges. Photographic Reproduction of a "Larva of Smicridea (S.) annulicornis (Blanchard) lateral; (Common name: Caddisfly); drawn by Elaine R.S. Hodges in carbon dust, graphite, and diluted ink on 00 Ross board." Ca. 1989. Entomology Department Scientific Illustrator's Collection I A.K.A. Elaine R.S. Hodges Collection (NH·26). Unnumbered.

Stanley Weitzman and W.L. Fink. "Nannostomus eques Steindachner (Common name: pencil fish), from Guyana, South America, freshwater; specimen length: 33.4 mm/female and 32.5 mm/male; collected in 1970; 35mm Panatomic-X film; Leicaflex camera, 100mm lens (macro), strobe light; specimens were alive." 1971. Silver gelatin photoprint. Fishes Division South American Freshwater Fishes Collection (NH·79). OPPS Negative #89-3772.

Stanley Weitzman and W.L. Fink. "Carnegiella strigata Günther (Common name: hatchet fish), from Peruvian Amazon, South America, freshwater; specimen length: 25.5 mm; collected in 1970; 35mm Panatomic-X film, Leicaflex camera, 100mm lens (macro), strobe light; specimen was alive." 1971. Silver gelatin photoprint. Fishes Division South American Freshwater Fishes Collection (NH·79). OPPS Negative #89-3773.

Anon. "Five mountain lions killed in three days by government hunter Cleve Miller and party." N.D. Silver gelatin photoprint. Biological Survey General Collection (NH·104). Bio-Survey #B-2170-b-M; OPPS Negative #88-19990.

W.H. Osgood. "Camp at base of Plateau Mt., Alaska." 1904. Silver gelatin photoprint. Biological Survey General Collection (NH·104). Bio-Survey #B-7402; OPPS Negative #88-19989.

Edward A. Goldman. "Rock camp under overhanging ledge, at about 2500 ft. on Bass Trail in Grand Canyon, Arizona; left to right, H.H.T. Jackson, W.P. Taylor, and Bert Luzon (guide)." September 9, 1916. Silver gelatin photoprint. Biological Survey General Collection (NH·104). Bio-Survey #B-17024; OPPS Negative #88-19993.

J.S. Ligon. "Lion hunter B.V. Lilly and his most famous dogs, Jack, Crook, Tip, and Queen on Members [Mimbres] River, New Mexico." 1919. Silver gelatin photoprint. Biological Survey General Collection (NH·104). Bio-Survey #B-20995; OPPS Negative #88-19986.

Anon. "I.L. Richie, government hunter since 1915; he has taken 17 lions and 7 bears with the six-shooter." N.D. *Silver gelatin photoprint. Biological Survey General Collection (NH·104). Bio-Survey #B-38907; OPPS Negative #88-19983.*

L.J. Goldman. "Mrs. Frank (Ada) Tingley, predatory animal huntress, for the Biological Survey—now the Fish and Wildlife Service—which directs the work of a large number of hunters engaged in destroying predatory wild animals of the West, such as wolves, coyotes, and mountain lions; several huntresses have been engaged in this work and have been as successful in it as the men employed for this purpose (Idaho)." 1919. Silver gelatin photoprint. Biological Survey General Collection (NH·104). Bio-Survey #B-24084; OPPS Negative #88-19980.

L.L. Laythe. "Trapper's cabin, Colorado." 1929. Silver gelatin photoprint. Biological Survey General Collection (NH·104). Bio-Survey #B-33883; OPPS Negative #88-19988.

Anon. "Bureau workers, camp on Burro Creek, Arizona." July 21, 1915. Silver gelatin photoprint. Biological Survey General Collection (NH·104). Bio-Survey #B-16541; OPPS Negative #88-19994.

Edward A. Goldman. "Parry century plant in full flower at 8,100 feet on top of the Big Hatchet Mountains, New Mexico." 1908. Silver gelatin photoprint. Biological Survey General Collection (NH·104). Bio-Survey #B-10896; OPPS Negative #88-19981.

Anon. "V. Bailey (left) and H.H.T. Jackson at Spring Pont [sic], Big Levels Game Refuge, Virginia." 1935. Silver gelatin photoprint. U.S. Biological Survey General Collection (NH·104). Bio-Survey #B-42039; OPPS Negative #88-19984.

Anon. "Vernon Bailey, Dr. C. Hart Merriam, T.S. Palmer, Dr. A.K. Fisher; at Lone Pine, Owen Valley, California on 1891 Death Valley Survey." June 13, 1891. U.S. Biological Survey General Collection (NH·104). Bio-Survey #B-1929; OPPS Negative #88-19991.

Anon. "Tasmanian wolves (Thylacinus cynocephalus), on exhibit at NZP; these animals are now extinct." 1904–1906. Silver gelatin photoprint from silver gelatin dry plate photonegative. Historical Photograph Collection (ZP·7). NZP Negative #139.

Anon. "The Monkey House, which is extant, is the oldest animal building in use at the Zoo." 1906. Silver gelatin photoprint. Historical Photograph Collection (ZP·7). NZP Negative #85.

Frances Benjamin Johnston. "School group viewing bison." 1899. Silver gelatin photoprint. Historical Photograph Collection (ZP·7). NZP Negative #FBJ-2.

Frances Benjamin Johnston. "School children at the Zoo, looking at birds in front of the old Lion House (now torn down)." 1899. Silver gelatin photoprint. Historical Photograph Collection (ZP·7). Negative #FBJ-10.

Anon. "Early zoo-goers relax at Rock Creek Park." N.D. *Silver gelatin photoprint. Historical Photograph Collection* (ZP·7). *Unnumbered.*

Anon. "Head Keeper William H. Blackburne bottle-feeding a young female Bactrian camel at the NZP; the camel was born in the Zoo." 1893. *Silver gelatin photoprint from silver gelatin dry plate photonegative. Historical Photograph Collection* (ZP·7). NZP *Negative* #269.

Anon. "Between 1889 and 1891 the NZP consisted of these bison and other American mammals and birds on public view near the Smithsonian Institution Building." 1889–1891. Silver gelatin photoprint. Historical Photograph Collection (ZP·7). Unnumbered.

Anon. "The Zoo's first Indian elephants (Elephants maximus), 'Dunk' and 'Gold Dust' with their keeper." 1891. Silver gelatin photoprint from silver gelatin dry plate photonegative. Historical Photograph Collection (ZP·7). NZP Negative #902.

Anon. "A yak near the Yak Barn; Parking Lot C now occupies this area." Early 1900s. Silver gelatin photoprint from silver gelatin dry plate photonegative. Historical Photograph Collection (ZP·7). NZP Negative #892.

Anon. "Keepers, part of the all-male staff, with a wooden horse-drawn cart used for moving animals; this site is near the present-day Parking Lot A." Ca. 1920. Silver gelatin photoprint from silver gelatin dry plate photonegative. Historical Photograph Collection (ZP·7). NZP Negative #532.

Anon. "Beatrix Henderson Bird Cage, which is extant; built in 1913." Ca. 1939. Silver gelatin photoprint from silver gelatin dry plate photonegative. Historical Photograph Collection (ZP·7). NZP Negative #405.

Anon. "Head Keeper William H. Blackburne (just right of the center) and Zoo visitors in the Reptile House." 1928–1943. Silver gelatin photoprint from silver gelatin photonegative. Historical Photograph Collection (ZP·7). NZP Negative #9800-H.

Anon. "Ringling Brother's Circus staff posing with the Indian elephant 'Babe', donated to NZP by the circus." Spring 1935. Silver gelatin photoprint from silver gelatin dry plate photonegative. Historical Photograph Collection (ZP·7). NZP Negative #1284.

Anon. "The animal commissary in the Reptile House basement; names of men: (second from left) Mr. Burdett, (third from left) Roy Jennier." Spring 1936. Silver gelatin photoprint from silver gelatin photonegative. Historical Photograph Collection (ZP·7). NZP Negative #2082.

Anon. "A Komodo dragon and Keeper Roy Jennier, probably in the Komodo exhibit in the Reptile House." Ca. 1938. Silver gelatin photoprint from silver gelatin photonegative. Historical Photograph Collection (ZP·7). NZP Negative #3371.

Anon. "William M. Mann (third from right) and Lucille Mann (standing) cross the St. Paul's River near Dobli's Island, Liberia, on the Firestone Expedition." 1940. Silver gelatin copy photoprint from silver gelatin dry plate lantern slide. Lantern Slide Collection A.K.A. William M. Mann Lantern Slide Collection (ZP·8). NZP Negative #89-6277.

Anon. "Children feeding the Hybrid (polar and Kodiak) bears; this exhibit is extant but the bars have been removed." 1949. Silver gelatin photoprint. Historical Photograph Collection (ZP·7). NZP Negative #3303-B.

Jessie Cohen. "Male leopard (Panthera pardus), 'Sam.' " 1979. Silver gelatin photoprint from silver gelatin photonegative. Design and Exhibit Planning Photograph Collection (ZP·6). Unnumbered.

Jessie Cohen. "Orangutans (Pongo pygmaeus), mother 'Pensi' and baby 'Tucker'." 1983. Silver gelatin photoprint from silver gelatin photonegative. Design and Exhibit Planning Photograph Collection (ZP·6). Unnumbered.

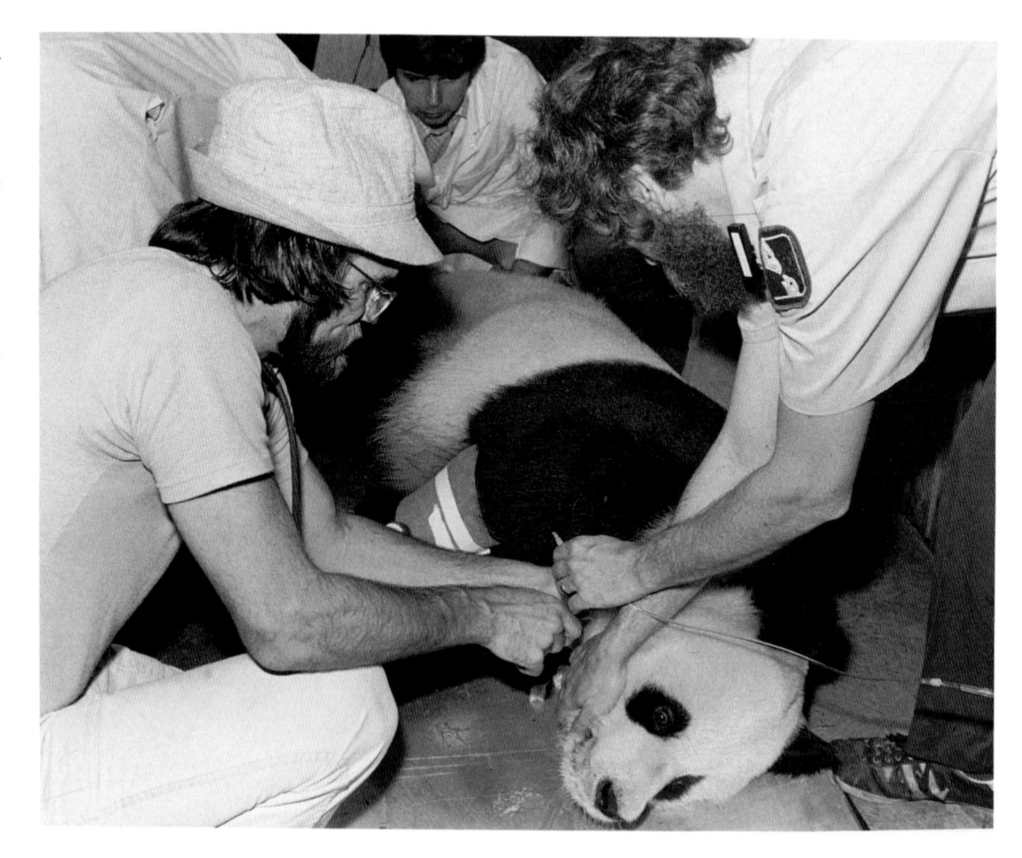

Jessie Cohen. "The first artificial insemination of giant panda in the U.S.; National Zoo veterinarians prepare male giant panda (Ailuropoda melanoleuca), Hsing-Hsing, for the procedure." 1980. Silver gelatin photoprint from silver gelatin photonegative. Design and Exhibit Planning Photograph Collection (ZP·6). Unnumbered.

Jessie Cohen. "Giant pandas, Hsing-Hsing (top) and Ling-Ling play on their furniture during an early Spring encounter." 1985. Silver gelatin photoprint from silver gelatin photonegative. Design and Exhibit Planning Photograph Collection (ZP·6). Unnumbered.

J.A. Whipple. "Daguerreotype of the Moon. Taken at the 15-inch refractor of the Harvard College Observatory in Cambridge, Mass." February 26, 1852. Silver gelatin copy photoprint from a daguerreotype. Original in the Harvard Plate Collection (SA·16). Copy in the Harvard College Observatory Historical Photograph Collection (SA·10). (Copies also available from SAO Publications Department.) HCO Negative #6806-18H.

Anonymous Harvard College Observatory staff member in Arequipa, Peru. "Halley's Comet; 30-minute exposure on blue-sensitive emulsion; photographed with 8-inch Bache photographic doublet at the Boyden Station of HCO in Arequipa, Peru." April 21, 1910. Silver gelatin photoprint. Original in the Harvard Plate Collection (SA·16). Copy in the Harvard College Observatory Historical Photograph Collection (SA·10). (Copies available from SAO Publications Department.) HCO Negative #B41215.

Anonymous Harvard College Obervatory staff member. "The Great Spiral Galaxy, Messier 31, in Andromeda; 150-minute exposure was made on blue-sensitive emulsion; photographed with the 36-inch Schmidt Telescope at the Agassiz Station of the Harvard College Observatory." September 6, 1945. Silver gelatin photoprint. Original in the Harvard Plate Collection (SA·16). Copy in the Harvard College Observatory Historical Photograph Collection (SA·10). (Copies available from SAO Publications Department.) HCO Negative #J482.

Joe Wrinn. "The 25-meter-diameter radio telescope at Oak Ridge Observatory, used for Project META, an automated search for extraterrestrial intelligence conducted by Paul Horowitz under a grant from the Planetary Society." N.D. *Silver gelatin photoprint. Harvard College Observatory Historical Photograph Collection (SA·10). (Copies available from SAO Publications Department.) Unnumbered.*

Anonymous SAO staff member. "A Smithsonian solar observatory at Montezuma, Chile." Ca. 1920. Silver gelatin photoprint. Publications Department Photoprint Collection (SA·12). SAO Negative #33668.

Anonymous SAO staff member. "The prototype for the Baker-Nunn Satellite Tracking Camera . . . While still in final testing . . . this camera photographed Sputnik 1 on the night of October 17, 1957, thus producing the Western World's first photograph of an artificial satellite." N.D. *Silver gelatin photoprint (chloro-bromide DOP Velox). Publications Department Photoprint Collection (SA·12). Unnumbered.*

Anonymous SAO staff member. "The Multiple Mirror Telescope's innovative design combines six 1.8-m mirrors around a central axis, with the light collected by each mirror brought to a common focus. The entire 500-ton building rotates with the telescope during observations. The MMT is a joint facility of the Smithsonian Astrophysical Observatory and the University of Arizona." N.D. *Silver gelatin photoprint. Publications Department Photoprint Collection (SA·12). Unnumbered.*

Anonymous SAO staff member. "Fred Lawrence Whipple Observatory on Mount Hopkins, Arizona, looking north toward Tucson. In the left foreground, site of the 10-m gamma-ray collector and 61-cm and 1.5-m telescopes; top center, the 8500-foot summit and site of the Multiple Mirror Telescope. A portion of the 18-mile road linking summit instruments with basecamp facilities in the Santa Cruz Valley below can also be seen." N.D. *Silver gelatin photoprint. Publications Department Photoprint Collection (SA·12). Unnumbered.*

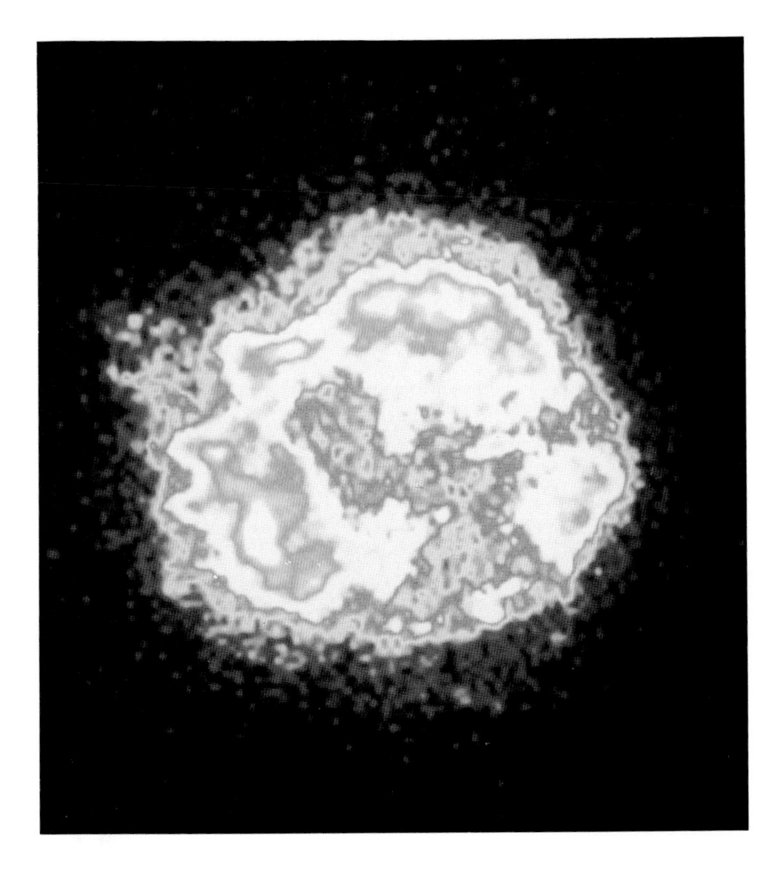

Anonymous Center for Astrophysics staff member. "The expanding remnant shell of gas and dust from the Cassiopeia A supernova seen in x-ray wavelengths." N.D. *Silver gelatin photoprint. Publications Department Photoprint Collection (SA·12). Unnumbered.*

Anonymous Center for Astrophysics–Mount Palomar Sky Survey staff member. "Contour lines define a giant halo of hot, hitherto invisible, x-ray-emitting gas surrounding the elliptical galaxy M86 in the Virgo cluster detected by Center for Astrophysics researchers from data obtained by the Einstein Observatory satellite." N.D. *Silver gelatin photoprint. Original in Einstein Satellite Photograph Collection (SA·1). Copy in Publications Department Photoprint Collection (SA·12). Unnumbered.*

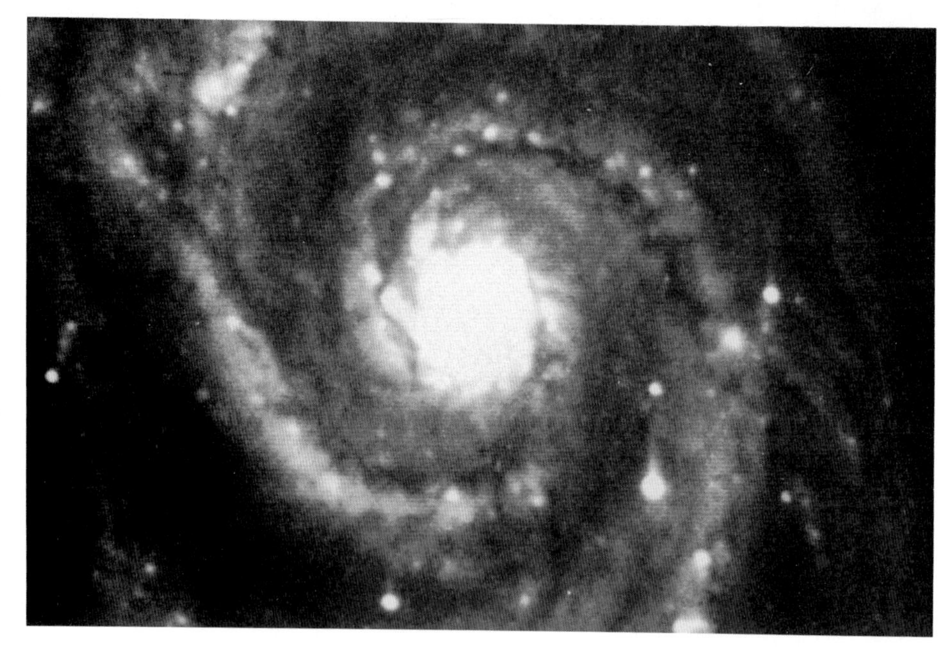

Rudolph Schild. "A spiral galaxy, photographed with a 61-cm telescope equipped with a charged-coupled device (CCD) electronic detector." N.D. *Silver gelatin photoprint. Original in Optical and Infrared Astronomy Collection A.K.A. Rudolph E. Schild Research Collection (SA·4). Copy in Publications Department Photoprint Collection (SA·12). Unnumbered.*

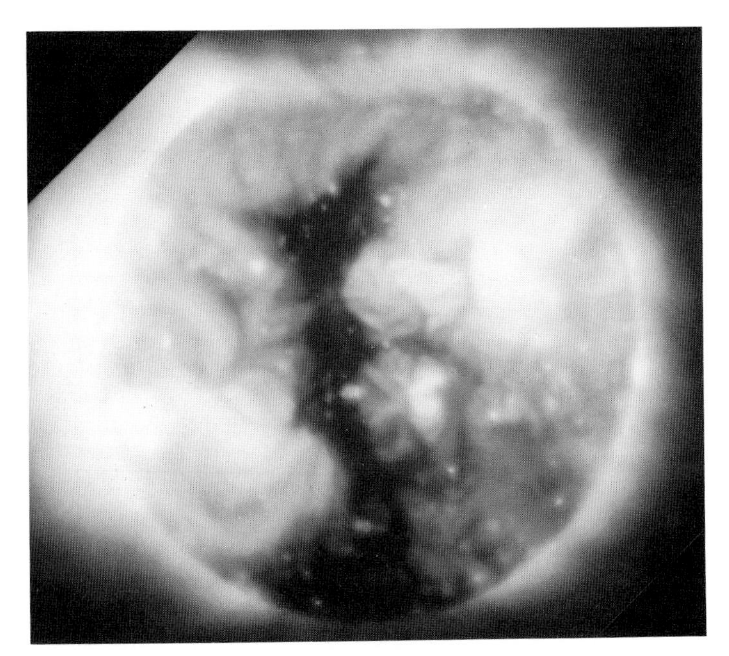

Skylab *Satellite. "Sun seen in x-rays, taken by camera aboard the* Skylab *Satellite. The large dark areas are 'coronal holes,' gaps in the Sun's hot outer atmosphere from which the solar wind spews forth."* N.D. *Silver gelatin photoprint. Original in* Skylab *Ultraviolet Solar Photograph Collection (SA·8). Copy in Publications Department Photoprint Collection (SA·12). Unnumbered.*

Joe Wrinn. "The 1.5-meter Wyeth Reflector at the Oak Ridge Observatory, at Harvard, in Cambridge, Massachussetts." N.D. *Silver gelatin photoprint. Publications Department Photoprint Collection (SA·12). Unnumbered.*

Carl Hansen. "Caterpillars eating a leaf; research by Phil DeVries." Ca. 1987. Silver gelatin photoprint from color dye coupler slide. STRI Photographic Services Collection (ST·15). OPPS Negative #90-2542.

Carl Hansen. "Three-toed sloth (Bradypus tridactylus)." Ca. 1987. Silver gelatin photoprint from color dye coupler slide. STRI Photographic Services Collection (ST·15). OPPS Negative #90-2543.

Carl Hansen. "Using a fish-eye lens to record the amount of light reaching the forest floor through the tropical forest canopy; research project of Alan Smith." Ca. 1987. Silver gelatin photoprint from color dye coupler slide. STRI Photographic Services Collection (ST·15). OPPS Negative #90-2545.

Carl Hansen. "Archeological excavation by STRI scientists in Panama." Ca. 1987. Silver gelatin photoprint from color dye coupler slide. STRI Photographic Services Collection (ST·15). OPPS Negative #90-2544.

Carl Hansen. "Plant beetles mating; project of Donald Windsor." Ca. 1987. Silver gelatin photoprint from color dye coupler slide. STRI Photographic Services Collection (ST·15). OPPS Negative #90-2547.

Carl Hansen. "Plant tendril with insect eggs." Ca. 1987. Silver gelatin photoprint from color dye coupler slide. STRI Photographic Services Collection (ST·15). OPPS Negative #90-2548.

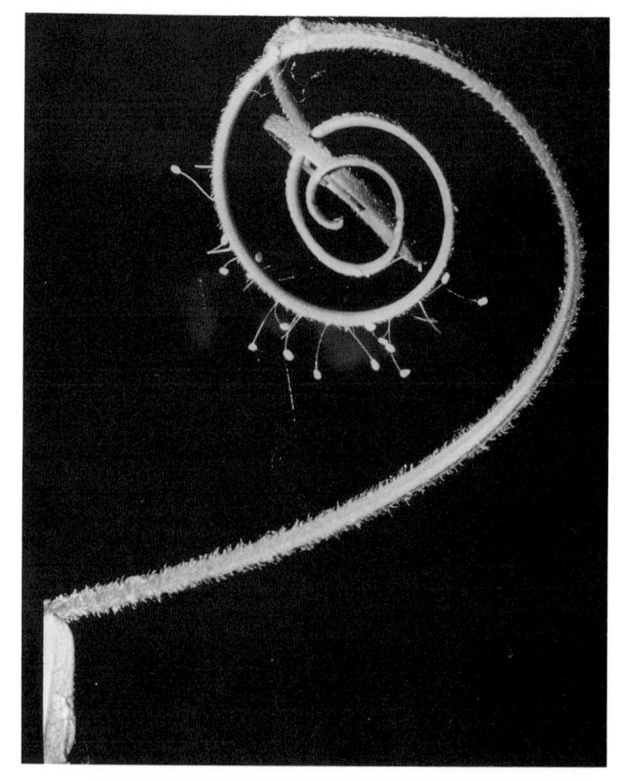

Carl Hansen. "Tropical deforestation in Panama." Ca. 1987. Silver gelatin photoprint from color dye coupler slide. STRI Photographic Services Collection (ST·15). OPPS Negative #90-2549.

Carl Hansen. "Oil spill on the coral reef at Galeta with Galeta Marine Lab visible at top; focus of major STRI research effort." Ca. 1987. Silver gelatin photoprint from color dye coupler slide. STRI Photographic Services Collection (ST·15). OPPS Negative #90-2551.

Carl Hansen. "Barro Colorado Island from the air." Ca. 1987. Silver gelatin photoprint from color dye coupler slide. STRI Photographic Services Collection (ST·15). OPPS Negative #90-2552.

Carl Hansen. "Young iguana hatched in captivity; Iguana Management Project of Dagmar Werner." Ca. 1987. Silver gelatin photoprint from color dye coupler slide. STRI Photographic Services Collection (ST·15). OPPS Negative #90-2553.

Carl Hansen. "Glass frog (Centrolenella colymbiphyllum)." Ca. 1987. Silver gelatin photoprint from color dye coupler slide. STRI Photographic Services Collection (ST·15). OPPS Negative #90-2555.

Carl Hansen. "Species of orchid." Ca. 1987. Silver gelatin photoprint from color dye coupler slide. STRI Photographic Services Collection (ST·15). OPPS Negative #90-2557.

Carl Hansen. "Yellow-bellied sea snake (Pelamis platurus) of the Pacific Ocean; subject of research by Ira Rubinoff and others on diving behavior." Ca. 1987. Silver gelatin photoprint from color dye coupler slide. STRI Photographic Services Collection (ST·15). OPPS Negative #90-2559.

Carl Hansen. "Researcher at STRI marine facilities recording data underwater using scuba gear." Ca. 1987. Silver gelatin photoprint from color dye coupler slide. STRI Photographic Services Collection (ST·15). OPPS Negative #90-2560.

NH

Department of Entomology

Department of Entomology
National Museum of Natural History
Smithsonian Institution
Washington, D.C. 20560
(202) 357-2317
Hours: Monday–Friday, 10 a.m.–4 p.m.

Scope of the Collections

There are 11 photographic collections with approximately 65,000 images.

Focus of the Collections

The collections document the Department of Entomology and its three divisions: Hemiptera and Hymenoptera; Lepidoptera; and Neuroptera and Diptera. The departmental photographs illustrate the behavior, bionomics, biosystematics, habitats, taxonomy, and zoogeography of arachnids and insects. There are also portraits of early and well-known entomologists, as well as the staff of the NMNH, U.S. Department of Agriculture, and USNM. Images of scientific illustrations, created for education, reproduction, and security purposes, are also included.

Photographic Processes and Formats Represented

There are albumen photoprints; color dye coupler photonegatives, photoprints, phototransparencies, and slides; dye diffusion transfer photoprints (SEMs and TEMs); platinum photoprints; and silver gelatin photonegatives, photoprints, and slides.

Other Materials Represented

The department also contains abstracts, correspondence, drawings, greeting cards, journals, newspaper clippings, notes, obituaries, photostatic copies, scientific illustrations, specimens, and xerographic copies.

Access and Usage Policies

The collections are open to scholarly researchers by appointment. Interested researchers should write to the department and describe their research topic, the type of material that interests them, and their research aim.

Publication Policies

Researchers must obtain permission from the Smithsonian Institution to reproduce a photograph and may also have to obtain permission from the copyright holder, which is not necessarily the Smithsonian Institution. The preferred credit line is "Courtesy of the Department of Entomology, National Museum of Natural History, Smithsonian Institution."

NH·26

Entomology Department Scientific Illustrator's Collection I *A.K.A.* Elaine R.S. Hodges Collection

Dates of Photographs: 1976–Present

Collection Origins

Scientific illustrator Elaine R.S. Hodges (1937–) and OPPS staff created the collection to document her scientific illustrations. Hodges studied English at Wilson Teacher's College (1954–1955) in Washington, D.C.; art education at Pratt Institute (1955–1956) in Brooklyn, New York; and entomology at the University of Maryland (1974–1976). Joining the Smithsonian Institution in 1965, Hodges has served as scientific illustrator for the Department of Entomology since 1976. Hodges has also been President of the Guild of Natural Science Illustrators and of the Maryland Entomological Society and a member of the executive council of the Lepidopterists Society and the Council of Biology Editors Subcommittee on Standards for Publication.

Photographers represented include OPPS photographer Harold E. Dougherty and Elaine R. S. Hodges. The collection also contains drawings by illustrator Carolyn B. Gast. The photographs have been used to illustrate research publications including the following: 1) Elaine R.S. Hodges. *The Guild Handbook of Scientific Illustration*. New York: Van Nostrand Reinhold, 1989. 2) Council of Biology Editors, Scientific Illustration Committee, eds. *Illustrating Science: Standards for Publication*. Bethesda, Maryland: Council of Biology Editors, 1988.

Physical Description

There are 850 photographs including color dye coupler photoprints, phototransparencies, and slides (Ektachrome and Kodachrome) and silver gelatin photonegatives, photoprints, and slides. Other materials include drawings, photostatic copies, and xerographic copies.

Subjects

The photographs reproduce drawings of entomological specimens by Elaine R.S. Hodges and other scientific illustrators, as well as the process of drawing a scientific illustration. Many of the drawings reproduced were done in carbon dust or on scratchboard. The drawings illustrate several insect orders, including Coleoptera (beetles), Diptera (gnats, midges, mosquitoes, true flies, and two-winged flies), and Hymenoptera (ants, bees, sawflies, and wasps). A caddis fly drawing by Hodges is reproduced in this volume's illustrations.

Arranged: No.

Captioned: With drawing medium, illustrator, and specimen name; some also with date.

Finding Aid: No.

Restrictions: No.

NH·27

Entomology Department Scientific Illustrator's Collection II *A.K.A.* Young T. Sohn Collection

Dates of Photographs: 1981–Present

Collection Origins

Scientific illustrator Young T. Sohn assembled the collection from OPPS photographic reproductions of his scientific illustrations for security purposes. Sohn, who received a masters degree from Sung Kyun Kwan University, has been with the department since 1972. The photographs have been used to illustrate articles in scientific journals.

Physical Description

There are six photographs including silver gelatin photonegatives and slides.

Subjects

The collection documents entomological illustrations by Young T. Sohn.

Arranged: No.

Captioned: With specimen name.

Finding Aid: No.

Restrictions: No.

NH·28

Entomology Department Scientific Illustrator's Collection III *A.K.A.* George L. Venable Collection

Dates of Photographs: 1971–Present

Collection Origins

Scientific illustrator George L. Venable, who joined the department in 1971, assembled the collection from OPPS photographic reproductions of his scientific illustrations for security purposes.

Physical Description

There are 75 photographs including color dye coupler phototransparencies and slides (Ektachrome and Kodachrome) and silver gelatin photoprints.

Subjects

The photographs document George L. Venable's drawings and illustrations of entomological specimens, including carabid beetles and walking sticks.

Arranged: No.

Captioned: Some with OPPS negative number and subject.

Finding Aid: No.

Restrictions: No.

NH·29

Hemiptera and Hymenoptera Division Miscellaneous Photograph Collection *A.K.A.* Karl V. Krombein Photograph Collection

Dates of Photographs: 1912–Present

Collection Origins

Karl V. Krombein (1912–) created the collection around 1950 as a working file. Krombein, who received Ph.D.s from Cornell University in entomology (1960) and from Sri Lanka's University of Peradeniya in zoology (1980), served as an Entomologist with the USDA Bureau of Entomology and Plant Quarantine (1941–1965), and as Chairman and Senior Entomologist of the NMNH Department of Entomology (1965–). Photographers and studios represented include Bolling Air Force Base; Colorfax Lab; Atelier W. Fleischer; Karl V. Krombein; Lockheed Aircraft Corporation; Medical Photography Department, U.S. Naval Medical School, National Naval Medical Center; National Institutes of Health; Office Provincial de Publicité; OPPS; Walter Reed Army Institute of Research; and Keizo Yasumatsu.

Physical Description

There are 750 photographs including color dye coupler photoprints and slides, dye diffusion transfer photoprints (Polaroid), and silver gelatin photonegatives and photoprints. Some photographs are SEMs and TEMs.

Subjects

The photographs document bees and wasps; bee and wasp eggs and nests; and entomologists and their activities, colleagues, friends, and meetings. Bees and wasps shown include bald-faced hornets, carpenter bees, and yellow jackets.

Entomologists portrayed include James C. Crawford, Donald R. Davis, Jacot Guillarmod, Ashley B. Gurney, Y. Hirashima, George L. Hutton, T. Ishihara, Karl V. Krombein, J.D. Lattin, Astrid Loken,

John Martin, P. Oman, V.V. Popov, O.W. Richards, C.W. Sabrosky, Reece I. Sailer, Grace A. Sandhouse, H. K. Townes, W. W. Wirth, K. Yano, and K. Yasumatsu.

Activities and meetings documented include the Agriculture Short Course, University of Maryland, June 1963; Bureau of Yards and Docks Conference on Pest Control and Wood Preservation, October 22–25, 1956; Entomologists at Cosmos Club luncheon, Washington, D.C., 1970; Forest Products Lab, Madison, Wisconsin; Military Entomologists Conference, Walter Reed Institute of Research, October 23, 1961; Military Entomology Training Program, July–August 1963; and the U.S.-Japan Cooperative Science Program Seminar, Smithsonian Institution, Washington, D.C., December 4–8, 1967. There is also one sheet of contact photoprints of Japanese military officers and planes just before Japan's surrender at the end of World War II (1945).

Arranged: No.

Captioned: Many with date and subject.

Finding Aid: No.

Restrictions: No.

NH·30

Hemiptera and Hymenoptera Division SEM Collection *A.K.A.* Karl V. Krombein SEM Collection

Dates of Photographs: 1975–Present

Collection Origins

Karl V. Krombein created the collection for personal research on the behavior, bionomics, ecology, and systematics of wasps and to illustrate scientific publications. For a biography of Krombein see the *Collection Origins* field of *NH·29*.

Physical Description

There are 1,500 photographs including dye diffusion transfer photoprints and silver gelatin photonegatives and photoprints. Many of the photographs are SEM microphotographs.

Subjects

The photographs are scanning electron microscope (SEM) images at different magnifications of wasps and wasp body segments.

Arranged: No.

Captioned: With scanning electron microscope information, including magnification and scientist.

Finding Aid: No.

Restrictions: No.

NH·31

Lepidoptera Division Manuscript Photograph File

Dates of Photographs: 1960–Present

Collection Origins

Curator Donald R. Davis (1934–) created the collection for his research and publications on New World primitive moths. Davis, who received a Ph.D. in entomology from Cornell University in 1962, joined NMNH in 1964. Photographers represented include Victor Krantz and other OPPS staff. Many of the photographs are published in books and scientific journals, including the following: Donald Ray Davis. *The North American Moths of the Genera Phaeoses, Opogona, and Oinophilia.* Washington, D.C.: Smithsonian Institution Press, 1978.

Physical Description

There are 27,300 photographs including dye diffusion transfer photoprints and silver gelatin photonegatives and photoprints. Many are SEM and TEM images. Other materials include notes and scientific illustrations.

Subjects

The photographs are scanning electron microscope (SEM) or transmitting electron microscope (TEM) images, including cross-sections, pigment, and wing scales of New World primitive moths. Habitat locations documented include Ceylon (now Sri Lanka), North America, the Philippines, South America, and the West Indies.

Arranged: By type of image: 1) SEM or 2) TEM; then alphabetically by family, then by genus and species.

Captioned: Many with date, description, name, and sex. Notebooks with family and the specimen collecting project title (country or specific area). Envelopes in file drawers with specimen name and whether a SEM or a TEM.

Finding Aid: No.

Restrictions: Available only to NMNH staff.

NH·32

Lepidoptera Division Slide File

Dates of Photographs: 1963–Present

Collection Origins

Curator Donald R. Davis created the collection for lecture and research purposes. For a biography of Davis see the *Collection Origins* field of *NH·31*. Photographers and studios represented include S. Claflin; Donald R. Davis; Mignon Davis; Victor Krantz; OPPS staff; and Andree Robinson, Phoenix, Arizona.

Physical Description

There are 12,200 photographs including color dye coupler (Agfachrome, Ektachrome, and Kodachrome) slides and silver gelatin slides.

Subjects

The photographs document habitats and specimens of New World primitive moths. There are also some travel photographs of anthropological sites, botanical gardens, cities, memorials, and museums, as well as images documenting speleology—the study of the biological, geological, and physical aspects of caves.

Habitats illustrated include Africa, Asia, Caribbean islands, Chile, China, Cuba, the Philippines, Taiwan, the United States, and Venezuela. Specific locations in China shown include Beijing's Institute of Zoology, Beijing's Peking Man Site, Datong, Nanjing Botanical Garden, Quindao, and Shanghai. Taiwanese photographs show the Chang Memorial, Lan Yu (now Hung-t'ou-Hsu), and the National Palace Museum. Other locations illustrated include Dominica; Martinique, France; Kenya; Nigeria; South Africa; Sri Lanka; and Cerro de la Neblina, Venezuela. Caves shown are in the Dominican Republic; Runaway Bay, Jamaica; Kenya; South Africa; and Texas, Virginia, and West Virginia in the United States.

Arranged: By geographic location.

Captioned: Many with subject, such as geographic location and specimen name.

Finding Aid: No.

Restrictions: Open by appointment only to Smithsonian staff and scholarly researchers.

NH·33

Lepidoptera Division Static Research File

Dates of Photographs: Circa 1970–Present

Collection Origins

The Lepidoptera Division staff created the research collection in the early 1970s to contain record copies of photographs that have been published in scientific journals. Photographers represented include Jack Clark, Donald R. Davis, William Field, John B. Heppner, OPPS staff, and W.Y. Watson.

Physical Description

There are 20,720 photographs including color dye coupler phototransparencies and silver gelatin photonegatives and photoprints. Most of the photographs are SEM and TEM images.

Subjects

Most of the photographs are scanning or transmitting electron microscope (SEM or TEM) images of Lepidoptera, the order of insects which includes butterflies and moths. The photographs document Lepidoptera type specimens, some in photomicrographs. A type specimen is a specimen chosen by taxonomists as the basis for naming and describing a new species. The collection also includes portraits of eminent lepidopterists, including Gaston Allard, Jules Culot, Antoine Guillemot, François-Clement Lafaury, Emmanuel Martin, Frederic Moore, Charles Oberthur, P. Rambur, William Schaus, Max Standfuss, Comte Emilio Turati, Roger Verity, and Theodore Vige. Most of the portraits are photographic reproductions of book illustrations including drawings, engravings, and etchings.

Arranged: Alphabetically by taxonomic order.

Captioned: On envelopes with location, scientist's name, and specimen name. Some are labeled "Oberthur Plates."

Finding Aid: No.

Restrictions: No.

NH·34

Neuroptera and Diptera Division Biographical File of Dipterists

Dates of Photographs: 1895–Present

Collection Origins

The Department of Entomology staff created this periodically updated obituary file to document the careers of international dipterists, who study insects of the order Diptera, including true flies and two-winged flies. Photographers and studios represented include Olaf M. Braunner, H.P. Eggan, Evans, L. Knutson, the National Archives, OPPS staff, and Spencer. The photographs have been published in the following article: Alan Stone. "History of Nearctic Dipterology." In *Flies of the Nearctic Region,* Vol. 1, edited by Graham C.D. Griffiths. Stuttgart, West Germany: E. Schweizerbart'sche Verlagsbuchhandlund (Nagele u. Obermiller), 1980.

Physical Description

There are 20 photographs including albumen photoprints (some cartes-de-visite), platinum photoprints, and silver gelatin photoprints. Other materials include abstracts, correspondence, greeting cards, journals, newspaper clippings, obituaries, and xerographic copies.

Subjects

The photographs are individual and group portraits of eminent international dipterists and their colleagues. Dipterists portrayed include Charles P. Alexander, Charles F. Baker, Conde Amadeu Amidei Barbiellini, T. Becker, C.H. Curran, Carl J. Drake, Henry E. Ewing, G.B. Fairchild, Arthur B. Gahan, Hermann A. Hagen, Walther Horn, John R. Malloch, Zeno P. Metcalf, Ralph L. Parker, Charles R. Osten Sacken, Robert E. Snodgrass, Alan Stone, Charles H.T. Townsend, William M. Wheeler, and S.W. Williston. Groups portrayed include British Museum of Natural History entomologists, an International Entomological Congress in 1928, and Soviet entomologists in Budapest.

Arranged: Alphabetically by name.

Captioned: Some with date, image source, and name of individual or group portrayed.

Finding Aid: No.

Restrictions: No.

NH·35

Neuroptera and Diptera Division Research Collection *A.K.A.* F. Christian Thompson Research Collection

Dates of Photographs: 19th Century–Present

Collection Origins

Research entomologist F. Christian Thompson (1944–) created the collection to document his research in the systematics and zoogeography of Syrphidae (drone flies, flower flies, hoverflies, sunflies, and sweat flies) and related groups. Thompson, who received a Ph.D. from the University of Massachusetts in 1969, joined the USDA Systematic Entomology Laboratory in 1974. Photographers and studios represented include the British Museum of Natural History, Metropolitan Museum of Art, OPPS staff, Ross, Curtis Sabrosky, Rudolf Schmidt, and Visual Media Corporation.

Physical Description

There are 850 photographs including color dye coupler slides (Kodachrome); dye diffusion transfer photoprints (Polaroid); and silver gelatin photonegatives, photoprints, and slides. Some of the photoprints are SEMs. Other materials include items used in slide presentations, such as artwork, computers, and screens.

Subjects

The photographs show entomologists and their surroundings, particularly entomologists in the British Museum and in Budapest, as well as a group portrait of Department of Entomology dipterists. There are also photographs of insect specimens, particularly type specimens of various flies, and tools. Type specimens are chosen by scientists as the basis for describing and naming a new species.

Arranged: In lecture presentation sequence.

Captioned: A few with location, photographer, and specimen name.

Finding Aid: No.

Restrictions: By appointment only.

NH·36

Neuroptera and Diptera Division Wasps Publication Collection

Dates of Photographs: 1954–1967

Collection Origins

Karl V. Krombein created the collection for his book: *Trap-Nesting Wasps and Bees: Life Histories, Nests, and Associates.* Washington, D.C.: Smithsonian Press, 1967. For a biography of Krombein see the *Collection Origins* field of *NH·29*. Photographers represented include Karl V. Krombein and OPPS staff.

Physical Description

There are 725 photographs including silver gelatin photonegatives and photoprints.

Subjects

The photographs document bee and wasp nest development and the trap-nesting techniques of solitary bees and wasps. Activities illustrated include nesting behavior, pupal development, and wasps' trap-building procedures, boring procedures, and trapping techniques. Habitats shown include Portal, Arizona; Florida; and Arlington, Virginia.

Arranged: No.

Captioned: Some photoprints with subject; most photonegatives with subject on the sleeves.

Finding Aid: No.

Restrictions: No.

NH

Department of Invertebrate Zoology

Department of Invertebrate Zoology
National Museum of Natural History
Smithsonian Institution
Washington, D.C. 20560
(202) 357-2030
Hours: Monday–Friday, 10 a.m.–4 p.m.

Scope of the Collections

There are 12 photographic collections with approximately 55,400 images.

Focus of the Collections

The collections document the activities, holdings, and staff of the Department of Invertebrate Zoology and its four divisions: Crustacea, Echinoderms, Mollusks, and Worms. There are images of fossil and modern marine invertebrates (animals lacking a spinal column or backbone). Many specimens shown are type specimens, which are used by taxonomists as a basis for naming and describing new species. There are also individual and group portraits of carcinologists (specialists who study crustaceans), malacologists (specialists who study mollusks), and other scientists.

Photographic Processes and Formats Represented

There are albumen photoprints; color dye coupler photonegatives, photoprints, phototransparencies, and slides; cyanotypes; dye diffusion transfer photoprints (many are SEMs); silver gelatin dry plate lantern slides and photonegatives; and silver gelatin photonegatives, photoprints, phototransparencies, and slides. Some photographs are in albums.

Other Materials Represented

The department also contains card indexes of species information, data sheets, etchings, literature, lists of species, maps (including collection site maps), microscope slide mounts, notebooks of species information, oil paintings, publications, reprints, specimens, and watercolors.

Access and Usage Policies

These collections are open to scholarly researchers by appointment. Interested researchers should write to the department and describe their research topic, the type of material that interests them, and their research aim.

Publication Policies

Researchers must obtain permission from the Smithsonian Institution to reproduce a photograph and may also have to obtain permission from the copyright holder, which is not necessarily the Smithsonian Institution. The preferred credit line is "Courtesy of the Department of Invertebrate Zoology, National Museum of Natural History, Smithsonian Institution."

NH·37

Crustacea Division Carcinologists' Portrait File *A.K.A.* Rogues' Gallery

Dates of Photographs: 1903–Present

Collection Origins

Waldo L. Schmitt (1887–1977) assembled this collection from newspaper obituaries and journals in the 1920s to document international carcinologists—scientists who study crustaceans such as barnacles, crabs, lobsters, and shrimp. Schmitt, who received a Ph.D. in zoology from George Washington University in 1922, worked as an aide for the U.S. Department of Agriculture from 1907 to 1910. Schmitt was associated with NMNH (1910–1977) as a Science Assistant on the U.S. Bureau of Fisheries steamer *Albatross* (1910–1913), Naturalist (1913–1914), Assistant Curator (1914–1920), Curator (1920–1943), Head Curator in Biology (1943–1947), Head Curator in Zoology (1947–1957), and Honorary Resident Associate in Zoology (1957–1977).

The collection was moved to NMNH's West Wing in 1963. Three years later Museum Specialist Colby A. Child took over the collection's upkeep, a responsibility that was transferred to Museum Specialist Patricia Nutter in 1988. Nutter arranged to have the portraits hung in the Department of Invertebrate Zoology in NMNH's West Wing. Photographers and studios represented include M.D. Burkenroad and OPPS staff.

Physical Description

There are 130 silver gelatin photoprints.

Subjects

The photographs portray scientists, primarily non-Smithsonian carcinologists, many from countries other than the U.S. Some images are photographic reproductions of drawings, engravings, etchings, and paintings. Scientists portrayed include Alfred W. Alcock, Heinrich Balss, Keppel H. Barnard, Carlos Berg, Edward A. Birre, C. Bocquet, Hilbrandt Borchma, L. Alexander Borradaile, George S. Brady, William T. Calman, Fenner A. Chace, Jr., B.F. Chapgar, Edouard Chevreux, Charles Chilton, Robert E. Coker, Edwin P. Creaser, Georges Cuvier, James D. Dana, Hugh H. Darby, Charles Darwin, J. Deguerne, W. De Haan, Jean-Baptise de Lamarck, Antonio Della Valle, Johannes G. De Man, Henri De Saussure, A.G. Desnarest, Franz Doflein, R.P. Dollfus, J. Eights, Calvin D. Esterly, Louis Fage, George P. Farran, Walter Faxon, Henry W. Fowler, Norma C. Furtos, Lewis Gibbes, Theodore N. Gill, Steve A. Glassell, Isabella Gordon, Charles-Joseph Gravier, Robert Gurney, Hermann A. Hagen, Hans J. Hansen, Josephine F.L. Hart, William A. Haswell, Oliver P. Hay, William P. Hay, Joel W. Hedgpeth, Janus A. Herklots, Horton H. Hobbs, Jr., Samuel J. Holmes, L.B. Holthuis, A.G. Humes, Martin W. Johnson, Chancey Juday, S.L. Karaman, S. Kemp, Friedrich Kiefer, K. Kishinouye, P.A. Latreille, Marie V. Lebour, Chanan Lewisohn, W. Lilljeborg, Carolus Linnaeus, William N. Lockington, Herman Luederwaldt, E. Marcus, C. Dwight Marsh, Frederik V.A. Meinert, Alphonse Milne-Edwards, Theodore Monod, Carlos Moreira, John Murdock, C. Naiynetr, Alfreda B. Needler, Canon Alfred M. Norman, Theodor Odhner, Bruno Parisi, Arthur S. Pearse, Robert W. Pennak, Otto Pesta, Georg J. Pfeffer, Rudolfo Philippi, N.K. Pillai, Carlos E. Porter, Emile G. Racovitza, Constantine S. Rafinesque, Mary Jane Rathbun, Richard Rathbun, R. Rhoades, Jean Roux, F. Russell, T. Sakai, Georg O. Sars, Thomas Say, Adolf Schellenberg, Waldo L. Schmitt, Thomas Scott, R. Serene, S.M. Shiino, Clarence R. Shoemaker, Sidney I. Smith, Thomas R.R. Stebbing, Knud H. Stephensen, Belle A. Stevens, J.H. Stock, Olive S. Tattersall, Walter M. Tattersall, George M. Thomson, Willard G. Van Name, Victor Van Straelen, Karl W. Verhoeff, Addison E. Verrill, Alejandro Villalobos-Figueroa, Jean Paul Visscher, Nils Von Hofstein, Charles B. Wilson, Richard Woltereck, and Carl W.E. Zimmer.

Arranged: Hung on the wall in NMNH's West Wing in the order they were received.

Captioned: With the name of the subject; some also with birth and death dates.

Finding Aid: Self-indexing duplicate negative file arranged alphabetically by subject's name.

Restrictions: No.

NH·38

Crustacea Division Crayfish Slide Collection *A.K.A.* Horton H. Hobbs, Jr., Slide Collection

Dates of Photographs: 1962–1985

Collection Origins

NMNH Zoologist Emeritus Horton H. Hobbs, Jr. (1914–) created the collection for research purposes. After receiving a Ph.D. in biology in 1940 from the University of Florida, Hobbs taught there until 1946. For the next 16 years, Hobbs taught at the University of Virginia, and then served as Director of the Mountain Lake Biological Station (1956–1960). In 1962 Hobbs joined the NMNH, where he served first as Head Curator for two years and then as Senior Zoologist (1964–). Hobbs studies crayfish in the southeastern United States, relying on photography to record their color patterns in different habitats. Hobbs, who has named more than 100 different crayfish species, has donated his collections to the Smithsonian, where they are maintained. Numerous papers by Hobbs containing line drawings based on these slides were published by the Biological Society of Washington, the Environmental Protection Agency, the Smithsonian Institution Press, and the University of Florida.

Physical Description

There are 1,730 color dye coupler slides.

Subjects

The slides depict crayfish found in the southeastern United States, including Alabama, Florida, and Georgia.

Arranged: Chronologically.

Captioned: With county and state, field number, genus and species, museum catalog specimen number, sex, and slide number.

Finding Aid: Card catalog tab-indexed by genus and filed by species, listing catalog number, county, field number, sex, slide number, and state.

Restrictions: No.

NH·39

Crustacea Division Research Collection *A.K.A.* Brian F. Kensley Research Collection

Dates of Photographs: 1970s–Present

Collection Origins

Brian F. Kensley created the private research collection, which documents the fields of invertebrate zoology and paleobiology. Kensley, who received a Ph.D. and D.Sc. from the University of Cape Town, South Africa, joined the NMNH in 1978 and specializes in crustacean systematics and tropical marine ecology.

Photographers represented include Mike Carpenter, Brian F. Kensley, Tony Rath, Marilyn J. Schotte, and Robert H. Sims. The photographs have been published in the following series: 1) Brian Frederick Kensley. *The Atlantic Barrier Reef Ecosystem at Carrie Bow Cay, Belize, III.* Smithsonian Contributions to the Marine Sciences, no. 24. Washington, D.C.: Smithsonian Institution Press, 1984. 2) Brian Frederick Kensley. *Deep-Water Atlantic Anthuridea.* Smithsonian Contributions to Zoology, no. 346. Washington, D.C.: Smithsonian Institution Press, 1982. 3) Brian Frederick Kensley and John Pether. *Late Tertiary and Early Quaternary Fossil Mollusca of the Hondeklip Area, Cape Province, South Africa.* Annals of the South African Museum, vol. 97, pt. 6. Cape Town: South African Museum, 1986. 4) Brian Frederick Kensley. *New Records of Bresiliid Shrimp From Australia, South Africa, Caribbean, and Gulf of Mexico.* Smithsonian Contributions to Zoology, no. 394. Washington, D.C.: Smithsonian Institution Press, 1983. 5) Brian Frederick Kensley. *On the Zoogeography of Southern African Decapod Crustacea.* Smithsonian Contributions to Zoology, no. 338. Washington, D.C.: Smithsonian Institution Press,

1981. 6) Brian Frederick Kensley and Ilse Walker. *Palaemonid Shrimps From the Amazon Basin, Brazil.* Smithsonian Contributions to Zoology, no. 362. Washington, D.C.: Smithsonian Institution Press, 1982.

Physical Description

There are 2,000 photographs including color dye coupler slides and silver gelatin photonegatives and photoprints. Many images are SEMs.

Subjects

The photographs illustrate fossil mollusks and specimens of the Decapoda order of crustaceans, such as crabs, crayfish, lobsters, and shrimp. Many images are scanning electron microscope (SEM) close-ups of crustaceans. The photographs document specimen color patterns, geological settings, habitat details, and nearby landscapes and seascapes including coral reefs and mangrove swamps. There are also a few informal portraits of Kensley's colleagues. Fieldwork research sites shown include Australia, Belize, Bermuda, Brazil, the Caribbean Islands, the Seychelles (Aldabra Island), South Africa, and the United States (Florida Keys).

Arranged: In two series by subject. 1) Decapoda. 2) Fossil Mollusks. Then by type of material: a) loose prints, b) SEM negatives and Polaroid prints, and c) slides. Finally, by taxonomic order.

Captioned: No.

Finding Aid: 1) Card catalog arranged by taxonomic groupings with accession, catalog, and specimen numbers for each lot. 2) Online database with associated fauna, expedition, habitat, and other data.

Restrictions: Portions of the collection are restricted private research materials. Write the departmental staff for further information.

NH·40

Echinoderms Division SEM Octocoral File

Dates of Photographs: 1971–Present

Collection Origins

NMNH Curator Frederick M. Bayer (1921–) assembled the collection for his personal taxonomic research on octocorals, which are sedentary colonial corals. Bayer, who earned a Ph.D. in zoology from George Washington University in 1958, was Assistant Director of the Florida State Museum (1942–1946), Assistant at the Marine Laboratory, University of Miami (1946–1947), Assistant and Associate Curator at USNM (1947–1961), Associate Professor and Professor at the Rosenstiel School of Marine and Atmospheric Science of the University of Miami (1962–1975), and Visiting Curator (1971) and Curator at NMNH (1975–). The photographs were used in the exhibition "Exploring Microspace" (1984) and appeared in the following publications: 1) Frederick M. Bayer and Harding Boehme Owre. *Free-Living Lower Invertebrates.* New York: Macmillan, 1968. 2) Frederick M. Bayer, Manfred Grasshoff, and Jakob Verseveldt, eds. *Illustrated Trilingual Glossary of Morphological and Anatomical Terms Applied to Octocorallia.* Leiden: E.J. Brill/Dr. W. Backhuys, 1983. 3) Frederick M. Bayer. *The Shallow-Water Octocorallia of the West Indian Region: A Manual for Marine Biologists.* The Hague: M. Nijhoff, 1961.

Physical Description

There are 20,000 silver gelatin photonegatives and photoprints (Polaroid) in SEM format.

Subjects

The photographs illustrate the characteristics and skeletal microstructures of octocoral specimens primarily from NMNH collections as seen through a scanning electron microscope. Octocorals include flexible corals, sea fans, sea pens, and soft corals.

Arranged: In chronological order.

Captioned: Micrographs of individual specimens are numbered in sequence as prepared for examination. The numbers correspond to complete specimen data in the department's records.

Finding Aid: 1) Alphabetical index and computer file arranged by species. 2) Document file in chronological order.

Restrictions: No.

NH·41

Mollusks Division Cyanotype Collection

Dates of Photographs: 1907

Collection Origins

Paul Bartsch (1871–1960) created the collection to document the taxonomic features of live mollusk specimens and mounted mollusk shells. Bartsch, who received a Ph.D. in 1905 from Iowa State University, served in the NMNH Division of Mollusks for approximately 50 years, working as an aide (1896–1905), Assistant Curator (1905–1914), and Curator (1920–1960), as well as serving as Curator in the Division of Marine Invertebrates. Bartsch was also Professor of Zoology at George Washington University (1899–1939) and Director of the Histology Laboratory and lecturer at Howard University Medical School (1901–1930). In 1907 Bartsch represented the Smithsonian Institution on the Philippine expedition aboard the U.S. Bureau of Fisheries steamer *Albatross*. This collection consists of photographs taken on this expedition and later published in various books on Filipino freshwater mollusks, shipworms, and West Indian land snails, including the following: Paul Bartsch. *Giant Species of the Molluscan Genus Lima Obtained in Philippine and Adjacent Waters*. Scientific Results of the Philippine Cruise of the Fisheries Steamer *Albatross*, 1907–1910, no. 26. Washington, D.C.: Smithsonian Institution Press, 1913.

Physical Description

There are 150 cyanotypes in two clothbound albums.

Subjects

Photographs show mollusks, invertebrates belonging to the phylum Mollusca, which includes chitons, cuttlefish, clams, nautiloids, octopus, slugs, snails, and squid. There are images of live mollusk specimens, mollusk shells, and published mollusk illustrations, as well as a few images of mollusk exhibit models.

Arranged: No.

Captioned: With negative number. A few with subject.

Finding Aid: No.

Restrictions: No.

NH·42

Mollusks Division Malacologist Portrait File

Dates of Photographs: 1904–Present

Collection Origins

The Mollusks Division staff began assembling the collection during the 1881 to 1927 tenure of honorary curator William Healey Dall to document eminent malacologists active from 1866 to the present. Dall (1845–1927) was a naturalist whose work included anthropology, malacology, paleontology, and zoology. He served as a naturalist on the Western Union Telegraph Expedition to Alaska in 1865 and in 1866 became its scientific director. Dall studied the Aleutian Islands and Cenozoic mollusks first while working for the U.S. Coastal Survey and the Coastal and Geodetic Survey and later as a Paleontologist for the U.S. Geological Survey.

Physical Description

There are 2,500 photographs including color dye coupler photoprints and silver gelatin photonegatives and photoprints.

Subjects

The photographs portray famous malacologists and their colleagues, both individually and in groups, including R. Tucker Abbott, H.B. Baker, Paul Bartsch, J. Hughes Bennett, Pedro Bermudez, S.S. Berry, Thomas E. Bowman, Philip Carpenter, M. Champion, John Cleland, William J. Clench, Timothy A. Conrad, Joseph P. Couthouy, Hugh Cuming, William Healey Dall, William K. Emerson, Carl Gegenbaur, Theodore N. Gill, George Robert Gray, P. Harting, C. Hedley, C. Helly, H. Hemphill, John B. Henderson, Jr., Y. Hirase, John Jay, A. Mayor, W. Newcomb, A. Olssem, Charles R. Orcutt, Richard Owen, Juan Parodiz, Charles T. Ramsden, Harald A. Rehder, Thomas San, Hans Schlesch, Anton Schneider, Charles T. Simpson, Edgar A. Smith, Robert E.C. Stearns, Leonhard Stejneger, Ruth Turner, W. Vrolik, August Weismann, Jeffries Wyman, James Zetch, and A. Zilsch. There are group portraits of the American Malacological Union (1966 and 1983), the NMNH Department of Zoology (1949), and the Pacific Science Congress (1966).

Arranged: Alphabetically by name.

Captioned: With the subject's name; some also with birth and death dates.

Finding Aid: No.

Restrictions: No.

NH·43

Mollusks Division Publication Collection

Dates of Photographs: 1916–Present

Collection Origins

The Mollusks Division staff created the collection during the 1881 to 1927 tenure of honorary curator William Healey Dall for publication purposes. For a biography of Dall see the *Collection Origins* field of *NH·42*. The photographs appear as figures, frontispieces, and plates in published articles, books, journals, and manuscripts generated by the NMNH Mollusks Division staff. Photographers and studios represented include T. Tucker Abbott, Paul Bartsch, Richard S. Houbrick, King Photo, and Joseph Rosewater.

Physical Description

There are 5,900 silver gelatin photoprints.

Subjects

Ninety-five percent of the photographs show mollusks, invertebrates belonging to the phylum Mollusca, which includes chitons, cuttlefish, clams, nautiloids, octopus, slugs, snails, and squid. There are photographs of freshwater and marine bivalves, land gastropods, loricates, marine gastropods, and mollusks from Ecuador and the Indopacific. There are also a few group portraits of the American Malacological Union.

Arranged: By subject.

Captioned: Half with subject.

Finding Aid: No.

Restrictions: No.

NH·44

Mollusks Division Slide Collection

Dates of Photographs: 20th Century

Collection Origins

The Mollusks Division staff created the research collection to document mollusk specimens worldwide. Photographers and studios represented include A/V Educational Products, D. Beach, T. Bratcher, D.M. Byrne, China Color Laboratories, D.A. Cobb, Neville Coleman, Treat Davidson, Bert Draper, Antonio J. Ferreira, Leiden Museum (Netherlands), G.M. Moore, OPPS, R. Poorman, Harald A. Rehder, Gordon A. Robilliard, Joseph Rosewater, Klaus Ruetzler, P.W. Signor, Allyn G. Smith, Tom E. Thompson, and R.G. Tuck, Jr.

Physical Description

There are 1,050 photographs including color dye coupler slides and silver gelatin photonegatives and phototransparencies (SEMs).

Subjects

The photographs document mollusk specimens, some as seen through a scanning electron microscope. There are images of holotype specimens from the phylum Mollusca, including chitons, clams, cuttlefish, nautiloids, octopus, slugs, snails, and squid. A holotype is the single specimen used as the basis of the original published description of a taxonomic species and later designated a type specimen. Specimens illustrated are from Australia, Belize, the Indian Ocean, the Philippines, and the United States (California, Hawaii, Massachusetts, and New Hampshire). The slides portray Mollusks Division staff and associates, including naturalist William Healey Dall, Alison Kay (at Congress), Alan Kohn, C.J. Maynard, and Joseph Rosewater. There are also photographic reproductions of species distribution charts.

Arranged: Alphabetically by family, then by genus and species.

Captioned: Each slide's cardboard mount with creator, date (if known), frame number, genus, museum number, negative number, row number, slide number, species, and type. SEM negatives with magnification number, museum number, and specimen.

Finding Aid: Card catalog, arranged alphabetically by family and then by genus and species, lists the frame, row, and slide numbers, and the type of process (35mm).

Restrictions: Some images are copyrighted and may not be reproduced. Contact the department staff for more information.

NH·45

Mollusks Division Specimen File

Dates of Photographs: 1890s–Present

Collection Origins

The Mollusks Division staff assembled this collection to document mollusks—particularly mollusk type specimens in NMNH collections—for research and taxonomic documentation purposes. Photographers and studios represented include Acme Newspictures, Inc., New York City; V.R. Boswell, Jr.; NMNH staff; and C.A. Weaver.

Physical Description

There are 13,350 photographs including albumen photoprints; color dye coupler photoprints and phototransparencies; silver gelatin dry plate lantern slides and photonegatives; and silver gelatin photonegatives and photoprints (some SEMs). Other materials include etchings, maps, oil paintings, reprints, and watercolors.

Subjects

The photographs document mollusk specimens and line drawings of mollusks. Mollusks are members of the phylum Mollusca, which includes chitons, clams, cuttlefish, nautiloids, octopus, slugs, snails, and squid. Many specimens shown are holotypes, which are single specimens used as the basis of the original published description of a taxonomic species and later designated a type specimen. Other specimens illustrated include fossils in the Colorado Desert, giant squid, and pearls. There are also images of the Smithsonian Institution Arts and Industries Building exhibition halls; maps of the Bahamas, Cuba, Fiji, and Hawaii; and pearl ornamentation.

Arranged: Alphabetically by family, then by genus and species.

Captioned: Most with genus and species names. Holotype specimens also with location and the USNM number.

Finding Aid: Card file with an alphabetical list of specimens by genus and species.

Restrictions: No.

NH·46

Worms Division Marine Nematode Photoprint and Photonegative Collection

Dates of Photographs: 1965–Present

Collection Origins

NMNH Curator W. Duane Hope (1935–) created the collection for personal research purposes. Hope, who received a Ph.D. in nematology from the University of California at Davis (1965), has worked at the NMNH as an Associate Curator (1964–1972), Curator (1972–1976, 1981–), and Department Chairman of Invertebrate Zoology (1976–1981). Hope conducts comparative and functional anatomical studies of marine nematodes, identifies nematodes, names and describes new nematode species, and studies evolutionary relationships of nematodes.

The photographs appear in the following publications: 1) A.C. Giese and John S. Pearse, eds. *Reproduction of Marine Invertebrates.* New York: Academic Press, 1974. 2) W. Duane Hope. *Structure of Head and Stoma in the Marine Nematode Genus Deontostoma.* Smithsonian Contributions to Zoology, no. 353. Washington, D.C.: Smithsonian Institution Press, 1982.

Physical Description

There are 1,450 photographs including color dye coupler slides and silver gelatin photonegatives, photoprints, and slides. Other materials include card indexes on nematode taxonomy, data sheets, maps of collection sites, notebooks of species descriptions arranged taxonomically, and publications on marine nematodes.

Subjects

The photographs document marine nematodes specimens, which are worms of the phylum Nematoda that have unsegmented thread-like bodies. Images show cross-sections of specimens' buccal cavity internal ridges, gland duct openings, muscles, nerve cells, and other anatomical features.

Arranged: No.

Captioned: Mounted on notebook pages with ASA number, date, file number, film speed and type, illumination, magnification, object dark/light ratio, objective, roll number, and subject.

Finding Aid: No.

Restrictions: No.

NH·47

Worms Division Marine Nematode SEM and TEM Collection

Dates of Photographs: 1964–Present

Collection Origins

Curator W. Duane Hope and NMNH scanning electron microscope (SEM) technicians created the collection for use in embryonic and genetic research. For a biography of Hope see the *Collection Origins* field of *NH·46*. These photomicrographs were taken under very high levels of magnification, using light microscopes for serial sections of whole mounted specimens; scanning electron microscopes (SEM) for surface studies; and transmitting electron microscopes (TEM) for studies of internal cross-sections.

The photographs have been published in many journals, including the following: 1) National Research Council of Canada. *Journal Canadien de Zoologie (Canadian Journal of Zoology).* Ottawa: National Research Council of Canada. 2) Society of

Nematologists. *Journal of Nematology.* Athens, Georgia: Society of Nematologists. 3) Biological Society of Washington. *Proceedings of the Biological Society of Washington.* Washington, D.C.: Biological Society of Washington. 4) Helminthological Society of Washington. *Proceedings of the Helminthological Society of Washington.* Washington, D.C.: The Society. 5) W. Duane Hope. *Structure of Head and Stoma in the Marine Nematode Genus Deontostoma.* Smithsonian Contributions to Zoology, no. 353. Washington, D.C.: Smithsonian Institution Press, 1982. 6) American Microscopical Society. *Transactions of the American Microscopical Society.* Lawrence, Kansas: American Microscopical Society.

Physical Description

There are 6,300 photographs including silver gelatin photonegatives, photoprints, and slides. The images are photomicrographs, highly magnified images taken using the aid of scanning electron microscopes (SEM), transmitting electron microscopes (TEM), and standard light microscopes.

Subjects

The photomicrographs show cross-sections, serial-sections, and the surface of nonparasitic marine nematodes, a phylum of free-living worms that have unsegmented thread-like bodies. The photographs document both type and non-type nematode specimens, many of which are mounted on slides. There are also some photographic reproductions of drawings of nematodes.

Arranged: In three series. 1) SEM series, alphabetically by genus and species. 2) Slides, unarranged. 3) TEM series, numerically by a five-digit number.

Captioned: With date, magnification, and name.

Finding Aid: 1) SEM log with magnification, name, sex, specimen number, and view. 2) TEM log with block number, date, grid number, location, magazine number, name, negative number, and section number. Later entries also include box and frame numbers.

Restrictions: No.

NH·48

Worms Division Marine Nematode Slide Collection

Dates of Photographs: 1965–Present

Collection Origins

Curator W. Duane Hope assembled the collection to assist him in identifying nematode species and in demonstrating their anatomical features for lectures and publications. For a biography of Hope see the *Collection Origins* field of *NH·46*. For a full list of publications in which these images have appeared see the *Collection Origins* field of *NH·47*. Photographers represented include NMNH and OPPS staff.

Physical Description

There are 800 color dye coupler slides, most of which were taken with light microscopes, scanning electron microscopes (SEM), or transmitting electron microscopes (TEM) at high magnifications. Other materials include a card index with references to every marine nematode species mentioned in the literature; microscope slide mounts of marine nematodes; notebooks with descriptions of the taxonomy of marine nematode species; and publications pertaining to the ecology, morphology, and systematics of marine nematodes.

Subjects

The photomicrographs are highly magnified views of marine nematodes, a phylum of free-living worms that have unsegmented thread-like bodies. There are photomicrographs, including SEMs and TEMs, of nematode morphological features, including the amphids, body wall muscles, buccal area, cuticle, digestive system, head, reproductive system, and sensory receptors in muscles.

Arranged: Alphabetically by species.

Captioned: Some with subject.

Finding Aid: No.

Restrictions: No.

NH

Department of Mineral Sciences

Department of Mineral Sciences
National Museum of Natural History
Smithsonian Institution
Washington, D.C. 20560
(202) 357-2060
Hours: Monday–Friday, 10 a.m.–4 p.m.

Scope of the Collections

There are eight photographic collections with approximately 42,500 images.

Focus of the Collections

The photographs document the specimen collections, equipment, research, and staff of the Department of Mineral Sciences. The department is composed of four divisions (Meteorites, Mineralogy, Petrology and Volcanology) and the Physical Sciences Laboratory. It also includes the Global Volcanism Program and the Scientific Event Alert Network, which do not have photographic collections described in this *Guide*. There are photographs of gems and jewelry, lunar materials, meteorite impact sites, meteorites (iron, stony, or stony-iron), and minerals and rocks. Photographs also document carved minerals, exhibit halls, laboratory equipment, mineral cross-sections and thin-sections (photomicrographs), mineral quarries, and staff members and other mineralogists.

Photographic Processes and Formats Represented

There are albumen photoprints; color dye coupler photonegatives, photoprints, and slides; dye diffusion transfer photonegatives and photoprints (SEMs); and silver gelatin photonegatives, photoprints, and slides.

Other Materials Represented

This department also contains clippings, correspondence, geological charts, maps, microscope sample slides, notebooks, photomechanical reproductions, press releases, and specimens.

Access and Usage Policies

These collections are open to scholarly researchers by appointment. Interested researchers should write to the division and describe their research topic, the type of material that interests them, and their research objective.

Publication Policies

In addition to obtaining permission from the Smithsonian Institution to reproduce a photograph, researchers may have to obtain permission from the copyright holder, which is not necessariy the Smithsonian Institution. The preferred credit line is "Courtesy of the Department of Mineral Sciences, National Museum of Natural History, Smithsonian Institution."

NH·49

Meteorite Division Photograph Collection I *A.K.A.* Kurt A.I. Fredriksson Photograph Collection

Dates of Photographs: 1960–Present

Collection Origins

Kurt A.I. Fredriksson (1926–) created the collection to document his research on lunar rocks from the *Apollo* missions, meteorite impact sites, and stony meteorites. Fredriksson, a geochemist and Supervisor of the Division of Meteorites, received a Ph.D. in geology and mineralogy from the University of Stockholm in 1957. Before joining the Smithsonian in 1964, Fredriksson was employed at Hagconsult Inc. in Sweden (1946–1952), the University of Gothenburg (1953–1955), the University of Stockholm (1955–1957), the Geological Survey of Sweden (1958–1960), and the University of California at San Diego (1960–1964). Many of these photographs were published in scientific books and journals by Fredriksson and his colleagues. Photographers represented include R. Beauchamp, Victor Krantz, and Sparkletone Photo Service.

Physical Description

There are 2,000 photographs including color dye coupler slides, dye diffusion transfer photoprints, and silver gelatin photonegatives and photoprints. A large part of the collection is composed of photomicrographs.

Subjects

These photographs document various types of meteorites including iron, stony (achondrite and chondrite), and stony-iron. There are photographs of ordinary chondrites and C-chondrites, especially those in ultra-thin-sections. Specific achondrite meteorites photographed include Aubrites, Diogenites, Eucrites, and Howardites. Stony-iron meteorites illustrated include Lodranite, Mesosiderite, and Pallasite. Lunar rock samples from the Apollo missions and meteorite impact sites are also documented. In addition, there are photographs of stony building materials and of "Vitrified Forts" in France and Scotland.

Arranged: In three series. 1) Photonegatives and photoprints, alphabetically by meteorite name. 2) Color slides, numerically by serial number. 3) Photomicrographs, by *Apollo* mission number.

Captioned: With date, description, meteorite name, and serial number.

Finding Aid: To the color slides, in three parts. 1) Slides—Key Words, alphabetically. 2) Slides—Key Word Glossary, alphabetically. 3) Slides, by reprint author or meteorite name and numerically by serial number.

Restrictions: No.

NH·50

Meteorite Division Photograph Collection II

Dates of Photographs: 1930s–Present

Collection Origins

The Division of Meteorites staff created the collection for scholarly publication and research purposes. The photographs document meteorites in the division's and other institutions' collections. Photographers represented include Victor Krantz, Stuart H. Perry, and Jack Scott. Some of the photoprints appear in the following publication: Stuart H. Perry. *Photo Micrographs of Meteoric Iron.* 9 vols. Adrian, Michigan: n.p., 1933–1942.

Physical Description

There are 13,000 photographs including color dye coupler slides, and silver gelatin photonegatives and photoprints. A portion of the collection is composed of photomicrographs.

Subjects

The photographs document meteorites and meteorite cross-sections from the Smithsonian and several other institutions.

Arranged: In four series, by type of material. 1) Photoprints, alphabetically by meteorite name. In two sequences: a) original prints in 25 boxes, and b) copy prints in 27 boxes. 2) Photonegatives, chronologically by division negative number, then by meteorite name and location. 3) Slides, alphabetically by meteorite name. 4) Photoprints, by type of meteorite and number, mounted in nine published volumes.

Captioned: Approximately 40 percent with meteorite name, OPPS or division negative number, and type of meteorite.

Finding Aid: A photographer's log book (index) to Series 2, arranged by negative number, lists meteorite name, number, and size.

Restrictions: Available only by appointment. Write the divisional staff at least two weeks in advance.

NH·51

Meteorite Division Polished Thin-Sections Photograph Collection

Dates of Photographs: 1985–Present

Collection Origins

Glenn J. MacPherson, Associate Curator of Meteorites, created this collection to document microscope polished thin-sections of stone meteorites in the Smithsonian specimen collection. MacPherson, who received a Ph.D. from Princeton University in 1981, joined NMNH in 1984. Theresa McGervey, an intern in the division during 1985, photographed a significant part of the collection.

Physical Description

There are 1,500 photographs including dye diffusion transfer photoprints and silver gelatin photonegatives and photoprints.

Subjects

The photographs are of polished microscope thin-sections of stony meteorites in the Smithsonian Institution specimen collection.

Arranged: Alphabetically by meteorite name and then numerically by specimen number.

Captioned: No.

Finding Aid: A catalog of the meteorite specimens, arranged chronologically; with specimen number, weight, time and date acquired, origin, and loan/transaction requests.

Restrictions: No access.

NH·52

Mineralogy Division Archival Photograph Collection *A.K.A.* John White Photograph Collection

Dates of Photographs: 1983–Present

Collection Origins

Smithsonian volunteer Martha Hartelberg created the collection to document gems in the mineralogy collections of NMNH. John White is the curator currently responsible for the collection.

Physical Description

There are 1,400 color dye coupler slides.

Subjects

These photographs are a record of gems in the Mineral Sciences Division specimen collections.

Arranged: By catalog number, color coded by type of mineral.

Captioned: No.

Finding Aid: 1) Card catalog. 2) Computer file.

Restrictions: No access.

NH·53

Mineralogy Division Gems, Minerals, and Jewelry Photograph Collection

Dates of Photographs: 1960s–Present

Collection Origins

The Division of Mineralogy staff assembled the collection to document gems, minerals, and other materials in the Smithsonian Institution, other museum, and private collections. Photographers and studios represented include Dan Behnke, Lee Bolton, Chip Clark, Victor Krantz, OPPS, Dane A. Penland, Jan Pett, Tiffany & Company, and Wendell Wilson. A slide set, "Gems of the Smithsonian," incorporates some of these images. It is available for purchase from OPPS, Smithsonian Institution, NMAH, CB054, Washington, D.C. 20560. Telephone: (202) 357-1933. The photographs appear in the following publications by Paul E. Desautels: 1) *Gems in the Smithsonian Institution*. Washington, D.C.: Smithsonian Press, 1965. 2) *Rocks and Minerals*. New York: Grosset and Dunlap, 1974. 3) *Treasures in the Smithsonian: The Gem Collection*. Washington, D.C.: Smithsonian Institution Press, 1979.

Physical Description

There are 20,750 photographs including albumen photoprints, color dye coupler phototransparencies and slides, and silver gelatin photoprints. There are copy, duplicate, and original photographs. Other materials include microscope sample slides and a photomechanical (Woodburytype) made from an albumen stereograph.

Subjects

The photographs document gems, minerals, and rocks from private, Smithsonian Institution, and other museum collections. Art pieces, carvings, and jewelry made from gems, minerals and rocks are also illustrated. Minerals shown include native elements, such as copper, gold, graphite, iron, platinum, and silver. Gems illustrated include beryl, diamond, garnet, jadeite, opal, peridot, spinel, spodumene, topaz, tourmaline, turquoise, and zircon. Other minerals and rocks photographed include actinolite, andradite, asbestos, azurite, barite, beryl, calcite, columbite, cryolite, epidote, fluorite, franklinite, gypsum, halite, hematite, limestone, malachite, muscovite, nephrite, orthoclase, pyrite (fool's gold), rutile, ulexite, wulfenite, and zoisite. Synthetic forms of corundum, quartz, and YAG are also shown.

Art pieces, carvings, and jewelry shown include objects made of diamond, ivory, jade, pearl, and quartz. Diamond objects illustrated include the Hope Diamond, the Jubilee Diamond, the Napoleon necklace, the Shepherd Diamond, and the Victoria-Transvaal Diamond. Jade objects shown include carvings from the Maude Monell Vetlesen Collection of Chinese jade, a desk set, and vases. Pearl objects documented include a seed pearl bag and the Van Buren Pearls. Quartz objects depicted include spheres on stands. Additional objects recorded include altar lanterns, carved birds, a chalice, and a Mogul tea set.

Arranged: In three series by subject. 1) Color slides of gems, by catalog number. 2) Notebooks and a file box of silver gelatin photoprints and color dye coupler phototransparencies and slides of gems and carvings, alphabetically. 3) Color dye coupler slides of minerals, alphabetically by mineral.

Captioned: Most with catalog number, gem or mineral name, locality, photographer, source, and sometimes magnification. Some with specimen labels.

Finding Aid: No.

Restrictions: Limited access. Slides by amateur or commercial photographers are restricted. Smithsonian slide sets are available for lectures, loans, and reproductions. Slide sets of major gems in the Smithsonian collection are sold through OPPS or the Smithsonian Museum Shop in the NMNH. All other reproductions are available through OPPS. Write

OPPS, Smithsonian Institution, NMAH, CB054, Washington, D.C. 20560. Telephone: (202) 357-1933.

NH·54

Mineralogy Division History Photograph File

Dates of Photographs: 1965–Present

Collection Origins

The Division of Mineralogy staff created the collection to document the division's exhibits, gem and mineral collections, and staff. Photographers represented include Paul E. Desautels, William G. Melson, and OPPS staff.

Physical Description

There are 1,700 photographs including color dye coupler phototransparencies and slides, dye diffusion transfer photoprints, and silver gelatin photonegatives and photoprints. Other materials include clippings, correspondence, and photomechanical prints.

Subjects

The photographs record the Division of Mineralogy's exhibits, gem and mineral collections, and staff, as well as a number of mineral quarries.

Staff members portrayed include J.J. Abert, Dan Appleman, Burton Ashley, Cynthia Barnes, Lazard Cahn, L.T. Chamberland, Esther Claffy, F.W. Clarke, Dorthey Clement, Paul E. Desautels, Pete Dunn, Charles Fiori, William Foshag, Margaret D. Foster, Kurt Fredericksson, Ed Geisler, E.P. Henderson, Esper Larsen, Mike Laskin, Isaac Lea, J.P. Marble, George Merrill, Ed Over, Nancy Perkins, W.T. Schaller, Benjamin Silliman, George Switzer, H.S. Washington, A.G. Werner, John S. White, and Mary Winters. Other people portrayed include Harold Banks, Pierre Bariand, Carol Bell, Phyllis Brenner, Julie Norberg Burrows, Roy Clarke, Peter Embrey, John Gurney, Richard Johnson, Fred Jones, Rusty Kothavala, Sydney Krandall, Carl Krotki, George F. Kunz, Werner Lieber, Art Roe, John Roebling, Washington Roebling, Hubert Seaman, Charles U. Shepard, George Vaux, Magnus Vonsen, and Herbert Whitlock.

Gems and jewelry documented include the Bismark sapphire, the Eugenie Blue Diamond, the Hope Diamond, a lapis lazuli necklace, Marie Antoinette's earrings, an opal peacock pin, the Portuguese Diamond (colorless), a tumbled emerald necklace, and the Van Buren Pearls. Mines and quarries documented include the Branford Quarry; emerald mine; Great Notch and Summit Quarry, New Jersey; and Strickland Quarry. Other subjects illustrated include gem cutting, including Harry Winston cutting a diamond; members of the Smithsonian Board of Regents with the Hope Diamond; the NMNH gem and mineral exhibit hall; and a presentation of a replica of the Cullinan Diamond. There are also travel photographs of Ceylon (now Sri Lanka) showing a Hindu temple.

Arranged: In three series by type of material. 1) Slides, alphabetically by subject (gems, exhibit, or locale). 2) Photonegatives, by published plate number order. 3) Photoprints, alphabetically by subject (name of an individual or a gem). 4) Phototransparencies, alphabetically by subject.

Captioned: Some with dates, name, and negative number of the individual or subject shown.

Finding Aid: No.

Restrictions: Available by appointment only. Call or write two weeks in advance.

NH·55

Petrology and Volcanology Division Metamorphic Rock Slide Collection

Dates of Photographs: 1978–Present

Collection Origins

Sorena S. Sorensen, Associate Curator of Metamorphic Petrology in the Division of Petrology and Volcanology, created this collection to document the origins and distribution of metamorphic rocks for personal lecture, publication, and research purposes. Sorenson, who received a Ph.D. in 1984 from the University of California, Los Angeles, joined NMNH in 1984.

Physical Description

There are 1,800 color dye coupler slides. Other materials include diazo reproductions, geological charts, maps, and notebooks.

Subjects

The photographs document metamorphic rock specimens, particularly their original locations and thin-section samples. There are also photographic reproductions of charts, graphs, and maps. The original landscape settings of the rock specimens shown include the north coast of the Dominican Republic; Santa Catalina Island and Sierra Madre in California; the Great Basin in Nevada; and the Skagit River in Washington.

Arranged: No.

Captioned: Some with grain, location, and size of the specimen photographed.

Finding Aid: No.

Restrictions: Available only to scholarly researchers.

NH·56

Physical Sciences Laboratory Collection

Dates of Photographs: 1965–Present

Collection Origins

Eugene Jarosewich and Joseph A. Nelen, analytical chemists in the Physical Sciences Laboratory of the Department of Mineral Sciences, created this collection to document the activities and equipment of the Physical Sciences Laboratory. Jarosewich and Nelen perform chemical investigations of lunar materials, meteorites, minerals, and rocks. Some of the photographs were taken by OPPS staff. Several images in this collection appeared in the following publication: Paul E. Desautels. *The Mineral Kingdom*. New York: Madison Square Press, 1968.

Physical Description

There are 300 photographs including color dye coupler slides, dye diffusion transfer photoprints, and silver gelatin photoprints (some mounted in notebooks). There are several scanning electron microscope (SEM) images. Other materials include press releases.

Subjects

The photographs document the activities, instruments, research, and staff of the Physical Sciences Laboratory since 1965. Most of the photographs are of laboratory instruments, lunar materials, meteorites, minerals, and rocks. A few photographs show other manmade and natural objects, including carbonates, ceramics, corals, medallions, pigments, and worms.

Arranged: In three series, by type of material. 1) Notebooks of notes and photographs, by subject and then chronologically by date of project. 2) Silver gelatin photoprints, unarranged. 3) Color dye coupler slides, unarranged.

Captioned: Some with description, meteorite name, OPPS negative number, and specimen number.

Finding Aid: No.

Restrictions: No.

NH

Department of Paleobiology

Department of Paleobiology
National Museum of Natural History
Smithsonian Institution
Washington, D.C. 20560
Frederick J. Collier, Collection Manager
(202) 357-2405
Hours: Monday–Friday, 10 a.m.–4 p.m.

Scope of the Collections

There are ten photographic collections with 195,000 images.

Focus of the Collections

The Department of Paleobiology has four divisions: Invertebrate Paleontology, Paleobotany, Sedimentology, and Vertebrate Paleontology. The photographs document fossil remains of animal and plant life from the Paleozoic to the Cenozoic era. Other images illustrate dinosaur skeletons and reconstructions; and NMNH events, exhibit construction, fieldwork sites, fossil restoration, and staff.

Photographic Processes and Formats Represented

There are albumen photoprints; color dye coupler photonegatives, photoprints, and slides; dye diffusion transfer photoprints; platinum photoprints; silver gelatin dry plate photonegatives and lantern slides; and silver gelatin photonegatives (some SEMs), photoprints (some SEMs), radiographs, and slides.

Other Materials Represented

The department also contains books, correspondence, diagrams, illustrations, manuscripts, maps, notes, photograph albums, photostats, postcards, publication plates, and specimens.

Access and Usage Policies

The collections are open to scholarly researchers by appointment. Interested researchers should write to the department and describe their research topic, the type of material that interests them, and their research aim.

Publication Policies

Researchers must obtain permission from the Smithsonian Institution to reproduce a photograph and may also have to obtain permission from the copyright holder, which is not necessarily the Smithsonian Institution. The preferred credit line is "Courtesy of the Department of Paleobiology, National Museum of Natural History, Smithsonian Institution."

NH·57

Invertebrate Paleontology Division Brachiopod Lantern Slide Collection

Dates of Photographs: 1932–1940s

Collection Origins

G. Arthur Cooper (1902–) created the collection to document his research in invertebrate fossils, modern and fossil brachiopods, and in paleontology and stratigraphy of the Hamilton Group of New York. In 1929 Cooper received a Ph.D. in geology from Yale University, where he served first as an assistant (1928–1929) and then as a research associate (1929–1930) at the Peabody Museum. He came to the USNM Department of Paleobiology in 1930 as a specialist in brachiopods (marine invertebrates) and became Assistant Curator of Invertebrate Fossils (1930–1939), Associate Curator (1939–1943), Curator (1943–1956), Head Curator of the Department of Geology (1956–1963), Chairman of the Department of Paleobiology (1963–1966), and Senior Paleobiologist (1967–1974). Cooper retired in 1974 and until 1988 held the title of Paleobiologist Emeritus.

Physical Description

There are 400 silver gelatin dry plate lantern slides.

Subjects

The slides depict brachiopod fossils and modern brachiopods and their habitats. Brachiopods are marine invertebrates which have bivalve shells and tentacled armlike structures alongside their mouths. The preparation of fossil brachiopods by USNM curators is shown. There are also diagrams and illustrations of brachiopods, as well as photographs of adventitious shells and shale. Fieldwork research sites illustrated include Glass Mountain, California; Cherry Valley, Lake Erie, Oneida, Port Jervis, and Union Springs, New York; and the Cascade Mountains, Washington.

Arranged: No.

Captioned: Most with subject.

Finding Aid: No.

Restrictions: No. Contact Richard E. Grant, Curator, Department of Paleobiology, NMNH, Room E205, MRC NHB121, Smithsonian Institution, Washington, D.C. 20560. (202) 357-2211.

NH·58

Invertebrate Paleontology Division Brachiopod Slide File

Dates of Photographs: 1960s–Present

Collection Origins

G. Arthur Cooper (1902–) created the collection for his research in invertebrate fossils, modern and fossil brachiopods, and in the paleontology and stratigraphy of the Hamilton Group of New York. For a biography of Cooper see the *Collection Origins* field of *NH·57*.

Physical Description

There are 2,500 color dye coupler slides.

Subjects

Brachiopods shown include fossils from the Cambrian to the Tertiary period and modern brachiopods (marine invertebrates which have bivalve shells and tentacled armlike structures alongside their mouths). There are also images of rock formations and layers including landscape images of west Texas.

Arranged: In four series by subject. 1) Geological slides. 2) Permian brachiopods. 3) Modern brachiopods. 4) Fossil brachiopods.

Captioned: No.

Finding Aid: Separate finding aids, listing species name and slide numbers, for each series in the collection.

Restrictions: No. Contact Richard E. Grant, Curator, Department of Paleobiology, NMNH, Room E205, MRC NHB121, Smithsonian Institution, Washington, D.C. 20560. (202) 357-2211.

NH·59

Invertebrate Paleontology Division Historical Photograph Collection

Dates of Photographs: 1905, 1906

Collection Origins

The collection documents the paleobiology research of Charles D. Walcott (1850–1927) and George R. Wieland (1865–1953). Wieland, who earned a Ph.D. from Yale University in 1900, was a botanist and paleontologist at Yale University and the Carnegie Institution. Walcott, who received a Ph.D. from Royal Fredericks University, Christiania, in 1911, worked as a geologist and paleontologist on Cambrian and Paleozoic faunas and rocks in Alberta, British Columbia, Newfoundland, and Québec in Canada; the Rocky Mountains in Canada and the United States; and Arizona, Montana, Nevada, New York, North Carolina, Tennessee, Utah, and Vermont in the United States. Walcott collected preserved trilobites with their appendages intact in New York at the age of 21, and in 1909, he discovered Canada's Cambrian Burgess shale deposit, which yielded many soft-bodied organisms that are rarely preserved as fossils. Walcott became the third Director of the U.S. Geological Survey in 1894 and held an honorary curator position at the USNM until 1907, when he became the fourth Secretary of the Smithsonian Institution.

Photographers represented include Charles D. Walcott, George R. Wieland, and Bailey Willis. Since 1964 the collection has been under the custodial care of Francis M. Hueber, Curator of Paleobiology. Walcott used these photographs in his lectures and presentations. Photoprints from the dry plate photonegatives were used in the following: George R. Wieland. *American Fossil Cycads.* Washington, D.C.: Carnegie Institution of Washington, 1906.

Physical Description

There are 100 photographs including silver gelatin dry plate lantern slides and photonegatives and silver gelatin photoprints made from these glass negatives. Other materials include notes.

Subjects

Most of the images are of Cambrian paleobiology specimens. The items documented include algae from the Burgess shale deposit; drawings of fossil specimens; landscapes near fossil discovery sites, particularly in Canada and New York; limestone; and trilobites.

Arranged: In two series. 1) Charles D. Walcott's lantern slides. 2) George R. Wieland's photonegatives and photoprints.

Captioned: Some lantern slides with subject.

Finding Aid: No.

Restrictions: No. Contact Francis M. Hueber, Curator, Department of Paleobiology, NMNH, Room W309, MRC NHB164, Smithsonian Institution, Washington, D.C. 20560. (202) 357-1801.

NH·60

Invertebrate Paleontology Division Photograph Album Collection *A.K.A.* Joseph A. Cushman Photograph Album Collection

Dates of Photographs: Late 1800s–Present

Collection Origins

Joseph A. Cushman (1881–1949) created the collection for his personal research and publications. Cushman, who received a Ph.D. from Harvard College in 1909, worked at the Woods Hole Oceanographic Institution with Mary Jane Rathbun of the USNM. Rathbun encouraged him to pursue the study of foraminifera, an order of amoeboid protozoa having chambered external shells. Cushman joined the U.S. Geological Survey in 1912 and established the Cushman Laboratory for Foraminiferal Research at Sharon, Massachusetts, in 1923. During his career Cushman published over 500 articles, monographs, reports, and manuals; he also assembled a collection of 12,000 primary and secondary type specimens of foraminifera. His collections and library were bequeathed to the Smithsonian Institution. For several years this photograph album was maintained by Cushman's colleague, M. Ruth Todd (1913–1981). The collection is now cared for by an assistant to Martin Buzas, Curator of Paleobiology. Photographers represented include Lotte Adametz, Alfred Bischoff, and Edith Vincent.

Physical Description

There are 185 photographs including albumen photoprints, color dye coupler photoprints, platinum photoprints, and silver gelatin photoprints housed in two albums. There is one oversize composite panorama.

Subjects

The photographs document people and events associated with the study of invertebrate paleontology from 1782 to the present. Some are photographic reproductions of drawings, engravings, and etchings. People portrayed include Harold V. Andersen, Jane Aubert, Lois Berggen, H. Bolli, Esteban Boltovskoy, Paul Bronnimann, Fritz Brotzen, Martin Buzas, Fred Collier, Ann Dorsey, Carl O. Dunbar, Patricia Edwards, Adolf Franke, Maria Lourdes Gamero, H. Pauline Gilbert, A. Goldfuss, Ernot Haeikel, Tan Sin Hok, Dick Jones, Doris Low, Nell Ludbrook, Cathy McNair, Margaret Moore, Ted Murphy, J.L. Neugeboren, Frances L. Parker, Mel Pechet, O. Pratje, Z. Reiss, Susan Richardson, Isabel Riobo, Arthur Rogers, Laurie Smith, Roberta Smith, Hugo Storm, Zoya Stschedrina, Helen Tappan, Ruth Todd, Edward O. Ulrich, W.C. Warner, Silvia Watanabe, Don Weir, and Keith Yenne. Events and facilities documented include the Cushman Laboratory and Library; the Ninth European Micropaleontology Colloquium, Switzerland, September 1965; and the USNM's Commonwealth Paleontology Laboratory.

Arranged: Chronologically.

Captioned: With subject.

Finding Aid: No.

Restrictions: No. Contact Martin A. Buzas, Curator, Department of Paleobiology, NMNH, Room E112, MRC NHB121, Smithsonian Institution, Washington, D.C. 20560. (202) 357-1390.

NH·61

Invertebrate Paleontology Division Publications Collection I *A.K.A.* G. Arthur Cooper Publications Collection

Dates of Photographs: 1930s–Present

Collection Origins

G. Arthur Cooper created the collection for his research in invertebrate fossils, modern and fossil brachiopods, and the paleontology and stratigraphy of the Hamilton Group of New York. For a biography of Cooper see the *Collection Origins* field of *NH·57*.

Photographers represented include OPPS staff and Jack Scott. Photographs from this collection have been published in books, exploration reports, and scientific journals, including the following: 1) G. Arthur Cooper. *Jurassic Brachiopods of Saudi Arabia*. Smithsonian Institution Contributions to Paleobiology, no. 65. Washington, D.C.: Smithsonian Institution Press, 1989. 2) G. Arthur Cooper. *New Brachiopoda from the Indian Ocean*. Smithsonian Institution Contributions to Paleobiology, no. 16. Washington, D.C.: Smithsonian Institution Press, 1973. 3) G. Arthur Cooper and Richard E. Grant. *New Permian Brachiopods from West Texas*. Smithsonian Institution Contributions to Paleobiology, no. 1. Washington, D.C.: Smithsonian Institution Press, 1969.

Physical Description

There are 151,100 photographs including silver gelatin dry plate lantern slides and photonegatives and silver gelatin photonegatives (some on nitrate) and photoprints. There is one oversize composite panorama.

Subjects

The photographs illustrate brachiopod specimens and G. Arthur Cooper's research on brachiopods, which are marine invertebrates with bivalve shells and tentacled armlike structures alongside their mouth. Collecting areas shown include New Brunswick and Québec (Gaspé) in Canada; the Fiji Islands in the Pacific Ocean; the Gulf of Mexico; the Indian Ocean; Israel; Paricutín Volcano and Sonora in Mexico; Saudi Arabia; and Florida, New Mexico, and Texas (the Glass Mountains) in the United States.

Arranged: Some either alphabetically by genus and species or by publication, then by plate number.

Captioned: Some with subject.

Finding Aid: A journal serves as an index for part of the collection with date, location, negative number, and subject noted on the illustrations.

Restrictions: No. Contact Richard E. Grant, Curator, Department of Paleobiology, NMNH, Room E205, MRC NHB121, Smithsonian Institution, Washington, D.C. 20560. (202) 357-2211.

NH·62

Invertebrate Paleontology Division Publications Collection II *A.K.A.* Richard E. Grant Publications Collection

Dates of Photographs: 1957–Present

Collection Origins

Richard E. Grant (1927–), Curator of Brachiopods, created this collection as part of his personal research file on brachiopods (marine invertebrates). Grant, who received a Ph.D. in geology from the University of Texas in 1958, came to the Smithsonian Institution in 1957. He has been a Research Assistant in Invertebrate Paleontology (1951–1961); Geologist with the U.S. Geological Survey (1961–1972); Chairman of the Department of Paleobiology (1972–1977); and Curator of Paleobiology (1977–). Photographers represented include G. Arthur Cooper and Richard E. Grant. The photographs have appeared in the following publications: 1) *Geological Survey Professional Papers*. Washington, D.C.: U.S. Government Printing Office. 2) David M. Raup and Steven M. Stanley. *Principles of Paleontology*. San Francisco: W.H. Freeman, 1971.

Physical Description

There are 25,350 photographs including silver gelatin dry plate lantern slides and silver gelatin photonegatives and photoprints. Other materials include correspondence, diagrams, maps, photostats, postcards, and publication plates.

Subjects

The photographs show brachiopod specimens, habitats, and specimen collecting areas. Brachiopods are marine invertebrates which have bivalve shells and tentacled armlike structures alongside their mouth. Specimen collecting areas shown include the North West Territories (Axel Heiberg Island) in Canada; Greece; Guatemala; Pakistan; Thailand; and Alaska, Arizona (Indian Wells), California, New Mexico (Sacramento Mountains), Texas (Glass Mountains), and New York (Bear Mountain) in the United States.

Arranged: By publication.

Captioned: Some with location and specimen name.

Finding Aid: No.

Restrictions: No. Contact Richard E. Grant, Curator, Department of Paleobiology, NMNH, Room E205, MRC NHB121, Smithsonian Institution, Washington, D.C. 20560. (202) 357-2211.

NH·63

Invertebrate Paleontology Division SEM Foram Collection

Dates of Photographs: 1970s–1980s

Collection Origins

Martin Buzas (1934–), Curator of Invertebrate Paleontology, created the collection for his personal research and publications. Buzas received a Ph.D. in geology from Yale University in 1963 and joined the Smithsonian Institution NMNH staff as Curator of Invertebrate Paleontology that same year. Concurrently, Buzas has been a member of the Cushman Foundation. Photographs from this collection appeared in two Smithsonian publications: 1) Bruce W. Hayword and Martin A. Buzas. *Taxonomy and Paleoecology of Early Miocene Benthic Foraminifera of Northern New Zealand and the North Tasman Sea.* Smithsonian Contributions to Paleobiology, no. 36. Washington: Smithsonian Institution Press, 1979. 2) Martin A. Buzas and Kenneth P. Severin. *Distribution and Systematics of Foraminifera in the Indian River, Florida.* Smithsonian Contributions to the Marine Sciences, no. 16. Washington, D.C.: Smithsonian Institution Press, 1982.

Physical Description

There are 200 silver gelatin photonegatives and photoprints (all SEMs), including an oversize photoprint.

Subjects

The SEM photographs show foraminifera specimens, an order of amoeboid protozoa with chambered external shells. There are also photographic illustrations of benthic (sea or lake bottom-living) foraminifera.

Arranged: No.

Captioned: Some with specimen name.

Finding Aid: No.

Restrictions: No. Contact Martin A. Buzas, Curator, Department of Paleobiology, NMNH, Room E112, MRC NHB121, Smithsonian Institution, Washington, D.C. 20560. (202) 357-1390.

NH·64

Paleobiology Department Exhibition File

Dates of Photographs: 1894–Present

Collection Origins

This collection is part of the NMNH Department of Paleobiology's working file created to document exhibitions designed and installed by the department, dating from the 19th century, when the Smithsonian Institution Building (Castle) was used as exhibit space, to the present. Photographers and studios represented include the American Museum of Natural History, New York City; Chip Clark, Victor Krantz, and Thomas Smillie of the Smithsonian Institution; and the Victoria Memorial Museum, Ottawa, Canada.

Physical Description

There are 2,500 photographs including color dye coupler slides and silver gelatin photonegatives and photoprints.

Subjects

The photographs record NMNH and USNM Department of Paleobiology exhibitions, dating from 1894 to the present, which were held in the Arts and Industries Building (previously USNM), the NMNH building, and the Smithsonian Institution Building (Castle). Exhibits shown deal with dinosaurs; fossil plants; geological periods including the Cretaceous, Jurassic, Late Jurassic, Mesozoic, Miocene, Mississippian, Pennsylvanian, Permian, Pliocene, Silurian, and Triassic periods; ice age mammals; and invertebrates.

Smithsonian Institution exhibits documented include the "Carboniferous Coal Swamp Forest"; "Dinosaur Bone"; "Giants of the Past"; "Mammals and Reptiles of Middle Eocene"; "Mesozoic-Tertiary Reptiles"; "Neanderthal Burial"; "Reptiles Adapted for Life in Sea"; "What is a Fossil?"; and "Would You Like to Touch a Dinosaur Bone?" NMNH dioramas of the Jurassic and Triassic, maps of the Cretaceous and Permian, and murals of the Eocene and Oligocene are also illustrated. Halls shown include the Dinosaur Hall; Paleontology Hall; Pteranadon-Dinosaur Hall; Vertebrate Paleontology Hall; and Woolly Mammoth-Ice Age Hall. Dinosaurs featured include allosaurus, antosaurus, ceratosaurus, ichthyosaurus, phytosaurus, plateosaurus, pterosaurus, stegosaurus, styracosaurus, thecodonts, triceratops, tyrannosaurus, and yaleosaurus. Other animals illustrated include giant beavers, ground sloths, pandas, saber-toothed cats, and woolly mammoths.

Arranged: In four series. 1) The Smithsonian Institution Building (Castle) and Arts and Industries Building. 2) Arts and Industries Building. 3) NMNH, 1910–late 1950s. 4) NMNH, 1961–1970s. Then by exhibit title or exhibit hall.

Captioned: Approximately 85 percent with negative number. About 15 percent include some subject information.

Finding Aid: A list of photographs of dinosaurs with format, negative numbers, and subject.

Restrictions: No. Contact Raymond T. Rye II, Museum Specialist, Department of Paleobiology, NMNH, Room E208, MRC NHB121, Smithsonian Institution, Washington, D.C. 20560. (202) 357-2229.

NH·65

Paleobiology Department Specimen File

Dates of Photographs: 1894–Present

Collection Origins

The NMNH Department of Paleobiology staff created the collection as part of its working files to document animal and plant fossil specimens from Smithsonian Institution collections, from other museums, and private collections; as well as specimens in their natural habitats. Photographers and studios represented include Chip Clark; Elite Studio, Butte, Montana; Victor Krantz, OPPS; the Library of Congress; and Ward's National Science Establishment.

Physical Description

There are 9,800 photographs including albumen photoprints, color dye coupler photoprints and slides, silver gelatin dry plate photonegatives, and silver gelatin photonegatives and photoprints.

Subjects

The photographs document fossil plants and invertebrate and vertebrate specimens, as well as staff activities, such as collections care and display. Among the fossils shown are birds, brachiopods (marine invertebrates), and insects such as a caddis fly in amber. Other specimens illustrated include ammonites, amphibians, corals, dinosaurs, fish, gastropods, and sponges. Activities shown include exhibit construction, fieldwork, laboratory work, and restoration of fossils. Field locations shown include British Columbia (Burgess Pass), Canada; Derbyshire, Great Britain; Montana (Yellowstone River), Utah (Dinosaur National Monument), and Virginia (Accomack County), United States; and the Wolkow River, USSR. NMNH staff portrayed include Ermin C. Case, G. Arthur Cooper, James W. Gidley, Charles W. Gilmore, O.P. May, Frank Pearce, and Frank C. Whitmore.

Arranged: In three series. 1) Fossil plants. 2) Invertebrate Zoology. 3) Vertebrate Zoology. Then by subject.

Captioned: Half with geological age, locality, negative number, and subject.

Finding Aid: A 1964 index listing format, negative number, and subject.

Restrictions: Yes. Contact Raymond T. Rye II, Museum Specialist, Department of Paleobiology, NMNH, Room E208, MRC NHB121, Smithsonian Institution, Washington, D.C. 20560. (202) 357-2229.

NH·66

Vertebrate Paleontology Division Tertiary Mammals Field Specimen Collection *A.K.A.* Robert Emry Field Specimen Collection

Dates of Photographs: 1971–Present

Collection Origins

Robert J. Emry (1940–), Curator of Fossil Mammals at the Department of Paleobiology, created the collection to document fossil mammals from the Cenozoic Era's Tertiary Period (between the Eocene and Oligocene epochs). Emry, who received a Ph.D. from Columbia University in 1970, has been a Vertebrate Paleontologist with the Smithsonian Institution since 1971. Photographers represented include Victor Krantz and other OPPS staff. Photographs from the collection have appeared in the following publication: Robert J. Emry and Richard J. Thorington, Jr. *Descriptive and Comparative Osteology of the Oldest Fossil Squirrel Protosciurus (Rodentia: Sciuridae).* Smithsonian Contributions to Paleobiology, no. 47. Washington, D.C.: Smithsonian Institution, 1982.

Physical Description

There are 2,850 photographs including color dye coupler photonegatives, photoprints, and slides; dye diffusion transfer photoprints; and silver gelatin photonegatives and photoprints (some radiographs and SEMs). There are two oversize composite panorama photoprints. Other materials include books, illustrations, manuscripts, maps, notes, and specimens.

Subjects

The photographs document fossil mammal specimens from the Eocene to the Oligocene epochs including bats, rodents, and tree squirrels. Field research locations shown include Beaver Creek; the Duchesne River; and Natrona County, Wyoming.

Arranged: Loosely by fossil genus, species, and type.

Captioned: A few with subject.

Finding Aid: No.

Restrictions: No. Contact Robert J. Emry, Curator, Department of Paleobiology, NMNH, Room E107, MRC NHB121, Smithsonian Institution, Washington, D.C. 20560. (202) 357-1774.

NH

Department of Vertebrate Zoology

Department of Vertebrate Zoology
National Museum of Natural History
Smithsonian Institution
Washington, D.C. 20560
(202) 357-2740
Hours: Monday–Friday, 10 a.m.–4 p.m.

Scope of the Collections

There are 19 photographic collections with approximately 123,500 images.

Focus of the Collections

The Department of Vertebrate Zoology is organized in four divisions: Amphibians and Reptiles, Birds, Fishes, and Mammals. Departmental photographs document algae, aquatic plants, blue crabs, catfish, fossil and modern birds from the Hawaiian Islands, lobsters, marine mammals, octopus, pearls, sharks, shrimp, skeletons and skulls, sponges, whalebones, and whales. Other subjects illustrated include fish breeding stations, the fishing industry, habitat sites, hunters in wilderness areas, the NMNH, the National Zoological Park (NZP), oyster shell use, portraits of ichthyologists, Smithsonian exhibit halls, the Smithsonian Tropical Research Institute (STRI), sport fishing, taxidermy, vertebrate collecting sites, and whaling stations.

Photographic Processes and Formats Represented

There are albumen photoprints (some cabinet cards and stereographs); collodion wet plate photonegatives; color dye coupler photonegatives, photoprints, phototransparencies, and slides; cyanotypes; silver gelatin dry plate lantern slides and photonegatives; and silver gelatin photonegatives (some on nitrate), photoprints (some cartes-de-visite), phototransparencies, radiographs (hard and soft), and slides.

Other Materials Represented

The department also contains charts, correspondence, diagrams, drawings, etchings, illustrations, log books, mammal measurements, manuscripts, maps, newspaper clippings, notes, photomechanicals, postcards, publications, publication plates, reprints, watercolors, woodblock prints, specimens, and xerographic copies.

Access and Usage Policies

These collections are open to scholarly researchers by appointment. Interested researchers should write to the department and describe their research topic, the type of material that interests them, and their research aim.

Publication Policies

Researchers must obtain permission from the Smithsonian Institution to reproduce a photograph and may also have to obtain permission from the copyright holder, which is not necessarily the Smithsonian Institution. The preferred credit line is "Courtesy of the Department of Vertebrate Zoology, National Museum of Natural History, Smithsonian Institution."

NH·67

Birds Division Hawaiian Birds Research Collection

Dates of Photographs: 1971–Present

Collection Origins

Helen F. James assembled and partially created this ongoing research collection to document birds of the Hawaiian Islands and other oceanic islands. James, who received a B.A. from the University of Arkansas, is a Museum Specialist in the Department of Vertebrate Zoology, Birds Division. Other photographers and studios represented include Joan Aidem; Diane Drigot; Victor Krantz; J.K. Obata; Storrs L. Olson; OPPS; Ben Patnoi, Bernice Pauahi Bishop Museum, Honolulu; Alan Ziegler; and other field associates in Hawaii.

Photographs from this collection have appeared in the following publications: 1) *Occasional Papers of the Bernice Pauahi Bishop Museum.* Honolulu, Hawaii: Bishop Museum Press, 1898–1984. 2) *Proceedings of the Biological Society of Washington.* Washington, D.C.: Biological Society of Washington. 3) Paul S. Martin and Richard G. Klein, eds. *Quaternary Extinctions: A Prehistoric Revolution.* Tucson, Arizona: University of Arizona Press, 1984. 5) *Smithsonian Contributions to Zoology.* Washington, D.C.: Smithsonian Institution Press.

Physical Description

There are 860 photographs including color dye coupler photoprints and slides and silver gelatin photonegatives, photoprints, and radiographs.

Subjects

The photographs document fossil and modern birds from the Hawaiian Archipelago and other oceanic islands, as well as avian habitats and fossil sites. There are also photographic reproductions of engravings from publications. Hawaiian collecting sites documented include South Cape, Hawaii; dunes near Poipu on Kauai; caves on Maui; dunes and Ilio Point on Molokai; and Barbers Point on Oahu. Fossil sites on Bermuda, St. Helena, and Trindade Island (Brazil) are also illustrated. Specimens shown include hummingbird bones and the Molokai goose.

Arranged: In two series. 1) Silver gelatin photonegatives and photoprints. 2) Color dye coupler photoprints and slides. Then chronologically by collecting trip, presentation, or publication.

Captioned: Some with date, description of scene, measurement, and specimen name.

Finding Aid: No.

Restrictions: No. Contact Helen F. James, Museum Specialist, Department of Vertebrate Zoology, Birds, NMNH, Room E611, Smithsonian Institution, Washington, D.C. 20560. (202) 357-2031.

NH·68

Birds Division Publication Collection *A.K.A.* Storrs L. Olson Publication Collection

Dates of Photographs: 1970–Present

Collection Origins

Curator of Ornithology Storrs L. Olson (1944–) assembled and partially created the collection for his research on the evolution, paleontology, and higher systematics of birds. Olson, who received an Sc.D. in biology from Johns Hopkins University in 1972, has been Curator of Orinithology at NMNH since then. Other photographers and studios represented include Victor Krantz, the National Geographic Society, Yoichi R. Okamoto, OPPS, and Douglas S. Rogers. These photographs were used in the 1978 NMNH exhibition "Fossil Birds" and have been published in many scientific journals and in the following book: Jean Christophe Balouet. *Fossil Birds From Late Quaternary Deposits in New Caledonia.* Washington, D.C.: Smithsonian Institution Press, 1989.

Physical Description

There are 775 photographs including color dye coupler photoprints and silver gelatin photonegatives, photoprints, and phototransparencies. Other materials include correspondence, diagrams, drawings, newspaper clippings, notes, photomechanicals, photostats, publications, publication plates, and xerographic copies.

Subjects

The photographs document the evolution of birds and the skeletons of fossil birds including Clapper rails, flamingos, Ladds owl, and the Mauritian rail. Other specimens illustrated include bird eggs and the structure of bird feathers. There are also photographs of a spelunking expedition and former Smithsonian Secretary Alexander Wetmore.

Arranged: Chronologically by publication.

Captioned: A few with subject.

Finding Aid: A bibliography of publications in which the images appeared.

Restrictions: No. Contact Storrs L. Olson, Curator, Department of Vertebrate Zoology, Birds, NMNH, Room E612, MRC NHB 116, Smithsonian Institution, Washington, D.C. 20560. (202) 357-2031.

NH·69

Birds Division Slide Collection *A.K.A.* Storrs L. Olson Slide Collection

Dates of Photographs: 1966–Present

Collection Origins

Storrs L. Olson assembled and partially created this collection to document his field research on the evolution, higher systematics, and paleontology of birds. For a biography of Olson see the *Collection Origins* field of *NH·68*. Other photographers and studios represented include East West Color Photo, Inc.; Helen F. James; Victor Krantz; National Geographic Society; Yoichi R. Okamoto, Bethesda, Maryland; and OPPS.

Physical Description

There are 2,100 photographs including color dye coupler slides and silver gelatin photoprints. Other materials include charts, illustrations, and maps.

Subjects

The photographs primarily document birds and bird habitats—particularly landscapes on islands in the Caribbean Sea and South Atlantic, including Ascension (Green Mountain), Bermuda, Fernando de Noronha, St. Helena (Egg Island and Prosperous Bay), Trindade (Brazil), and the West Indies. Other bird habitats illustrated include Atalaia, Dois Irmaos, and Pão de Açúcar, Brazil.

Bird specimens pictured include loons, red-throated divers, South African fossils, white-bellied frigates, wideawake birds, and wirebirds. Other photographs show crabs, dunes, ferns, fish, snail tracks in a pool, snakes, turtles, and whalebones. There are informal portraits of Storrs L. Olson and William Stopforth.

Arranged: In four series by collecting trip. 1) St. Helena. 2) Ascension. 3) Fernando de Noronha. 4) Trindade.

Captioned: With date, description, location, photographer, and slide number.

Finding Aid: No.

Restrictions: No. Contact Storrs L. Olson, Curator, Department of Vertebrate Zoology, Birds, NMNH, Room E612, MRC NHB 116, Smithsonian Institution, Washington, D.C. 20560. (202) 357-2031.

NH·70

Fishes Division Ariidae Radiograph Collection *A.K.A.* W.R. Taylor Radiograph Collection

Dates of Photographs: ND

Collection Origins

William R. Taylor (1919–), NMNH Curator of Fishes, created the collection for his research in fish distribution, systematics, and taxonomy. Taylor, who received a Ph.D. in zoology from the University of Michigan in 1955, joined NMNH as an Associate Curator in 1956. Prior to his work at NMNH, Taylor worked at the Museum of Zoology at the University of Michigan (1947–1951) and as an aquatic biologist at the State Wildlife and Fisheries Commission in Louisiana (1954–1956). In 1979 Taylor became NMNH Curator Emeritus of Fishes.

Physical Description

There are 300 silver gelatin radiographs.

Subjects

The radiographs document many species of the Ariidae family of sea catfish found in subtropical and tropical waters worldwide.

Arranged: Alphabetically by genus.

Captioned: No.

Finding Aid: No.

Restrictions: For staff use only.

NH·71

Fishes Division Assessment Radiography Collection

Dates of Photographs: ND

Collection Origins

Departmental staff created the collection to document fish found in Canada and the United States.

Physical Description

There are 400 silver gelatin radiographs.

Subjects

The photographs are x-ray images of American and Canadian fish families such as Apogonidae (cardinal fish), Balistidae (triggerfish and filefish), Batrachoididae (toadfish), Lutjanidae (snapper), Synaphobranchidae (cut-throat eel), and Uranoscopidae (stargazer).

Arranged: Alphabetically by family.

Captioned: No.

Finding Aid: No.

Restrictions: Available only for staff use.

NH·72

Fishes Division Bulletin Collection

Dates of Photographs: 1890s–1960s

Collection Origins

The collection, created for publication and research purposes by the U.S. Department of Fisheries (now the U.S. Fish and Wildlife Service) and the U.S. National Oceanic and Atmospheric Administration

(NOAA), was transferred to the Smithsonian Institution from the U.S. Department of the Interior. Photographers represented include John N. Cobb; R.E. Coker; E. Ehrenbaum; L.C. Handy, Washington, D.C.; Morrison, Chicago; Howard Resler, West Palm Beach, Florida; Morris Rosenfeld, New York City; Robert W. Shufeldt, Washington, D.C.; H.W. Spooner, Gloucester, Massachusetts; and N.L. Stebbins, Boston, Massachusetts. Studios represented include the American Museum of Natural History, New York City; John G. Shedd Aquarium, Chicago; New York Zoological Society; and Tiffany & Company.

Physical Description

There are 4,500 photographs including albumen photoprints (some cartes-de-visite), silver gelatin dry plate photonegatives, and silver gelatin photonegatives and photoprints. Other materials include correspondence, illustrations including graphic prints and photomechanicals, and manuscripts.

Subjects

The photographs document fish-related research published from the 1890s to the 1960s in the U.S. National Oceanic and Atmospheric Administration (NOAA) journal *Fisheries Bulletin*. Topics illustrated include fish diseases, fish food products, fish and shellfish culture, fishery industries, fish migration, fish physiology, fish types and habits, spawning fishes, and sport fishing.

Fish culture and fisheries documented include crab canning; a fishing schooner from Gloucester, Massachusetts; fouling of ships' bottoms; the goldfish industry; lobster culture; the manufacture of mussel hooks; the oyster industry in Texas; pearl culture; salmon fisheries in Alaska and the Pacific; scallop fishing; sponge culture; trout farms; and the use of oyster shells. Fish habits shown include freshwater mussels feeding, intertidal spawning of pink salmon, and fish migration. Fish research shown includes Alaskan cod on the deck of the U.S. Bureau of Fisheries steamer *Albatross,* fish disease research (particularly contagious diseases of salmon and gas diseases of fish), propagation of bait fish studies, sea lion research, studies of hearing in fish, underwater photography of fish, and research at the Woods Hole Oceanographic Institution, Woods Hole, Massachusetts.

Fish research sites are shown in the Bahamas, Canada, Cuba, Mexico, Japan, and Alaska, California, Florida, Massachusetts, North Carolina, Oregon, and Texas in the United States. Types of fish illustrated include black angelfish, black cod, goldfish, goosefish, haddock, herring, oarfish, salmon, sea bass, trout, tuna, and wolffish. Other marine animals and plants shown include barnacles, blue crabs, coral reefs, lobster, marine algae, mussels, octopus, oysters, scallops, sea horses, sea lions, sea turtles, seaweed, shipworms, sponges (Cuban reef sponges, Honduran wool sponges, and Rock Island sheepswool sponges), starfish, and whalebones.

Arranged: Chronologically.

Captioned: Many with subject and date.

Finding Aid: No.

Restrictions: Available only for staff use.

NH·73

Fishes Division Ichthyologist Portrait File

Dates of Photographs: 1890–Present

Collection Origins

Leonard P. Schultz (1901–), who received a Ph.D. in icthyology from the University of Washington at Seattle in 1932, assembled most of this ongoing collection between 1938 and the 1950s to serve as a NMNH Fishes Division research file. He served as Assistant Professor and Instructor of Fisheries and Ichthyology at the University of Washington from 1928 to 1936 before joining the USNM in 1936. At the USNM Schultz served as assistant curator (1936–1938), Curator-in-Charge (1938–1965), Senior Zoologist (1965–1968), and Zoologist Emeritus (1968–).

Physical Description

There are 8,200 photographs including albumen photoprints and silver gelatin photonegatives and photoprints. Other materials include clippings, correspondence, publications, and xerographic copies.

Subjects

The photographs portray, singly and in groups, ichthyologists who have published articles in their field.

Individuals portrayed include Alexander Agassiz, John J. Audubon, Spencer F. Baird, Elinor Behre, M.E. Bloch, V.K. Brajnikov, D.C. Chandler, John N. Cobb, R.E. Coker, F. Daiber, Charles Darwin, H. De Vries, G. Duncker, M.P. Fish, Theodore N. Gill, C.E. Grunsky, J.J. Heckel, J.R. Hogan, Laura C. Hubbs, Reizo Ishiyama, Robert Jenkins, David S. Jordon, Clancey Juday, W.C. Kendall, Kiyu Kobayoshi, Karl Lagler, G.N. Lawrence, G. Lindgery, Carolus Linnaeus, Rose MacDonald, W.R. Martin, Seth Eugene Meek, Robert Miller, Merriman, Kakichi Mitsukuri, J.P. Morrison, J.R. Norman, F.C.W. Olson, Clarence Patzke, J. Pellegrin, Constantine S. Rafinesque (*A.K.A.* Constantine S. Rafinesque-Schmaltz), Edward C. Raney, L.R. Rivas, Theodore Roosevelt, J. Schmidt, Leonard P. Schultz, E.A. Seaman, W.A. Spoor, Leonhard Stejneger, R.O. Sweeney, Frank H. Talbot, M.B. Trautman, H.E. Warfel, Dwight Webster, and Charles Wilkes.

Groups portrayed include the Ahlstrom Memorial Symposium, 1983; American Canadian Fisheries Conference, 1918; American Fisheries Society; A.I.B.S. Meeting, Washington, D.C., 1951; American Museum of Natural History, 1953; American Society of Ichthyologists and Herpetologists, 1940 and 1979; College of Fisheries Graduates with U.S. Bureau of Fisheries, 1931; Division of Fishes staff, 1955; East African Marine Fisheries Research Association, 1960; 50th Anniversary of the American Society of Ichthyologists and Herpetologists, Vancouver, British Columbia, 1963; Institute of Fishery, Vienna, Austria, 1905; Japanese ichthyologists, 1963; Shark Research Panel, 1965; U.S. Bureau of Fish faculty, University of Washington, Seattle, 1928 to 1930; and University of Washington Scientists at Bikini Atoll, 1947.

Arranged: In two series, then alphabetically. 1) Individual portraits. 2) Group portraits.

Captioned: No.

Finding Aid: Alphabetical list of names.

Restrictions: No.

NH·74

Fishes Division Illustration File

Dates of Photographs: 1870s–Present

Collection Origins

The U.S. Department of the Interior donated this collection to the NMNH. The Division of Fishes staff and the NMNH illustrators continue to add to it. Photographers and studios represented include Spencer F. Baird; Bleeker; W.M. Chapman; Davis Studio, Washington, D.C.; Gibbs and Wilimorsky; Albert Greenberg Everglades Aquatic Nurseries; E.B. Ives, Niles, Michigan; Longley; David G. Mead; OPPS; S. Powell; Harold Schultz; Leonard P. Schultz; Seafoods Laboratory, Oregon; Robert W. Shufeldt; T. Soot-Ryan, Tromso, Norway; the U.S. Army Medical Museum; and the U.S. Navy.

Images from the collection have been reproduced in the following publications: 1) Hypzi Aoyagi. *Coral Fishes*. Tokyo: Maruzen Company, Ltd., n.d. 2) California Division of Fish and Game. *Fish Bulletin*. Sacramento: California Department of Fish and Game. 3) Leonard J.V. Compagno. *Sharks of the Order Carcharhiniformes*. Princeton, N.J.: Princeton University Press, 1988. 4) *Proceedings of the United States National Museum*. Washington, D.C.: Smithsonian Institution Press.

Physical Description

There are 20,000 photographs including color dye coupler photonegatives and phototransparencies and silver gelatin photonegatives, photoprints, phototransparencies, and radiographs. Other materials include correspondence, drawings, publications, and watercolors.

Subjects

The photographs document fish from all over the world, for example, anchovies, cardinal fish, croakers, and surfperch. Some images are reproductions of graphic prints.

Arranged: By taxonomic order, then alphabetically.

Captioned: With genus and species.

Finding Aid: The "Fish Illustrations Inventory" includes a history sheet for each of the first 669 folders in the collection. These sheets, arranged by serial number, list the artist; collection location; correspondence; expedition; field notes; fish genus, species, sub-species, and type; kind of illustration and number; publication citation; original numbers; remarks; and serial number.

Restrictions: For staff use only.

NH·75

Fishes Division Publications Collection

Dates of Photographs: 1876–Present

Collection Origins

The Fishes Division staff assembled the collection to serve as a reference file of miscellaneous published photographs. Photographers represented include Thomas Houseworth, San Francisco, California.

Physical Description

There are 160 photographs including albumen photoprints; collodion wet plate photonegatives; and silver gelatin photonegatives, photoprints, and radiographs. Other materials include manuscripts and woodblock print plates.

Subjects

The photographs illustrate fish breeding stations, fish specimens (including some from Engu Island at Bikini Atoll), oyster culture, and sport fishing. Specific facilities and habitats shown include an oyster culture ground; U.S. Fish Commission fish ponds located west of the Washington Monument in Washington, D.C.; and a U.S. Fish Commission Salmon Breeding Station at McCloud River, California.

Arranged: No.

Captioned: With date and subject.

Finding Aid: No.

Restrictions: For staff use only.

NH·76

Fishes Division Radiograph Collection I

Dates of Photographs: 20th Century

Collection Origins

The NMNH's Department of Vertebrate Zoology Fishes Division staff assembled the collection from visiting scientists' donations for fish documentation and research purposes.

Physical Description

There are 2,050 silver gelatin hard and soft radiographs.

Subjects

The radiographs document fish from all over the world, such as cardinal fishes, gobies, mojarras, right-eye flounders, and squalids.

Arranged: By taxonomic order, then alphabetically.

Captioned: Some with catalog number, collection, family, original field number, locality, and species number.

Finding Aid: No.

Restrictions: Available only for staff use. Reproduction is prohibited.

NH·77

Fishes Division Radiograph Collection II *A.K.A.* Robert H. Gibbs Radiograph Collection

Dates of Photographs: 20th Century

Collection Origins

Robert H. Gibbs (1929–), NMNH Curator of Fishes, created the collection to document the internal structure of the Stomiatidae family of fish. Gibbs, who received a Ph.D. in vertebrate zoology from Cornell University in 1955, specializes in biological oceanography and systematic ichthyology. Before coming to NMNH in 1963, Gibbs was associated with Boston University, the New York State Teachers College in Plattsburgh, and Woods Hole Oceanographic Institution in Woods Hole, Massachusetts.

Physical Description

There are 235 silver gelatin radiographs.

Subjects

These x-ray images document the internal structure of the family Stomiatidae—small, slender, deep-sea fish that have short heads and large mouths of powerful teeth. Research locations documented include Africa (particularly West Africa), the Atlantic Ocean, New South Wales in Australia, Bermuda, Brazil, Formosa (now Taiwan), the Gulf of Mexico, the Indo-Pacific, the Mediterranean, San Felix Island in Chile, and Delaware, Hawaii, and Puerto Rico in the United States.

Arranged: Taxonomically.

Captioned: With geographical location and species.

Finding Aid: No.

Restrictions: Available only for staff use.

NH·78

Fishes Division Shark Radiograph Collection *A.K.A.* Stewart Springer Radiograph Collection

Dates of Photographs: 20th Century

Collection Origins

Stewart Springer (1906–) created most of the collection while he was working at the California Academy of Sciences (1963–1967), the George Vanderbilt Academy, the Smithsonian Institution USNM (1967–1971), and the Stanford University International Indian Ocean Expedition. Springer, who received a B.A. from George Washington University in 1963, also worked for the U.S. Fish and Wildlife Service (1950–1967). Other materials were transferred from the Charles E. Dawson Collection and the U.S. Department of the Interior.

Physical Description

There are 1,600 silver gelatin radiographs. Many are cut into irregular shapes and may contain more than one image.

Subjects

The radiographs (x-ray images) show sharks, many from the Indian Ocean, including cat sharks, hound sharks, requiem sharks, and thresher sharks.

Arranged: Most numerically by serial number; a few alphabetically by species.

Captioned: With film, length and sex of specimen, museum number, register number, remarks, screen, serial number, species name, tank number, and various other unidentified numbers (KV, MA, sec). Date and location may also be recorded.

Finding Aid: 1) Inactive card catalog arranged alphabetically by genus and species, with location, museum number, radiograph number, registration number (which may relate to specimens now at the California Academy of Sciences, San Francisco), and station number. 2) Photographer's log book with film number, fx number, lighting, results, shutter, speed number, stop, and subject.

Restrictions: For staff use only.

NH·79

Fishes Division South American Freshwater Fishes Collection

Dates of Photographs: 1953–Present

Collection Origins

NMNH Curator Stanley H. Weitzman and his predecessor, Hicks Thompson, created the collection as part of their private research materials. Weitzman (1927–), who received a Ph.D. from Stanford University in 1960 with a specialty in the evolution, morphology, and taxonomy of fish, joined the Fishes Division in 1963. Weitzman took most of the photographs in this collection. Other photographers represented include W.L. Fink. Many of the photographs have been used in lectures and have been published in the following journal: 1) *Proceedings of the Biological Society of Washington*. Washington, D.C.: Biological Society of Washington. 2) *Smithsonian Institution Contributions to Zoology*. Washington, D.C.: Smithsonian Institution Press.

Physical Description

There are 5,000 photographs including color dye coupler photonegatives and slides and silver gelatin photoprints and radiographs. Other materials include correspondence, drawings, notes, and reprints.

Subjects

The photographs show South American fresh water fish, primarily Characiform, and their habitats. Most of the photographs were taken in the streams of coastal Brazil and Venezuela. Some images are of holotypes. Sample images of hatchet fish and pencil fish from this collection are reproduced in this volume's illustrations.

Arranged: By genus and species, then alphabetically.

Captioned: With image source, specimen name, and USNM number. Half the slides and prints with genus and species.

Finding Aid: No.

Restrictions: Available only for staff use.

NH·80

Mammals Division Marine Mammals Active Research File

Dates of Photographs: 1972–Present

Collection Origins

Curator James G. Mead created this collection to serve as part of his active research file on marine mammals. Mead, who received a Ph.D. from the University of Chicago in 1972, specializes in the biology, distribution, evolution, functional anatomy, and interrelationship of cetaceous organisms in the western and northern Atlantic. Photographers and studios represented include Balcomb, the Carnegie Museum of Natural History, Charleston Museum, Paul Finnegan, F.W. Fitzsimmons, Natalie Goodall, G. Joyce, Kellogg, Basil Lustig, William McLellan, Charles W. Potter, Randy Reeves, Richard Rowlette, and the University of Mexico.

Physical Description

There are 34,000 photographs including color dye coupler photonegatives (internegatives) and slides, silver gelatin dry plate photonegatives, and silver gelatin photonegatives and photoprints. Other materials include correspondence, notes, reprints, and skull specimen measurement sheets.

Subjects

Most of the photographs show whales. One of the dry plate photonegatives shows the construction of the first USNM blue whale model. There are also informal portraits of Ed Mitchell, Roger Payne, Steve Ratona, Clayton E. Ray, W.E. Schevill, and S. Skinder.

Arranged: Two-thirds of the collection by family, then by genus and species in alphabetical order. One-third by assigned roll number. Note: The dry plate photonegatives are housed together.

Captioned: Most with family, genus, and species. Portraits with personal name.

Finding Aid: No.

Restrictions: For staff use only.

NH·81

Mammals Division Marine Mammals Static Research File

Dates of Photographs: 1880s–1985

Collection Origins

The Mammals Division staff assembled the collection as a reference file on marine mammals. Many of the photographs have been published in scientific journals such as the following: 1) *Proceedings of the United States National Museum*. Washington, D.C.: Smithsonian Institution Press. 2) *Smithsonian Contributions to Knowledge*. Washington, D.C.: Smithsonian Institution.

Photographers represented include Glover H. Allen; J. Lawrence Angel; Dorothy Armstrong, Montreal; Stanley C. Arthur, New Orleans; F.G. Ashbrook; Dave Bratten; Henry B. Collins, Jr.; J.G. Crawford, Albany, Oregon; William H. Dall; Henry Dawson; Arthur Fisher; F.W. Fitzsimmons; Gus Gillas; Brendan Herlihy; W.H. Hesse; Pete Laurie; E. Lawton; J.S. Leatherwood; Basil Lustig; James G. Mead; Paul Meier; Gerrit S. Miller, Jr.; Nancy Orem; William Palmer; Pat E. Pittman; Samuel Powell; J.J. Ramkin; Louis Schwartz, Charleston; Charles H.T. Townsend; Frederick W. True; Ernest P. Walker; Bill Waller; A.G. Wallihan, Lay, Colorado; G.M. Wellington; Elizabeth Whitney; D.L. Wray; and M. Yamada, Okayama University. Studios represented include the Library of Congress; *Los Angeles Examiner;* National Geographic Society; OPPS; J.W. Slipp Collection; Taber Photographs, San Francisco; and Thors, San Francisco.

Physical Description

There are 30,000 photographs including albumen photoprints (some cabinet cards and stereographs), color dye coupler photoprints and slides, cyanotypes, silver gelatin dry plate photonegatives, and silver gelatin photonegatives, photoprints, and radiographs. There are several oversize composite panorama photoprints measuring up to 7″ × 49″. Other materials include graphic prints, newspaper clippings, notes, photomechanicals, and postcards.

Subjects

The photographs show marine mammals such as dolphins, seals, and whales; marine mammal habitats; specimens and specimen reconstructions including jawbones and skulls; skeletons in Smithsonian exhibit halls; and whaling stations.

Whales and dolphins illustrated include Baird's beaked whale, Bering Sea beaked whale, blue whale, false killer whale, humpback whale, killer whale, Layards beaked whale, narrow-snouted dolphin, saddleback dolphin, spinning dolphin, and sulphur-bottom whale. Marine mammal habitats and research locations represented include Antarctica; Santa Cruz Province and the Straits of Magellan in Argentina; Hermitage Bay and Notre Dame Bay in Canada; Guadalupe in Mexico; Mossel Bay, South Africa; and Alaska, Maryland (Ocean City), New York (the New York Aquarium in New York City), and South Carolina (Charleston) in the United States. Islands represented include the Falkland Islands in Great Britain; the Pribilof Islands (St. George Island and St. Paul Island) in the United States; and Lobos Island in Uruguay.

Arranged: In three series. 1) Alphabetically by genus and species. 2) Loosely by type of material. 3) By collector's name.

Captioned: With OPPS number, USNM number, and/or subject information. Envelopes with date, description, length, genus and species, location, negative number, photographer, sex, and USNM number.

Finding Aid: Two card catalogs. 1) Photo file by negative number. 2) Photo file by species. Cards in both catalogs include number, genus, species, and publication data.

Restrictions: For scholarly research only. Contact James G. Mead, Curator, Department of Vertebrate Zoology, Mammals, Marine Mammal Project, NMNH, Room 394, MRC NHB 108, Smithsonian Institution, Washington, D.C. 20560. (202) 357-1920.

NH·82

Mammals Division NMNH Published History Copyright File

Dates of Photographs: 1985

Collection Origins

OPPS created this copy photoprint collection in 1985 for Ellis L. Yochelson's book in honor of NMNH's Diamond Jubilee: *The National Museum of Natural History: 75 Years in the Natural History Building*. Washington, D.C.: Smithsonian Institution Press, 1985. Yochelson (1928–), who received a Ph.D. in paleontology from Columbia University in 1955, worked with the U.S. Geological Survey from 1952 until his retirement in 1985. Yochelson assembled the original photographs for his book and gave this collection of copy photoprints to the Division of Mammals.

Physical Description

There are 220 silver gelatin photoprints. All are copy images.

Subjects

The photographs record the NMNH building exterior and interior and the NMNH staff from 1910 to 1985. The collection focuses on the building's construction; museum staff changes; and the renovations of exhibit areas, offices, and storage areas. Photographs document the USNM (now the Arts and Industries Building) and the NMNH building, including construction of NMNH's east and west wings; exhibit halls; installation of the Fenykovi elephant; museum administration; the museum during World Wars I and II; museum facilities and maintenance; museum staff changes; new programs (Discovery Room, Insect Zoo); plans and construction of the NMNH building; shops and maintenance; and visitors to the museum. There are also photographs of organizations affiliated with the museum, such as the Biological Survey, the Bureau of American Ethnology, the U.S. Commission on Fish and Fisheries, the U.S. Department of Agriculture, and the U.S. Geological Survey.

Arranged: Chronologically.

Captioned: Some with OPPS negative number and subject.

Finding Aid: No.

Restrictions: No. Contact Francis M. Greenwell, Museum Specialist, Department of Vertebrate Zoology, Mammals, NMNH, Room 390, MRC NHB 108, Smithsonian Institution, Washington, D.C. 20560. (202) 357-1920.

NH·83

Mammals Division Photograph Collection

Dates of Photographs: 1886–Present

Collection Origins

The Mammals Division staff created the collection as part of their working files. Materials have been contributed by division curators since the 19th century and reflect their collecting and research interests. Photographers and studios represented include George W. Brady and Co., Chicago, Illinois; Ernest L. Crandall; Aleš Hrdlička; Edgar A. Mearns; G. Miller; Mitchell and Baer, Prescott, Arizona; New York Zoological Society; Public Library, Museum, and Art Gallery of South Australia; Elwin R. Sanborn; S. Schwenland, Albany Institute of History and Art; H.H. Smith; A.G. Wallihan; and OPPS staff. Some of the photographs appeared in the following journal: *American Journal of Physical Anthropology*,

New York: A.R. Liss, vol. 1–29, Jan./Mar. 1918–1942; new series vol. 1, Mar. 1943.

Physical Description

There are 12,350 photographs including albumen photoprints; color dye coupler photoprints, phototransparencies, and slides; cyanotypes; silver gelatin dry plate lantern slides and photonegatives (some oversize); and silver gelatin photonegatives (some on nitrate), photoprints, and radiographs. Other materials include correspondence, drawings, etchings, log book, maps, newspaper clippings, photomechanicals, postcards, reprints, and watercolors.

Subjects

The photographs illustrate animals from the National Zoological Park (NZP); animal habitats; mammal brains, skeletons, skins, skulls, and teeth; mammal type specimens; and NMNH exhibits. There are also studies of albino or deformed mammals taken for genetic research purposes.

Mammals illustrated include the aardvark, African lion, Alaskan wolf, American bison, American elk, anteater, ape, armadillo, bear, beaver, bighorn sheep, buffalo, caribou, elephant, flying kangaroo, fox, giraffe, gorilla, hartebeest, hippopotamus, hyena, jerboa, mink, moose, mountain goat, mice, musk ox, opossum, orangutan, panther, platypus, porcupine, pronghorn antelope, puma, rabbit, red wolf, rhinoceros, Rocky Mountain goat, rodents, squirrel, tiger, white-tailed deer, wild pigs, wolf, and zebra. Animal habitats illustrated include the Aleutian Islands and the Altai Mountains. There are also photographs of William T. Hornaday on Smithsonian grounds with a buffalo calf and of the Robinson-Lyon Venezuela trip, 1900.

NMNH exhibits and exhibit halls shown include "Adaptions for Hearing and Fleeing Danger," "Albinism and Melanism," "Bluffing the Enemy," "Cats of the World," "Concealment," "Destructive Mammals," "Fur-Bearing Mammals," "Lemming Cycles," "Locomotion," "Mammal Sonar," "Migratory Mammals," Osteology Hall, "Poisonous Mammals," and "Subspecies and Subspeciation."

Arranged: Part of the collection by genus.

Captioned: Many with accession number; date of accession; source of acquisition; and subject information, including specimen's common name, taxonomic name, and native habitat.

Finding Aid: Caption lists to several parts of the collection.

Restrictions: For scholarly research only. Contact James G. Mead, Curator, Department of Vertebrate Zoology, Mammals, Marine Mammal Project, NMNH, Room 394, MRC NHB 108, Smithsonian Institution, Washington, D.C. 20560. (202) 357-1923.

NH·84

Mammals Division STRI Nitrate Photonegative Collection *A.K.A.* John H. Welsh Nitrate Photonegative Collection

Dates of Photographs: August 1929

Collection Origins

John H. Welsh (1901–), Professor Emeritus of Zoology at Harvard University, created the collection during a trip to the Smithsonian Tropical Research Institute (STRI) in Panama. Welsh earned a Ph.D. in 1929 from Harvard University, where he served as a biology tutor (1928–1947), Zoology Instructor (1929–1932), Faculty Instructor (1932–1940), Associate Professor (1940–1955), Professor (1955–1968), Chairman of the Department of Biology (1947–1950), Director of the Biology Laboratories (1956–1959), and Emeritus Professor of Zoology (1968–).

Physical Description

There are 55 silver gelatin photonegatives on nitrate.

Subjects

The photographs are of Panama's Barro Colorado Island and the Canal Zone in August 1929. There are images of the Cathedral in Old Panama, the Miraflores Locks, and a ship in Gatun Lock. Creatures illustrated include an egret in Panama City and a spider.

Arranged: By assigned number.

Captioned: With subject information on sleeves.

Finding Aid: No.

Restrictions: No. Contact James G. Mead, Curator, Department of Vertebrate Zoology, Mammals, Marine Mammal Project, NMNH, Room 394, MRC NHB 108, Smithsonian Institution, Washington, D.C. 20560. (202) 357-1920.

NH·85

Mammals Division Taxidermy Research File

Dates of Photographs: 1887–1950s

Collection Origins

Smithsonian Institution taxidermists assembled the collection from diverse sources to document the taxidermic process. Taxidermists who assembled the collection include Charles Aschmire, William L. Brown, Charles East, William T. Hornaday, Watson M. Perrygo, and Julian S. Warmbath. Note: Taxidermy is now used at the Smithsonian only in the conservation of mammals already mounted.

Photographers and studios represented include the Arnold Studio, First National Bank Building, Waynesboro, Virginia; the Frank K.G. Carpenter Collection; Jas. L. Clark; Clinedinst, Washington D.C.; the Clive Studio, Chattanooga, Tennessee; H.J. Cole; M.E. Cowen; Arthur Fisher; F. Gutekunst, Philadelphia, Pennsylvania; Marshall Harvey; G. Hills, Hudson, Columbia County, New York; Martin and Osa Johnson; Karl W. Kenyon; Harry B. Leopold, Baltimore, Maryland; the Library of Congress; the Los Angeles Museum of History, Science, and Art; McClasky; Edgar A. Mearns; the Milwaukee Public Museum; Henry L. Moreland; the National Geographic Society; the New York Zoological Society, 1905; OPPS; Elwin R. Sanborn; Robert W. Shufeldt, Washington, D.C.; H.A. Strohmeyer, Sr., New York; Underwood and Underwood, New York; the Utah Parks Co.; Edward P. Walker; *Washington Post Magazine;* H.B. Welch, New Haven, Connecticut; Raymond A. Wohlrabe; F. York; and the Zoological Society of London.

Physical Description

There are 625 photographs including albumen photoprints and silver gelatin photonegatives and photoprints. Other materials include drawings, graphic prints, mammal specimen measurement sheets, newspaper clippings, photomechanical illustrations, and postcards.

Subjects

The photographs document the taxidermic process and taxidermists, as well as animals from zoological parks and hunters in the wild. Photographs show the construction of mammal exhibit cases; the mammal exhibit halls, 1935; models for mounting animals; a mounted walrus, 1890; the mounting of the Fenykovi elephant; and the USNM taxidermy shop (south shed). Taxidermists and hunters shown include Andrew Forney, William T. Hornaday, Martin and Osa Johnson, Edgar A. Mearns, H.H. Meer, Jr., William Palmer, Watson M. Perrygo, Theodore Roosevelt, and Julian S. Warmbath. Zoological specimens and mounted animals illustrated include African buffalos, American bison, anteaters, Asiatic leopards, Barbary wild sheep, bighorn rams, black bears, blue whales, Brazilian tapirs, camels, cheetahs, chickens, chimpanzees, domestic cats, eagles, earth bears, Great Danes, hippopotamuses, horses (Fancy Peavine #1), hyenas, jaguars, kangaroos, lions, martens, moose, mountain goats, Mulligan bulls, okapis, opossums, orangutans, ostriches, peacocks, penguins, reticulated giraffes, rhesus monkeys, Russian greyhounds, snakes, Syrian golden hamsters, Tasmanian wolves, tigers, turkeys, turtles, walruses, white alpacas, white Orphington hens, and zebras.

Arranged: No.

Captioned: Many with date and subject.

Finding Aid: No.

Restrictions: No. Contact Francis M. Greenwell, Museum Specialist, Department of Vertebrate Zoology, Mammals, NMNH, Room 390, MRC NHB 108, Smithsonian Institution, Washington, D.C. 20560. (202) 357-2487.

NH

Office of the Director

Office of the Director
Public Information Office
National Museum of Natural History
Smithsonian Institution
Washington, D.C. 20560
Thomas R. Harney, Public Information Officer
(202) 357-2458
Hours: Monday–Friday, 10 a.m.–5 p.m.

Scope of the Collections

There are three photographic collections with approximately 5,150 images.

Focus of the Collections

The collections document NMNH exhibit installations and openings, special events, and past and present staff members.

Photographic Processes and Formats Represented

There are color dye coupler phototransparencies and slides and silver gelatin photonegatives and photoprints.

Other Materials Represented

This office also contains articles, biographical information, caption lists, curriculum vitae, exhibit catalogs, exhibit opening invitations, fact sheets, memos, motion-picture films, newspaper clippings, pamphlets, press releases, proposals, reports, slide scripts, *Smithsonian Research Reports*, videotapes, and xerographic copies.

Access and Usage Policies

These collections are open to scholarly researchers by appointment. Interested researchers should write to the office and describe their research topic, the type of material that interests them, and their research aim.

Publication Policies

Researchers must obtain permission from the Smithsonian Institution to reproduce a photograph and may also have to obtain permission from the copyright holder, which is not necessarily the Smithsonian Institution. The preferred credit line is "Courtesy of the National Museum of Natural History, Smithsonian Institution."

NH·86

Public Information Office Biographical Information File

Dates of Photographs: 1970s–Present

Collection Origins

Thomas R. Harney, who has been with the NMNH Public Information Office since 1969, assembled the collection to document past and present NMNH researchers, scientists, and staff for future publications. Photographers represented include Chip Clark and Victor Krantz.

Physical Description

There are 250 photographs including color dye coupler slides and silver gelatin photonegatives and photoprints. Other materials include articles, caption lists, curriculum vitae, fact sheets, memos, newspaper clippings, notes, pamphlets, press releases, proposals, reports, slide scripts, and xerographic copies.

Subjects

The photographs portray both past and present NMNH researchers, scientists, and staff including Walter H. Adney, J. Laurens Barnard, Frederick M. Bayer, John M. Burns, Mary Agnes Chase, Henry B. Collins, Jr., Paul E. Desautels, Clifford Evans, Jr., William W. Fitzhugh, Theodore Gary Gautier, Mason E. Hale, Meredith L. Jones, Porter M. Kier, Samuel P. Langley, Brian H. Mason, James G. Mead, James N. Norris, Storrs L. Olson, David L. Pawson, Robert W. Purdy, Clayton E. Ray, Raymond T. Rye, Margaret A. Santiago, Waldo L. Schmitt, Stanwyn G. Shetler, Dennis J. Stanford, Thomas Dale Steward, Gus W. Van Beek, Herman J. Viola, Thomas R. Waller, Waldo R. Wedel, Frank C. Whitmore, Vincent Wilcox, and Richard L. Zusi.

Arranged: Alphabetically by name.

Captioned: Some with subject's names.

Finding Aid: No.

Restrictions: No.

NH·87

Public Information Office General Reference File

Dates of Photographs: 1970s–Present

Collection Origins

Thomas R. Harney of the Public Information Office created this collection as a general reference file on NMNH events, exhibitions, and staff. Photographers represented include Chip Clark, Walter Jahn, and Victor Krantz. The images were used to accompany newspaper articles about NMNH in the *Washington Post* and the *Washington Star* and in the following book: 1) Smithsonian Institution. *Seeing the Smithsonian: The Official Guidebook to the Smithsonian Institution, Its Museums and Galleries.* New York: Columbia Broadcasting System, 1973. Note: Some of the photographs are stills from the television program "Smithsonian World."

Physical Description

There are 4,000 photographs including color dye coupler phototransparencies and slides and silver gelatin photonegatives and photoprints. Other materials include articles, biographical information, exhibit information, fact sheets, a motion-picture film on NMNH by Cherzekian and American Image Productions (1973), newspaper clippings, slide scripts, and a David Wolper videotape production on the Hope Diamond (1974).

Subjects

The photographs document the history of NMNH including exhibit halls, installations and openings; projects; and the Secretaries of the Smithsonian Institution. NMNH exhibit halls documented include Earth, Moon, and Meteorites; Gems; Human Origin and Variation; the Insect Zoo; Minerals; Pacific Cultures; South America; and Western Civilization. NMNH exhibits documented are "Alfred Russell Wallace's Malay Archipelago"; "Birds of the District of Columbia"; "Blue Whale"; "Dead Sea Scrolls from Jordan"; "Exploring Microspace"; "Himbas of the Angola-Namibia Border"; "The Japan Expedition of Commodore Matthew C. Perry, 1852–1855"; "Splendors of Nature"; "Treasures of Mexico: From the Mexican National Museums"; "Tribal

Costumes of Southern Africa"; "Underwater Photographs by Walter Jahn"; and "Volcanoes and Volcanism."

There are also photographs of the Anthropology Conservation Laboratory, the installation of a slab of petrified wood on the Mall entrance steps of NMNH, the SI Museum Support Center, the 75th anniversary of NMNH, and U.S. Biological Survey staff. People shown include the Emperor of Japan and Smithsonian Institution Secretaries Robert McCormick Adams, Spencer F. Baird, and Joseph Henry. Artifacts and specimens shown include classical ceramics and glass, dinosaurs, and passenger pigeons.

Arranged: By subject.

Captioned: With subject.

Finding Aid: No.

Restrictions: No.

NH·88

Public Information Office Temporary Exhibits Collection

Dates of Photographs: 1966–Present

Collection Origins

Thomas R. Harney of the NMNH Public Information Office assembled the collection to document temporary exhibits in the NMNH foyer, rotunda, and the Thomas M. Evans Gallery. Photographers represented include Marilyn Anderson, Susanne Anderson, Ed S. Ayers, Tupper Ansel Blake, Joel Breger, Chip Clark, Edward S. Curtis, Mignon Davis, Doc Dougherty, Joseph Farber, Mark Gulezian, Peter Hasselrot, Ogawa Isshin, Walter Jahn, Sumner Matteson, Susan Middleton, Kim Nielsen, Jyoti Rath, Kjell B. Sandved, Dilip Sinha, Donald and Elizabeth Wiechee, and Ray Witlin. Studios represented include the Field Museum of Natural History, Chicago, Illinois; NAA; Quicksilver Photographers; SITES; the State Jewish Museum, Prague, Czechoslovakia; and the World Bank, Washington, D.C.

Many of these photographs appear in specific exhibit catalogs such as the following: 1) David A. Altshuler. *Precious Legacy: Judaic Treasures From the Czechoslovak State Collections*. New York: Summit Books, 1983. 2) Christopher M. Lyman. *The Vanishing Race and Other Illusions: Photographs of Indians by Edward S. Curtis*. Washington, D.C.: Smithsonian Institution Press, 1982. 3) Tamana Northern. *The Art of Cameroon*. Washington, D.C.: Smithsonian Institution Traveling Exhibition Service, 1984. 4) Dorothy Kosler Washburn. *Hopi Kachina: Spirit of Life*. San Francisco: California Academy of Sciences, 1980. 5) Joyce C. White. *Ban Chiang: Discovery of a Lost Bronze Age*. Washington, D.C.: Smithsonian Institution Traveling Exhibition Service Press, 1982.

Physical Description

There are 900 photographs including color dye coupler phototransparencies and slides and silver gelatin photonegatives and photoprints. Other materials include articles, exhibit catalogs, exhibit opening invitations, newspaper clippings, slide scripts, *Smithsonian Research Reports*, and xerographic copies.

Subjects

The photographs document temporary exhibits in the Thomas M. Evans Gallery, the foyer, and the rotunda areas of the NMNH since 1974, as well as NMNH events since 1966. Also included are images of award ceremonies, exhibit openings, the installation of permanent objects such as the Bengal tiger, and visitors.

Exhibits in the Thomas M. Evans Gallery illustrated include "Aditi: A Celebration of Life"; "Art of Cameroon"; "Ban Chiang: Discovery of a Lost Bronze Age"; "Brazilian Feather Art"; "Deep Ocean Photography"; "Exploring Microspace"; "Five Thousand Years of Korean Art"; "Heritage of Islam"; "Hopi Kachina: Spirit of Life"; "Inua: Spirit World of the Bering Sea Eskimo"; "Japanese Ceramics Today"; "Masterworks from the Kikuchi Collection"; "Precious Legacy: Judaic Treasures from the Czechoslovak State Collection"; "Silk Route and Diamond Path"; "Treasures from the Shanghai Museum, 6,000 Years of Chinese Art"; "Vanishing Frontiers"; and "Vanishing Race and Other Illusions: A New Look at the Work of Edward Curtis."

Exhibits in the foyer and rotunda areas of NMNH documented include "African Insects: Nature Photographs by Mignon Davis"; "Alaskan Sealherd Paintings by Henry Wood Elliott"; "Birds of the Galápagos Islands"; "Birds of Prey: Rediscovered Paintings by Louis Fuertes"; "Chinese Children's Art"; "Cycles of Sustenance"; "Diplomats in Buckskin"; "The Farallon Islands"; "Geological Art of W.H. Holmes"; "Paintings of Asian Birds by Elizabeth Gwillin"; "Palms of the Lesser Antilles"; "Photographs of China, Japan, and Korea in the Late 19th and Early 20th Centuries"; "Photographs of Galápagos Wildlife by Feodor Pitcairn"; "Pre-Columbian Skull Engravings by Peter Hasselrot"; "Pressed on Paper: Fish Rubbings and Nature Prints"; "Scenes of Contemporary Egypt"; "Sculptures by Jean Ann Whiteman"; and "Traditional Watercolors by Lee Marc Steadman."

Other exhibits illustrated include "The Art of the Rock: Micro Images from the Earth's Crust"; "Beyond the Ocean, Beneath a Leaf, Photographs by Kjell Sandved"; "Botanical Prints by Henry Evans"; "Dance Masks of Mexico"; "It All Depends"; "National Anthropological Archives Exhibition, 1970"; "Native Americans, Photographs by Susanne Anderson and Joseph Farber"; "Our Changing Land"; "Paintings of California Flora by Mary Foly Barson"; "Paintings of Kenya by Linda Hoyle Gill"; "Photographs of Tropical Blossoms by Ed S. Ayers"; "Shadows of a Stone Age Man"; and "Wetheisfold Meteorite."

Arranged: In two series. 1) Press release notebooks. 2) Temporary exhibits information. Both series are then in chronological order.

Captioned: Some with date or OPPS number and subject.

Finding Aid: No.

Restrictions: No.

NH

Office of Education

Office of Education
National Museum of Natural History
Smithsonian Institution
Washington, D.C. 20560
Laura McKie, Acting Director
(202) 357-2066
Hours: Monday–Friday, 10 a.m.–5 p.m.

Scope of the Collections

There are 13 photographic collections with approximately 10,800 images.

Focus of the Collections

The collections document the Office of Education and its three divisions: Discovery Room, Docent Program, and Naturalist Center. There are images of past and present NMNH artifacts and specimens, exhibit installations, exhibit openings, special events, staff members, and visitors.

Photographic Processes and Formats Represented

There are color dye coupler photonegatives, photoprints, and slides and silver gelatin photonegatives, photoprints, and slides.

Other Materials Represented

The office also contains articles, audiotape cassettes, caption lists, glossaries, maps, posters, slide scripts, slide sets, slide set study questions, suggested reading lists, and teachers' guides.

Access and Usage Policies

These collections are open to scholarly researchers by appointment. Interested researchers should write to the office and describe their research topic, the type of material that interests them, and their research aim.

Publication Policies

Researchers must obtain permission from the Smithsonian Institution to reproduce a photograph and may also have to obtain permission from the copyright holder, which is not necessarily the Smithsonian Institution. The preferred credit line is "Courtesy of the National Museum of Natural History, Smithsonian Institution."

NH·89

Discovery Room Photoprint Collection

Dates of Photographs: 1980–Present

Collection Origins

The NMNH and OPPS staff created the photographic collection to document Discovery Room events and to serve as a browsing file for people who wish to purchase duplicate images from OPPS. The Discovery Room is a hands-on learning center for children.

Physical Description

There are 600 photographs including silver gelatin photonegatives and photoprints.

Subjects

The photographs document daily activities, events, and programs that take place in the NMNH Discovery Room. Many photographs show children handling natural history specimens.

Arranged: No.

Captioned: With OPPS number.

Finding Aid: No.

Restrictions: No. Contact Linda C. Stevens, Acting Manager, Discovery Room, Office of Education, NMNH, Room C219, MRC NHB 158, Smithsonian Institution, Washington, D.C. 20560. (202) 357-2288.

NH·90

Discovery Room Slide Collection

Dates of Photographs: 1974–Present

Collection Origins

The Discovery Room staff created the collection as an archival record of the collection boxes, docent programs, special events, and visitors in the Discovery Room, a hands-on learning center for children. There is a slide set, "Discovery Room: An Introduction," by Roberta Diemer and Janet D. Pawlukiewicz, that is for sale through OPPS. Write OPPS, Smithsonian Institution, NMAH, CB054, Washington, D.C. 20560, or call (202) 357-1933. Two scripts accompany the slides—one is geared to teachers planning a trip to the Discovery Room, the other to museum personnel planning to build a similar exhibit. There is also a slide set illustrating Smithsonian artifacts for use with the following book: Mary Ann Hoberman. *A House is a House for Me.* New York: Viking Press, 1978. Photographers represented include Chip Clark, Roberta Diemer, Eliot Elisofon, Kim Nielsen, Janet D. Pawlukiewicz, Kjell B. Sandved, and Linda Stevens.

Physical Description

There are 950 color dye coupler slides.

Subjects

Most of the photographs show specimens found in the NMNH Discovery Room or in Smithsonian Institution holdings, such as beaver and rodent teeth, cephalopods, minerals, a minke whale, mollusks, paper wasps, sea apples, a Seminole doll, and worm snails. There are also photographs of the Smithsonian Institution Building (Castle).

Arranged: In six series. 1) Discovery Room collection box contents. 2) "Discovery Room: An Introduction." 3) Docent archival record. 4) General Discovery Room slides. 5) "A House is a House for Me." 6) Visitor archival record.

Captioned: Most with OPPS number and subject.

Finding Aid: No.

Restrictions: No. Contact Linda C. Stevens, Acting Manager, Discovery Room, Office of Education, NMNH, Room C219, MRC NHB 158, Smithsonian Institution, Washington, D.C. 20560. (202) 357-2288.

NH·91

Docent Programs Photograph Collection

Dates of Photographs: 1974–Present

Collection Origins

Magdalene C. Schremp, Coordinator of the NMNH Docent Program, assembled the collection to record Docent Program special events. Photographers represented include Robert S. Harding, Richard K. Hoffmeister, OPPS staff, and Dane A. Penland.

Physical Description

There are 325 silver gelatin photoprints.

Subjects

The photographs are of special events connected with the Docent Program, such as docents in front of the Bicentennial exhibitions; docents shaking First Lady Patricia Nixon's hand at the White House in 1974; docents visiting D.C. public schools with touchable objects in 1977; a group portrait of the 300 NMNH docents in 1985; and a picnic with Porter M. Kier at Carderock, Maryland, in 1975.

Arranged: No.

Captioned: Many with OPPS number and subject.

Finding Aid: No.

Restrictions: No. Contact Magdalene C. Schremp, Coordinator, NMNH Docent Program/Internship, Office of Education, NMNH, Room 210, MRC NHB 158, Smithsonian Institution, Washington, D.C. 20560. (202) 357-3045.

NH·92

Education Office Lecture Collection

Dates of Photographs: 1970–Present

Collection Origins

Margery E. Gordon, NMNH Education Specialist, created the collection to augment lectures she gives to the public and at teacher workshops. Photographers represented include Margery Gordon, Victor Krantz, Erica Long, OPPS staff, Jeffrey Ploskonka, Kjell B. Sandved, and John S. Steiner.

Physical Description

There are 760 photographs including color dye coupler slides and silver gelatin photoprints.

Subjects

The photographs illustrate topics covered in NMNH educational lectures, such as African dancers, bronzeware, Children's Day at the National Museum of American Art in 1975, docents with children, Egyptian mummies, glassware, Greek pottery, Japanese children, Mexico, Pueblo pottery, and Roman coins. Exhibit halls and exhibits illustrated include "Chinese Writing"; the Dinosaur Hall; "Neanderthal"; "SEM"; the South American Hall; and "Splendors of Nature."

Arranged: By subject.

Captioned: Some with date and subject or OPPS negative number.

Finding Aid: No.

Restrictions: No. Contact Margery E. Gordon, Education Specialist, Office of Education, NMNH, Room 212, MRC NHB 158, Smithsonian Institution, Washington, D.C. 20560. (202) 357-2481.

NH·93

Education Office Photoprint Collection

Dates of Photographs: 1973–Present

Collection Origins

NMNH Acting Assistant Director for Education Laura L. McKie assembled the collection as a research file to document collections, events, special exhibitions, and visitors at NMNH. Photographers represented include Chip Clark, Victor Krantz, and OPPS and Time-Life staff.

Physical Description

There are 820 silver gelatin photoprints.

Subjects

NMNH events illustrated include African Heritage Week, 1977; the Chinese Opera, November 4, 1985; the Indian Walkabout, fall 1983; the 75th Anniversary of NMNH; and the Shanghai Chinese Festival. The NMNH collections and exhibit halls shown include the Discovery Room, 1976; Physical Anthropology Hall; and skull sets.

Arranged: Chronologically and by subject.

Captioned: With date, OPPS number, and subject.

Finding Aid: No.

Restrictions: No. Contact Laura L. McKie, Acting Assistant Director for Education, Office of Education, NMNH, Room 212, MRC NHB 158, Smithsonian Institution, Washington, D.C. 20560. (202) 357-2066.

NH·94

Education Office Published Slide Sets Collection

Dates of Photographs: 1970s–Present

Collection Origins

The NMNH and OPPS staff created the collection, which consists of four slide sets, for loan to elementary school classrooms. Each set includes a script to be read with the slide presentation. Photographers and studios represented include C. Sissie Brimberg, Laura L. McKie, OPPS staff, and Woodfin Camp, Inc.

Physical Description

There are 270 color dye coupler slides. Other materials include a glossary, a list of suggested reading for each slide set, scripts, and a set of study questions.

Subjects

The four slide sets are as follows: 1) "Dinosaurs and the Age of Reptiles"; 2) "Glaciers"; 3) "Introduction to Natural History: Learning About the Museum"; and 4) "Native Peoples of North America." Dinosaurs illustrated include camptosaurus, stegosaurus, triceratops, and tylosaurus. There are also photographs of an unidentified fossil dinosaur being mounted. Buildings, exhibits, and objects illustrated include a tarantula at the Insect Zoo, the Polar Eskimo Hall, and the Smithsonian Institution Building (Castle). Staff and visitors shown include children in the NMNH Discovery Room and staff studying minerals and whales. American Indian-related images represented include informal portraits of people assembling potshards and building canoes, as well as images of artifacts such as a travois and wampum.

Arranged: In four slide sets. 1) "Dinosaurs and the Age of Reptiles." 2) "Glaciers." 3) "Introduction to Natural History: Learning About the Museum." 4) "Native Peoples of North America."

Captioned: With negative number and subject.

Finding Aid: An index with negative number, source, and subject.

Restrictions: No. Contact Laura L. McKie, Acting Assistant Director of Education, Office of Education, NMNH, Room 212, MRC NHB 158, Smithsonian Institution, Washington, D.C. 20560. (202) 357-2066.

NH·95

Education Office Slide Sets Collection

Dates of Photographs: 1970s–Present

Collection Origins

Acting Assistant Director of Education Laura L. McKie assembled the collection from a variety of sources for docent projects, in-house teaching sessions, and public programs. Outside educators may use these slides for research at NMNH. Although these slides do not circulate, they are occasionally lent to schools before their visits to NMNH. Photographers represented include Shirley Adams, Kitty Brown, Eliot Elisofon, Whitney Halstead, B. Hunter, Marsha Mirsky, H. Wes Pratt, Kjell B. Sandved, and Geza Teleki. Studios represented include Finley-Holiday Film, Whittier, California; Herbert E. Budek Co., Inc., Hackensack, New Jersey; the Japanese Embassy; the Milwaukee Public Museum, Milwaukee, Wisconsin; Museo Nacional de Antropologia, Mexico City; the National Geographic Society, Washington, D.C.; OPPS; Photo Lab, Inc., Washington, D.C.; SK Color Co., Ltd., Tokyo; UNICEF; and Wolfe Worldwide Films, Los Angeles.

Physical Description

There are 2,000 color dye coupler slides.

Subjects

Photographs document material culture and peoples worldwide, including China, Egypt, India, Korea, Latin America, and the United States. Specific locations and research sites illustrated include an Algonquin village, Roanoke Island Historical Park, North Carolina; architecture, Latin America; Buddhist caves, Lo Yang (now Luoyang), China; Chinese flower pagoda, Canton (now Guangzhou), China; Mayan ruins, Central America; and the Taj Mahal, India. Objects illustrated include Ashanti drums; an Egyptian coffin, c. 1000 B.C.; Japanese dolls in the NMNH Learning Center; Peruvian textiles; and Southwestern American Indian pottery and basketry. People portrayed include American Indians (in drawings by John White), Bushmen, Chinese acrobatic dancers, and Japanese families at home. NMNH exhibitions photographed include "Aditi: A Celebration of Life," "Brown Coal Forest (Cenozoic era)," "Indian Costume," and "Magnificent Voyagers." Smithsonian activities shown include African Heritage Week, February 1976; the American Folklife Festival, 1974; a demonstration of deerstalking with stone arrow points; docent tours, spring 1976; the Discovery Room; and a fossil collecting and hunting trip. Animals illustrated include chimpanzees, Cuban tree snails, and sharks.

Arranged: By subject.

Captioned: Some with subject.

Finding Aid: Two finding aids to part of the collection. 1) A 12-page guide to the chimpanzee slides by Geza Telecki. 2) A manual accompanying "The Culture of the American Southwest" set.

Restrictions: No. Contact Laura L. McKie, Acting Assistant Director of Education, Office of Education, NMNH, Room 212, MRC NHB 158, Smithsonian Institution, Washington, D.C. 20560. (202) 357-2066.

NH·96

General Education Photograph Collection *A.K.A.* Rebecca Mead Photograph Collection

Dates of Photographs: 1960s–Present

Collection Origins

Education Specialist Rebecca G. Mead created the collection as a working file to use in educational programs for children, lectures, published pamphlets, and teacher workshops. Photographers and studios represented include J. Lawrence Angel; Denver Museum of Natural History; Friends of the National Zoo; Rebecca G. Mead; Ernest G. Meyers; National Wildlife Federation; OPPS; Photo Lab, Inc., Washington, D.C.; Roloc Color Slides, Washington, D.C.; Kjell B. Sandved; Pat Vosburgh; and Thomas R. Waller.

Physical Description

There are 2,650 photographs including color dye coupler slides and silver gelatin photonegatives and photoprints.

Subjects

The photographs document Washington, D.C., architecture and Smithsonian Institution artifacts, exhibits, staff, and staff activities. Washington, D.C., architecture shown includes Ford's Theatre, the National Gallery of Art, and the U.S. Supreme Court. Smithsonian exhibits and exhibit halls shown include the "African Great Plains Animals"; Ecology Hall, 1976; "Eskimo Life"; Fossil Mammal Hall; "Graves of the Steppes"; Osteology Hall; "Our Changing Land"; "Prehistoric Life"; "Trojan Daily Life"; and "Woodland Indian Crafts." Objects illustrated include dinosaur skeletons, Greek vases, grave goods, mummies, and pottery.

There are informal portraits of Smithsonian curators and staff including John C. Ewers, Francis M. Greenwell, Raymond B. Manning, Joan W. Nowicke, Mary E. Rice, S. Dillon Ripley, Clyde F. Roper, Waldo L. Schmidt, and George R. Zug. There are also photographs of children's educational programs, docent field trips, and geological maps of the Washington, D.C., area.

Arranged: Some by type of material, then by subject.

Captioned: Most with OPPS number and subject.

Finding Aid: No.

Restrictions: No. Contact Rebecca G. Mead, Education Specialist, Office of Education, NMNH, Room 212, MRC NHB 158, Smithsonian Institution, Washington, D.C. 20560. (202) 357-2811.

NH·97

Naturalist Center Anthropological Photoprint Collection

Dates of Photographs: 1976–Present

Collection Origins

The Naturalist Center staff created the photographic collection to document the Center's holdings of more than 20,000 specimens which are available for hands-on examination and research. The Center emphasizes local (within a 90-mile radius of Washington, D.C.) anthropology and natural history but includes some worldwide specimens. There are anthropological artifacts, photographs, and specimens of fossils, insects, invertebrates, minerals, plants, rocks, and vertebrates. The photograph collection includes copy photoprints from the NMNH's National Anthropological Archives (NAA). Photographers and studios represented include David F. Barry, Christian Barthelmess, Charles M. Bell, Samuel M. Brookes, G. John Bryson, J.N. Chamberlain, Charles Barney Cory, Sr., Frances Densmore, William Dinwiddie, A.W. Ericson, Thomas M. Galey, Alexander Gardener, Dwight R. Gardin, De Lancey Gill, John M. Goggin, C.O. Hastings, F. Jay Haynes, H.W. Henshaw, John K. Hiller, H.L. Hime, Irwin and Mankins, G. Wharton James, William Libbey, R. Maynard, James Mooney, Stanley Morrow, Timothy H. O'Sullivan, William S. Prettyman, Frank Randall, Roland Reed, Robertson & Co., Frank A. Robinson,

Frank Russell, Harlen I. Smith, William S. Soule, Matilda Coxe Stevenson, Adam Clark Vroman, J.E. Whitney, and Winter and Pond.

Physical Description

There are 430 silver gelatin photoprints, all recent copies of originals.

Subjects

The photographs document North American Indians from the 1860s through the 1920s and their body ornamentation, clothing, dancing, housing, and tools. Some photographs are reproductions of engravings, lithographs, paintings, and pencil sketches.

Arranged: In three series. 1) Four notebooks labeled "Life of North American Indians," arranged by geographic location. 2) Two notebooks labeled "Indian Photographs by W.S. Soule (1867–1874)," arranged by Indian tribe. 3) Four notebooks labeled "Portraits of Famous Indians," arranged alphabetically by subject's name.

Captioned: With date, location, NAA number, photographer's name, and subject, including activity shown, location, and tribal name.

Finding Aid: No.

Restrictions: No. Contact Richard H. Efthim, Manager, or Helene Lisy, Assistant Manager, Naturalist Center, Office of Education, NMNH, Room C219, MRC NHB 158, Smithsonian Institution, Washington, D.C. 20560. (202) 357-2804.

NH·98

Naturalist Center Biological and Geological Slide Collection

Dates of Photographs: 1976–Present

Collection Origins

The Naturalist Center staff created the collection of slide sets to document the Center's holdings. For a description of the Center see the *Collection Origins* field of *NH·97*. Studios represented include Oxford Scientific Films, Ltd., and Carolina Biological Supply Company, Burlington, North Carolina, from whom the Center purchased slides.

Physical Description

There are 650 color dye coupler slides.

Subjects

The photographs form four slide shows on annelids; fishes; the life cycle of stickleback fish; and the 1980 eruption of Mount St. Helens, Washington. Annelids include earthworms, leeches, and other cylindrical segmented worms. Also shown are invertebrates such as arachnids, crustaceans, echinoderms, insects, and mollusks; minerals; and vertebrates such as amphibians, birds, and reptiles.

Arranged: By slide show subject. 1) "Our Mount St. Helens Story." 2) "Representative Annelids." 3) "Representative Fishes." 4) "Stickleback Life Cycle."

Captioned: With subject information.

Finding Aid: A caption list and text for each slide set.

Restrictions: No. Contact Richard H. Efthim, Manager, or Helene Lisy, Assistant Manager, Naturalist Center, Office of Education, NMNH, Room C219, MRC NHB 158, Smithsonian Institution, Washington, D.C. 20560. (202) 357-2804.

NH·99

Naturalist Center Photoprint Collection

Dates of Photographs: 1972–Present

Collection Origins

The staff of the Naturalist Center assembled the collection as an inventory of the Center's displays, special projects, specimens, and staff members. For a description of the Center see the *Collection Origins* field of *NH·97*. Photographers represented include Chip Clark and Naturalist Center and OPPS staff.

Physical Description

There are 760 silver gelatin photonegatives and photoprints. Many are photomicrographs.

Subjects

Photographs show NMNH Naturalist Center displays and specimens, students and staff at work, and thin-sections of specimens.

Arranged: In four series by subject. 1) Photomicrographs of specimens (thin-sections). 2) Specimens and displays. 3) Staff members at work. 4) Students using the Naturalist Center.

Captioned: Some with date, Naturalist Center number, and specimen name.

Finding Aid: No.

Restrictions: No. Contact Richard H. Efthim, Manager, or Helene Lisy, Assistant Manager, Naturalist Center, Office of Education, NMNH, Room C219, MRC NHB 158, Smithsonian Institution, Washington, D.C. 20560. (202) 357-2804.

NH·100

Naturalist Center SI Slide Sets

Dates of Photographs: 1976–1980

Collection Origins

The Naturalist Center staff assembled the collection, which consists of four slide sets based on materials in Smithsonian Institution collections. The sets are produced and sold by OPPS. Write OPPS, Smithsonian Institution, NMAH, CB054, Washington, D.C. 20560, or call (202) 357-1933. For a description of the Center see the *Collection Origins* field of *NH·97*. Photographers represented include Karen K. Bigelow, Marion F. Briggs, Chip Clark, and Ruth O. Selig.

Physical Description

There are 250 color dye coupler slides. Other materials include an audiotape cassette, caption list, maps, posters, and a teachers' guide.

Subjects

The slides document both biological specimens, such as insects and pandas, and North American Indian historical events and movements including the Battle of the Little Bighorn (Montana), the Battle at Wounded Knee (South Dakota), and the Ghost Dance.

Arranged: In four slide set series by subject. 1) "Arthropods! An Introduction to Insects and Their Relatives." 2) "The Battle of the Little Bighorn." 3) "The Ghost Dance Tragedy at Wounded Knee." 4) "Pandas."

Captioned: With subject information.

Finding Aid: Each slide set includes caption information, an introduction, and a list of suggested readings.

Restrictions: No. Contact Richard H. Efthim, Manager, or Helene Lisy, Assistant Manager, Naturalist Center, Office of Education, NMNH, Room C219, MRC NHB 158, Smithsonian Institution, Washington, D.C. 20560. (202) 357-2804.

NH·101

Naturalist Center Slide Collection

Dates of Photographs: 1977–1981

Collection Origins

Naturalist Center staff assembled the collection to be used in slide shows documenting the Naturalist Center events, history, holdings, and visitors. For a description of the Center see the *Collection Origins* field of *NH·97*. Photographers represented include Naturalist Center and OPPS staff and Meg Silver.

Physical Description

There are 330 color dye coupler slides.

Subjects

The photographs document archeological artifacts, fossil insects and vertebrate specimens, minerals, Naturalist Center facilities including the Teacher Resource Area, and Naturalist Center staff.

Arranged: By subject.

Captioned: A few with subject.

Finding Aid: No.

Restrictions: No. Contact Richard H. Efthim, Manager, Naturalist Center, Office of Education, NMNH, Room C219, MRC NHB 158, Smithsonian Institution, Washington, D.C. 20560. (202) 357-2804.

NH

Office of Exhibits

Office of Exhibits
National Museum of Natural History
Smithsonian Institution
Washington, D.C. 20560
Chip Clark, Staff Photographer
(202) 357-2760
Hours: Monday–Friday, 10 a.m.–5 p.m.

Scope of the Collections

There is one photographic collection with approximately 24,500 images.

Focus of the Collections

The collection documents past and present NMNH exhibits, exhibit halls, exhibit installations, exhibit openings, specimens, and staff. Many of the images were used in exhibit catalogs, guide books, and press releases.

Photographic Processes and Formats Represented

There are color dye coupler photonegatives, phototransparencies, and slides and silver gelatin photonegatives (some infrared test film) and photoprints.

Other Materials Represented

None.

Access and Usage Policies

This collection is open to scholarly researchers by appointment. Interested researchers should write to the office and describe their research topic, the type of material that interests them, and their research aim.

Publication Policies

Researchers must obtain permission from the Smithsonian Institution to reproduce a photograph and may also have to obtain permission from the copyright holder, which is not necessarily the Smithsonian Institution. The preferred credit line is "Courtesy of the National Museum of Natural History, Smithsonian Institution."

NH·102

Exhibits Office Photograph Collection *A.K.A.* Chip Clark Photograph Collection

Dates of Photographs: 1975–Present

Collection Origins

NMNH Staff Photographer Chip Clark created this collection to document NMNH collections, events, exhibits, and staff. Clark has worked at NMNH since 1973. Many of the photographs are reproduced in NMNH catalogs, press releases, and exhibit guide books such as the following publications: 1) Herman J. Viola. *The Magnificent Voyagers, the U.S. Exploring Expedition, 1838–1842.* Washington, D.C.: Smithsonian Institution Press, 1985. 2) Thomas M. Evans Gallery. *Aditi, the Living Arts of India.* Washington, D.C.: Smithsonian Institution Press, 1985.

Physical Description

There are 24,500 photographs including color dye coupler photonegatives, phototransparencies, and slides; and silver gelatin photonegatives (some infrared test film) and photoprints. Many images are duplicates.

Subjects

The photographs document NMNH collections, exhibit construction, exhibit openings, exhibits, facilities, staff, and visitors. NMNH exhibit halls and exhibits illustrated include the "Conquest of Land"; Dinosaur Hall; Discovery Room; Evolution Hall; Ice Age Mammals Hall; Insect Zoo; "It All Depends"; "Legacy of History"; "Magnificent Voyagers"; "Microspace"; Naturalist Center; "South America: Continent and Culture"; Thomas M. Evans Gallery exhibits of Japanese ceramics and Korean art; "Views of the Vanishing Frontier"; and Western Civilization Hall. Unidentified NMNH exhibits on fish, lunar geology, and squid are also documented. Other images show crowded storage conditions, exhibit banners, exhibit preparations, fieldwork, Folklife Festivals, projects (e.g., the Burgess Shale Project, Canada); and seminars.

Arranged: By subject into volumes.

Captioned: With OPPS number and Clark's stamp.

Finding Aid: No.

Restrictions: The photographs of the murals in the NMNH exhibit halls are restricted because the murals are copyrighted.

NH

Smithsonian Oceanographic Sorting Center

Smithsonian Oceanographic Sorting Center
Museum Support Center
Smithsonian Institution
Washington, D.C. 20560
Kristin Murphy, Museum Technician
(202) 238-3604
Hours: Monday–Friday, 10 a.m.–5 p.m.

Scope of the Collection

There is one photographic collection with approximately 63,300 images.

Focus of the Collection

This collection documents currents on the floors of antarctic and subantarctic waters.

Photographic Processes and Formats Represented

There are color dye coupler slides and silver gelatin photonegatives, photoprints, and slides.

Other Materials Represented

None.

Access and Usage Policies

This collection is open to scholarly researchers by appointment. Interested researchers should write to the Center and describe their research topic, the type of material that interests them, and their research aim.

Publication Policies

Researchers must obtain permission from the Smithsonian Institution to reproduce a photograph and may also have to obtain permission from the copyright holder, which is not necessarily the Smithsonian Institution. The preferred credit line is "Courtesy of the National Museum of Natural History, Smithsonian Institution."

NH·103

U.S. Antarctic Research Program Photograph Collection

Dates of Photographs: 1963–1973

Collection Origins

This collection was created by grantees and contractors aboard research vessels operating in antarctic and subantarctic waters from 1963 to 1973 under the U.S. Antarctic Research Program of the National Science Foundation. The primary vessel was the USNS *Eltanin,* with minor contributions from the R/V *Herd* and U.S. Coast Guard Service Vessel *Glacier.* Photographs were taken at about 1,000 locations in the Atlantic and Pacific Oceans. Data on a variety of biological, geological, and oceanographic features can be determined and analyzed from the photographs.

Physical Description

There are 63,300 photographs including color dye coupler slides and silver gelatin photonegatives, photoprints, and slides.

Subjects

These photographs show biological, geological, and oceanographic features including ocean currents on the ocean bottom in antarctic and subantarctic waters.

Arranged: Alphabetically by ship name, then by cruise number.

Captioned: With camera station, cruise of ship, depth, frame number, latitude, longitude, and ship station.

Finding Aid: A computerized master list with biological and geological materials collected, bottom type, fauna density, film size, homogeneity of materials, instrumentation, location's longitude and latitude, negatives copied, photography type, ocean current strength and direction, print quality, and other biological and physical features.

Restrictions: Restricted to qualified investigators. The National Science Foundation must be acknowledged if the material is used in published or unpublished reports.

NH

U.S. Biological Survey

U.S. Biological Survey
U.S. Fish and Wildlife Service
U.S. Department of the Interior
National Museum of Natural History
Smithsonian Institution
Washington, D.C. 20560
(202) 357-1930
Hours: Monday–Friday, 10 a.m.–5 p.m., by appointment only.

Scope of the Collections

There are seven photographic collections with approximately 33,200 images.

Focus of the Collections

The U.S. Biological Survey (USBS) is a research unit of the U.S. Fish and Wildlife Service of the U.S. Department of the Interior. Four USBS sections (Birds, Curatorial Services, Mammals, and Reptiles and Amphibians) are housed in the NMNH building. USBS staff share curatorial responsibilities and collections with the NMNH Division of Mammals. The USBS collections are described here as a courtesy to researchers, although the USBS is not formally part of the Smithsonian Institution.

In 1885 the Section of Economic Ornithology was established under the U.S. Department of Agriculture's Division of Entomology to study bird distribution, food habits, and migration in the United States in relation to insects and plants. In 1886 founding director C. Hart Merriam expanded the section to include mammals. Renamed the Bureau of the Biological Survey in 1896, the bureau joined the U.S. Department of the Interior in 1939 and the Bureau of Fisheries in 1940, when the USBS became a research unit of the U.S. Fish and Wildlife Service. The USBS acquired permanent collections, conducted biological expeditions, and studied American plant and animal distributions and the physical factors that influenced them. Since 1889 the Smithsonian Institution has been the official repository for specimens gathered for distributional, identification, and taxonomic studies by the staff of the USBS Bird and Mammal Laboratories. Many of the early scientists active in the USBS were also affiliated with the Smithsonian.

Note: Several related collections are housed in the Smithsonian Institution Archives, including Record Units 7146, 7171, 1070101, and 1070201, which document the Bird and Mammal Laboratories of the U.S. Fish and Wildlife Service; Record Unit 45, the Records of the Office of the Secretary (Charles D. Walcott), 1903-1924; Record Unit 7267, the Vernon Orlando Bailey Papers; Record Unit 7168, the Bureau of Biological Survey, U.S. Department of the Interior Big Game Estimates and Inventories; Record Unit 7172, the Hartley H.T. Jackson Papers; Record Unit 7170, the A. Remington Kellogg Papers; Record Unit 7252, the Edward Alexander Preble Papers; Record Unit 7176, the U.S. Fish and Wildlife Service Field Reports; Record Unit 7174, the Stanley Paul Young Papers; Record Unit 9507, the Paul H. Oehser Interviews; and Record Unit 9504, the Alexander Wetmore Interviews.

The photographs reflect the collecting and research interests of the USBS, including the Red Wolf Recovery Program, and are used to identify specimens (including holotypes), document habitats and wildlife refuges, and record site conditions and survey expeditions. A holotype is a specimen that is the basis for the original description of a species and later is designated a type specimen.

Photographic Processes and Formats Represented

There are albumen photoprints; color dye coupler photonegatives, photoprints, and slides; holograms; platinum photoprints; silver gelatin dry plate photonegatives; and silver gelatin photonegatives, photoprints, and slides.

Other Materials Represented

The USBS also contains charts, correspondence, maps, pamphlets, photomechanicals (photogravures), postcards, and specimens.

Access and Usage Policies

The collections are open to scholarly researchers by appointment only. Interested researchers should write to USBS and describe their research topic, the type of material that interests them, and their research aim.

Publication Policies

Researchers must obtain permission from the Smithsonian Institution to reproduce a photograph and may also have to obtain permission from the copyright holder, which is not necessarily the Smithsonian Institution. The preferred credit line is "Courtesy of the U.S. Biological Survey, National Museum of Natural History, Smithsonian Institution."

NH·104

Biological Survey General Collection

Dates of Photographs: 1885–Present

Collection Origins

The U.S. Biological Survey (USBS) staff created the collection to document its collecting and research interests. The photographs are used to identify specimens (including holotypes), document habitats and wildlife refuges, and record research site conditions and survey expeditions.

Photographers and collectors represented include the Alaska Railroad, Ansel Adams, Vernon Bailey, R.E. Bateman, W.B. Campbell, P.N. Chase, C. Cottam, L.K. Crouch, Paul Dalke, Ben East, Harriet Ewing, Frank Flack, L.A. Gehr, Edward A. Goldman, Luther C. Goldman, L.J. Goldman, J. Malcolm Greany, E.P. Haddon, Henry Haddon, B.M. Hazeltine, H.W. Hicks, Jay Higgins, Hileman, John M. Hopkins, Arthur H. Howell, Hartley H.T. Jackson, S.G. Jewett, J.C. Jones, N. Kent, W.F. Kubichek, L.L. Laythe, J.S. Ligon, J.S. Lundgeen, J.M. Madsen, David Marshall, Norman McClintock, C. Hart Merriam, Laura E. Mills, Olaus J. Murie, OPPS staff, L.W. Orr, W.H. Osgood, L.J. Palmer, Joseph H. Riley, Theo. H. Scheffer, V.B. Scheffer, Schultz Photo, W.M. Sharp, F. Sheldon, H.H. Sheldon, J. Silver, Robert H. Smith, Winston E. Steverward, A.W. Susott, S.M. Sutton, W.P. Taylor, J. Van Huizen, A. Walker, Alexander Wetmore, Cecil Williams, Stanley P. Young, and Howard Zahniser. The photographs are published in scientific journals including the following: 1) American Society of Mammalogists. *Journal of Mammalogy.* Baltimore, Maryland: American Society of Mammalogists, 1919– . 2) Biological Society of Washington. *Proceedings of the Biological Society of Washington.* Washington, D.C.: The Society, 1885– .

Physical Description

There are 3,400 photographs including albumen photoprints, holograms, platinum photoprints, silver gelatin dry plate lantern slides and photonegatives, and silver gelatin photonegatives (some on nitrate) and photoprints. Other materials represented include charts, correspondence, maps, pamphlets, and postcards.

Subjects

The photographs document animal habitats, animal specimens, expeditions, field parties, research activities, survey site conditions, and wildlife refuges as well as hunters, scientists, trappers, and USBS associates.

Survey expedition camp and field party locations shown include Canada (the rapids of the Athabaska River); Baja California, Cerro de Tancitario (Nelson's camp, 1919), and Michoacan (Nelson's camp, La Salada, 1903), Mexico; and Alaska, New Mexico (Dulee and Moreno camps, 1919), Virginia (High Levels camp), and Washington (Barron, Cascade Mountains, and Mt. Rainier, 1919), in the United States. The photographs also document conditions of survey sites.

Hunters and trappers portrayed include Vernon Bailey and Hartley H.T. Jackson in Virginia (1935); Mrs. Vernon Bailey holding beaver trapped at a Michigan beaver farm (1927); C.E. Beebe and dog with mountain lions; Robb K. Euders; J.H. Gant in New Mexico camp (1904); Hartley H.T. Jackson and E.E. Ritter examining grasses in Florida; Alaskan hunter, pioneer, and trapper Nellie Neal Lawing; Benjamin V. Lilly with a mountain lion and dogs; mountain lion hunters northwest of Silver City, New Mexico; and I.L. Richie. Several of these images are reproduced in the illustrations in this volume.

Animal specimens shown include badgers, bats, bears and bear scratches on an aspen tree, beavers, birds, bison, caribou, chipmunks, deer, elk, gophers, hares, lynx, martens, mice, mink, moles, moose, mountain lions (pumas), muskrats, opossums, otters, porcupines, rabbits, raccoons, rats, red foxes, reindeer, rodents, salmon, sea lions, seals, shrews, skunks, squirrels, weasels, and wolves.

Animal habitats and wildlife refuges illustrated include the Calaveras Reservation (1900) and Sacramento, California; the Okefenokee Swamp, Georgia; Laysan Island, Hawaii; Kentucky; Medicine Rocks, Montana; Valentine, Nebraska; Bosque, New Mexico; Chautauqua, New York; Des Lacs River, North Dakota; Wichita Mountains, Oklahoma; Hart Mountain, Klamath Falls (forest fire), and Malheur, Oregon; Cape Romain, South Carolina; Bear River City, Utah; and Olympic National Park, Washington. Mexican animal habitats, research sites, and villages illustrated include San Vicente, Baja California; Campeche; Chiapas; Hidalgo del Parral, Chihuahua; Colima; Durango; Guerrero; Lake Chapala, Jalisco; Michoacan; Oaxaca; Cozumel Island, Quintana Roo; Sonora; Tabasco; and the Yucatán. USBS colleagues and staff portrayed include C.H.M. Barret and Harold Vars in the taxidermy shop; Cliff Berryman; biological investigators at work in the laboratory; G.G. Cantwell preparing specimens at Mt. Rainier, Washington; Colorado pioneer naturalist Edwin Carter (1830–1900); Mrs. Christianson with young mountain lions near Columbia Falls, Montana; USBS Chief Jay N. Darling (1934–1935); Edward A. Preble, L.J. Goldman, and a game management agent on a waterfowl investigation (1934); researchers at Patuxent Wildlife Research Center in Bowie, Maryland; and past USBS employees shown in both group and individual portraits.

Arranged: In three series. 1) Lantern slides and photoprints made from lantern slides. 2) Employee and specimen file, containing framed images. 3) Habitat, survey site, and wildlife refuge file.

Captioned: Many with date, location, photographer, and subject.

Finding Aid: No.

Restrictions: No. Contact Robert Fisher, Collection Manager, or Thomas Fritts, Chief of Biological Survey, U.S. Fish and Wildlife Service, NMNH, Rooms 378 and 400, Smithsonian Institution, Washington, D.C. 20560. (202) 357-1865 (Fisher) and 357-1930 (Fritts).

NH·105

Biological Survey Mammal Skull Collection

Dates of Photographs: 1905–Present

Collection Origins

The USBS staff assembled the collection to reflect the research interests of the Mammals section, emphasizing the distributional, ecological, geographical, historical, and systematical studies of amphibians, birds, mammals, and reptiles. Photographers and studios represented include the Academy of Natural Sciences of Philadelphia, Pennsylvania; American Museum of Natural History, New York City; McHaney, Paragould, Arkansas; OPPS; Carl Rungins; and Carolyn Sheldon.

Physical Description

There are 315 silver gelatin photoprints (some mounted on board).

Subjects

The photographs document the skulls of mammals in the Americas and the Antarctic including caribou, dogs, foxes, musk oxen, rats, reindeer, and seals. Many of the skulls are type specimens found in museums in Europe and the United States. Type specimens are specimens chosen by taxonomists as the basis for describing and naming new species.

Arranged: No.

Captioned: With specimen name.

Finding Aid: No.

Restrictions: No. Contact Thomas Fritts, Chief of Biological Survey, U.S. Fish and Wildlife Service, NMNH, Room 378, Smithsonian Institution, Washington, D.C. 20560. (202) 357-1930.

NH·106

Biological Survey Photonegative Collection *A.K.A.* Ernest P. Walker Photonegative Collection

Dates of Photographs: 1940–1958

Collection Origins

Vertebrate Zoologist Ernest P. Walker (1891–1969) assembled the collection as part of his research materials. Walker worked for the Bureau of Fisheries in Alaska (1913–1919) and served as U.S. Game Warden in Arizona and southern California (1919–1921); Alaskan Fur and Game Warden (1921–1925); Chief Representative of the Bureau of the Biological Survey, U.S. Department of Agriculture in Alaska (1925–1927); and Assistant to Reservations and Senior Biologist of the U.S. Biological Survey (USBS) in Washington, D.C. (1927–1930). Walker was the Assistant Director of the National Zoological Park (NZP) from 1930 to 1956.

Walker studied the birds of Wyoming and the mammals of the world, as well as the administration and protection of wildlife such as fur-bearing land animals. He was a member of the Cooper Ornithological Club and the Pacific Northwest Bird and Mammal Society. Walker took all the photographs in this collection.

Physical Description

There are 23,330 silver gelatin photonegatives. Many are copy photonegatives.

Subjects

The photographs document animals worldwide and birds of Wyoming. Approximately half of the images are photographic reproductions of book and journal illustrations; the other half were taken of animals at the National Zoological Park (NZP) or in the wild. People portrayed include NZP and USBS scientists, Mr. and Mrs. M.E. Mugrave, and Esther S. Walker. Animals shown include anteaters, bats, bison, horses, moles, monkeys, mountain lions, red pandas, rhinoceros, squirrels, tarsiers, weasels, wombats, and woodchucks. Other photographs show the old bear cage at NZP; an old mill near Leesburg, Virginia; and staff preparing food in the basement of the NZP Reptile House.

Arranged: By assigned negative number (from 1431 to 5319).

Captioned: Photonegatives with negative number; photograph envelopes with animal name, date, location, and negative number.

Finding Aid: No.

Restrictions: Due to asbestos contamination the collection is restricted. Contact Thomas Fritts, Chief of Biological Survey, U.S. Fish and Wildlife Service, NMNH, Room 378, Smithsonian Institution, Washington, D.C. 20560. (202) 357-1930.

NH·107

Biological Survey Staff Collection *A.K.A.* C. Hart Merriam Family Collection

Dates of Photographs: 1855–Present

Collection Origins

The U.S. Biological Survey (USBS) staff assembled the portrait collection to document Clinton Hart Merriam (1855–1942), founding director of the USBS, and his family. Merriam, who attended Yale University from 1874 to 1877, received an M.D. from the College of Physicians and Surgeons (now Columbia) in 1879, after which he practiced medicine for six years. Merriam participated in several expeditions including the U.S. Geological and Geographical Survey of the Territories (the Hayden Survey) which he joined when he was 16, as a collector of bird skins and eggs. From 1885 to 1910 Merriam was Chief of the USBS. Under Merriam's guidance, the Biological Survey acquired permanent collections, conducted expeditions and general survey work, and studied American plant and animal distributions and the physical factors that influenced them. For a history of the USBS see the *Focus of Collections* section in the introduction to the U.S. Biological Survey.

Merriam surveyed Alaska and California's Death Valley and San Francisco Mountain areas. He wrote many books and treatises including articles on the vast USBS mammal specimen collection. When he retired in 1910, a trust fund provided by Mrs. E.H. Harriman allowed him to pursue, through the Smithsonian, independent research projects on the Indians of California. Merriam was a founder of the National Geographic Society and member of the American Ornithologists Union, the American Society of Mammalogists, the Biological Society of Washington, the National Academy of Sciences, and the Washington Academy of Sciences.

Photographers and studios represented include Associated News; Bachrach; Brady's National Photographic Portrait Galleries; G.V. Buck; Clinedinst Studio; Crandall; Davis and Sanford; Bernard DeWeese; Dall DeWeese; The Fine Arts Studio; Wm. Hubbell Fisher; Frizell; Gardner and Pray; Gessford; Harris and Ewing; Haynes Photo; N. Jenks; Lewis; Mandeville; National Cyclopedia of American Biography, James T. White and Co.; Notman Photo Company; Photographic Service, Inc.; J.E. Purdy and Company; Sarony, New York City; Taber; F. Valeche; and Williamson and Brookland.

The photographs have been used in the following publications by Merriam: 1) *Life Zones and Crop Zones of the United States.* Washington, D.C.: Government Printing Office, 1898. 2) *The Mammals of the Adirondack Region, Northeastern New York.* New York: Henry Holt and Co., 1886. 3) *Results of a Biological Survey of the San Francisco Mountain Region and Desert of the Little Colorado, Arizona.* U.S. Department of Agriculture, Division of Ornithology and Mammalogy, North American Fauna, no. 3. Washington, D.C.: Government Printing Office, 1890. 4) *A Review of the Birds of Connecticut.* New Haven: Tuttle, Morehouse & Taylor, 1877. The photographs have also appeared in the following recent publication: *Fish and Wildlife News Special Edition—Research.* U.S. Department of the Interior, April–May 1981.

Physical Description

There are 100 photographs including albumen photoprints, platinum photoprints, silver gelatin photoprints, and a tintype. Formats include cabinet cards, cartes-de-visite, and unfinished proofs. Other materials include a photogravure.

Subjects

Most of the photographs portray the C. Hart Merriam family, particularly ornithologist and writer Florence Merriam Bailey, who was the sister of C. Hart Merriam and the wife of Vernon Bailey. Other family members and friends portrayed include Helen Bagg (aunt), Vernon Bailey, Fred and Augusta Merriam Houe as children, C. Hart Merriam, Gustave Merriam (uncle), Helen Merriam, James S. Merriam, and Carolyn Sheldon. There are also some illustrations of Alaskan expeditionary field camps and research sites, as well as guides and trappers of the American West. A series of Alaskan landscape views (16 cabinet cards) show early exploration expeditions in the Kenai Mountains.

Arranged: By subject.

Captioned: With subject, and some with date.

Finding Aid: No.

Restrictions: No. Contact Thomas Fritts, Chief of Biological Survey, U.S. Fish and Wildlife Service, NMNH, Room 378, Smithsonian Institution, Washington, D.C. 20560. (202) 357-1930.

NH·108

Karyotype Research Collection *A.K.A.* Alfred L. Gardner Research Collection

Dates of Photographs: 1973–Present

Collection Origins

Curator of Mammals Alfred L. Gardner created the collection for personal research purposes. Gardner, who received a Ph.D. from Louisiana State University, joined the U.S. Fish and Wildlife Service in 1973 as a Biologist. Photographers represented include Alfred L. Gardner and OPPS staff.

Physical Description

There are 1,900 photographs including silver gelatin photonegatives and photoprints.

Subjects

The photographs document mammal karyotypes of bats, marsupials, and rodents. A karyotype is the entire chromosomal complement of an individual or cell, observable during mitotic metaphase, the second phase of cell division.

Arranged: Alphabetically by family, then by genus and species.

Captioned: With location and species.

Finding Aid: No.

Restrictions: Yes. Contact Alfred L. Gardner, Curator of Mammals, U.S. Fish and Wildlife Service, NMNH, Room 386, Smithsonian Institution, Washington, D.C. 20560. (202) 357-2876.

NH·109

Mammalogist Portrait File

Dates of Photographs: 20th Century

Collection Origins

The U.S. Biological Survey (USBS) staff created the portrait collection to document USBS mammalogists who have worked at NMNH. Photographers represented include B & M Laboratories, Luther C. Goldman, N.H. Kent, William Schmidtman, and the U.S. Department of Agriculture.

Physical Description

There are 815 silver gelatin photoprints (some mounted or framed).

Subjects

The photographs portray USBS mammalogists who have worked at the NMNH between 1855 and the present, including Vernon O. Bailey, Edward A. Goldman, Arthur H. Howell, Hartley H.T. Jackson, C. Hart Merriam, Edward W. Nelson, Wilfred H. Osgood, Theodore S. Palmer, Edward A. Preble, and Walter P. Taylor. Other individuals, including historians and scientists, portrayed include John W. Aldrich, Richard C. Banks, Thomas D. Burleigh, Jay N. Darling, A.H. Howell, Clyde Jones, Richard H. Manville, John L. Paradiso, John Pearce, Ernest P. Walker, and Stanley P. Young. There is also a photograph of the first meeting of the American Society of Mammalogists, held on April 4, 1919.

Arranged: Most alphabetically. One group of 12 photoprints arranged chronologically.

Captioned: Some with negative number and occasionally with employment dates or signature.

Finding Aid: An incomplete finding aid titled "Portraits in Bird and Mammal Laboratories of Former Workers" for 20 subjects lists life dates, name, and USBS employment dates.

Restrictions: No. Contact Thomas Fritts, Chief of Biological Survey, U.S. Fish and Wildlife Service, NMNH, Room 378, Smithsonian Institution, Washington, D.C. 20560. (202) 357-2930.

NH·110

Red Wolf Recovery Program Collection

Dates of Photographs: 1974–1980

Collection Origins

The staff of the Red Wolf Recovery Program of the U.S. Fish and Wildlife Service created the collection between 1974 and 1980 in Beaumont, Texas, for documentation and research purposes. The program was established in 1967 to save endangered red wolves by breeding and reestablishing them in the wild or in zoos.

Physical Description

There are 3,300 photographs including color dye coupler slides and silver gelatin radiographs.

Subjects

The photographs depict red wolf skulls and red wolves, some seen under x-rays.

Arranged: In two series, unarranged. 1) Color dye coupler slides. 2) Radiographs.

Captioned: Radiographs with age, brain ratio, date, location, number, photographer, and sex. Slides with number and sex.

Finding Aid: No.

Restrictions: No. Contact Thomas Fritts, Chief of Biological Survey, U.S. Fish and Wildlife Service, NMNH, Room 378, Smithsonian Institution, Washington, D.C. 20560. (202) 357-1930.

NH

Research Office of the Assistant Secretary for Research

Research Office of the Assistant Secretary for Research
National Museum of Natural History
Smithsonian Institution
Washington, D.C. 20560
Mary McCutcheon, Special Assistant to the Assistant Secretary
(202) 243-3643
Hours: Monday–Friday, 10 a.m.–6 p.m. or by appointment.

Scope of the Collection

There is one photographic collection with approximately 16,400 images.

Focus of the Collection

The photographs document the geography and vegetation of Indo-Pacific islands, including Clipperton Island, the Marshall Islands, and the Polynesian Islands. The majority of images are aerial photographs showing atolls, parts of larger islands, and reef systems. Landscape images illustrate geological features, plants, and vegetation zones, as well as erosion, typhoon damage, and volcanic activity. Some photographs portray island residents and their activities, especially people at work in boats and in villages.

Photographic Processes and Formats Represented

The collection contains color dye coupler photonegatives (Kodachrome) and silver gelatin photonegatives and photoprints.

Other Materials Represented

The Research Office also contains bibliographic reference cards, books, brochures, contracts, correspondence, diaries, field notes, government documents, journals, manuscripts, maps, memorandums, newspaper clippings, proposals, and reprints.

Access and Usage Policies

The files are open to the public by appointment only. There are partial finding aids to the collection. Certain materials are restricted due to their copyright status. Xerographic and photographic copies may be made of unrestricted images. There is a charge for photographic copies which is determined by OPPS.

Publication Policies

Researchers must obtain permission from the Smithsonian Institution to reproduce a photograph and may also have to obtain permission from the copyright holder, which is not necessarily the Smithsonian Institution. The preferred credit line is "Courtesy of the Biogeography Files, Smithsonian Institution."

NH·111

Biogeography Files *A.K.A.* World Biogeography Files

Dates of Photographs: 1916–Present

Collection Origins

The collection was assembled by former NMNH Botany Department curators Francis Raymond Fosberg (1908–) and Marie-Helene Sachet (ca. 1922–1986), who studied tropical islands and atolls in the Indian and Pacific Oceans. After receiving a Ph.D. in botany from the University of Pennsylvania in 1939, Fosberg worked for various government and private organizations, including the Catholic University of America (1948–1950), U.S. Geological Survey (1951–1966), UNESCO (1957–1964), and the Smithsonian Institution (1966–1978). Sachet, who studied botany at the University of Montpellier in France and at Smith College in Northampton, Massachusetts, became Fosberg's assistant at Catholic University in 1949. Later they worked together at the U.S. Geological Survey and the Smithsonian Institution. Their projects included studies of Sri Lanka and Clipperton Island and the successful prevention of the construction of an air base on Aldabra Atoll. Since retiring in 1978, Fosberg has continued his field work as well as his additions to the collection.

Most of the aerial photographs were taken by the U.S. Navy during World War II and the 1950s. Fosberg obtained the images of atolls and areas north of the equator when they were declassified in 1958, while the remainder went to the Bernice Pauahi Bishop Museum in Honolulu, Hawaii. Photographers and studios represented include F. Cohic, F. Raymond Fosberg, Helen Foster, J.L. Gressitt, Institutio Geografico de Colombia, F.S. MacNeill, L. Quate, E.S. Reese, L.P. Schultz, and W.R. Taylor. The photographs have appeared in the following books: 1) Francis Raymond Fosberg and Marie-Helene Sachet. *Manual for Tropical Herbaria.* Utrecht, Netherlands: International Bureau for Plant Taxonomy and Nomenclature, 1965. 2) U.S. Army. Forces in the Far East. *Military Geography of the Northern Marshalls.* n.p., 1956. They have also appeared in serials including the following: Smithsonian Institution. *Smithsonian Contributions to Botany.* Washington, D.C.: Smithsonian Institution Press, 1967–

Physical Description

There are 16,400 photographs including color dye coupler photonegatives (Kodachrome) and silver gelatin photonegatives and photoprints. Other materials include bibliographic reference cards, books, brochures, contracts, correspondence, diaries, field notes, government documents, journals, manuscripts, maps, memorandums, newspaper clippings, proposals, and reprints.

Subjects

The majority of photographs are aerial photographs documenting the geography and vegetation of Indo-Pacific islands including atolls, parts of larger islands, and reef systems. The remaining photographs show geological features, plants, and vegetation zones including erosion, typhoon damage, and volcanic activity. Animals shown include birds, cattle, donkeys, fish, horses, an ox, and turtles. There are some photographs of island residents, their architecture, and their material culture.

The largest group of photographs depicts Clipperton Island. Other atolls and islands shown include the Caroline Islands (Ifalik Atoll, Oroluk Atoll, and Woleai Atoll), Dominica, the Galapágos Islands, the Hawaiian Islands, Heron Island, Kiribati (Abemama Atoll, Kuria Island, and Maiana Atoll), the Marquesas Islands, the Marshall Islands (Bikini Atoll, Erikub Atoll, Jaluit Atoll, Jemo Atoll, Lae Atoll, Rongelap Atoll, Taka Atoll, and Utirik Atoll), New Britain, New Guinea (Tauu Island), Swain's Island, and Wake Island. There are also images of vegetation, particularly forests, in Asian countries including Indonesia, Japan, and Thailand; in Central and South American countries including Colombia, Jamaica, Trinidad, and Venezuela; in European countries including France, Germany, Great Britain (Scotland and Wales), and Spain; and in North America including Canada (Manitoba) and the United States (Colorado, Florida, Maryland, New Hampshire, North Carolina, Tennessee, Texas, Virginia, and Washington, D.C.).

People portrayed include Caroline Islanders in boats; Clipperton Islanders working with fish; Ifalik Atoll inhabitants building a pit, cutting breadfruit, cutting and planting crops in a swamp, and gathering coconuts; Jaluit Atoll inhabitants cleaning wells, rowing boats, and walking on beaches and in forests; Japanese crewmen aboard a ship; Japanese surveyors; a Jemo Atoll boy riding a turtle; a Lae Atoll baby receiving an injection from a medic; Marquesas Islanders working in boats and villages; Marshall

Islanders in boats and in villages, performing a dance, playing a game, and pounding food; and Polynesians slaughtering a pig. Scientists portrayed include Ted Arnow, F. Raymond Fosberg, Charles Fray, C.G. Johnson, and H. Wahl.

Structures shown include a bamboo fence and thatched huts in Colombia; cemeteries, a concrete pier, houses, Japanese buildings and gun emplacements, rain cisterns, a seawall, and thatched huts in the Marshall Islands (Ifalik, Jaluit, and Rongelap Atolls); and thatched huts in New Guinea. There are photographs of Hawaii in 1916 which show architectural and recreational sites including ancient stone structures, a barn, bridges, churches, a cigar factory, corncribs, a duck farm, gardens, government offices, grass huts, parks, piers, a playground, a ranch, roads, schools, a sugar mill, a tennis court, and U.S. barracks. Farm and transportation vehicles shown include boats, a car, an outrigger canoe, a plow, and tractors. Images of the natural environment include cactus, canyons, lava flows, ponds, trees, volcanoes, and waterfalls. There are portraits of a boy on a tricycle, boys with a baseball bat, Japanese picnickers in a park, local families, and men climbing mountains. Photographs of Japan in the 1950s primarily illustrate agricultural and architectural topics such as a farm, a pole bridge, rice drying racks, rice fields, a stadium, a statue, temples, terraced slopes, and villages. Japan's natural environment is documented with photographs of mountains and erupting volcanoes. There are also portraits of Japanese children, men, and women waving at a ship and of Japanese university professors.

Arranged: In two parts. 1) Manuscripts, maps, and photographs, by geographic location and subject. 2) Published material, by type of material and author or title.

Captioned: Most with date, location, photographer, and subject.

Finding Aid: 1) A three-part index card file to books; cards are filed by author, geographic code, and topical code. 2) A computer index to one journal. 3) A partial list of shelf and file cabinet contents.

Restrictions: No.

ZP

NATIONAL ZOOLOGICAL PARK

Michael H. Robinson, Director

The National Zoological Park (NZP) breeds, collects, exhibits, maintains, and studies animals, while advancing research in the biological and veterinary sciences, educating the public, and providing a recreational setting for visitors. The Zoo also breeds captive endangered species, preserves animal habitats, and trains Third World wildlife biologists.

The 328,600 photographs in the NZP's ten photographic collections document the Zoo's animals and their enclosures, collecting expeditions, education programs, pathology and veterinary procedures, programs, special projects, research, staff, and visitors from 1889 to the present. Zoo captive-breeding programs, grounds, and veterinary facilities worldwide are also documented.

The Zoo also has 2,500 animals representing more than 425 species including amphibians, birds, invertebrates, mammals, and reptiles. Databases, education programs, a library, registrar's records, and other research resources are also available for the study of animal behavior, comparative medicine, comparative pathology, conservation, ecology, evolutionary biology, nutrition, and reproductive physiology.

The NZP has an exhibition facility in Washington, D.C.'s Rock Creek Park and a 3,150 acre Conservation and Research Center (CRC) in Front Royal, Virginia, which breeds and researches endangered and rare species.

ZP

Department of Animal Health

Department of Animal Health
National Zoological Park
Smithsonian Institution
Washington, D.C. 20008
R. Mitchell Bush, Chief Veterinarian
(202) 673-4793
Hours: By appointment.

Scope of the Collection

There is one photographic collection with approximately 10,000 radiographs.

Focus of the Collection

The photographs document veterinary cases and programs at the National Zoological Park's Rock Creek Park facility in Washington, D.C., and the Conservation and Research Center at Front Royal, Virginia. The programs include animal examinations, medical and surgical treatment, quarantine and screening procedures, and routine preventative care. The department's work encompasses research in applied clinical techniques designed to improve the medical and surgical care of animals including anesthesiology, artificial insemination, clinical and diagnostic laparoscopy, establishing hematological normal values for exotic animals, and radiological evaluation of disease.

Photographic Processes and Formats Represented

There are silver gelatin radiographs.

Other Materials Represented

The department also maintains an online database for the radiograph collection.

Access and Usage Policies

The collection is open by appointment to scholarly researchers, who should write to the department and describe their research topic, the type of material that interests them, and their research aim.

Publication Policies

Researchers must obtain permission from the Smithsonian Institution to reproduce a photograph and may also have to obtain permission from the copyright holder, which is not necessarily the Smithsonian Institution. The preferred credit line is "Courtesy of the National Zoological Park, Smithsonian Institution."

ZP·1

Animal Care Radiograph Collection

Dates of Photographs: 1972–Present

Collection Origins

R. Mitchell Bush, Chief Veterinarian of the NZP, created the collection to document NZP veterinary work from 1972 to the present for diagnostic and teaching purposes. Bush received a doctorate in veterinary medicine from the University of California at Davis in 1965 and interned at Boston's Angell Memorial Animal Hospital from 1965 to 1966. He held appointments between 1967 and 1972 at Johns Hopkins University, Vanderbilt University, and the Baltimore Zoo. In 1972 Bush joined NZP, and in 1975 he became head of the Office of Animal Health. His research specialities are anesthesia, investigative medicine, radiology of exotic animals, reproductive physiology, and surgery. Some of the photographs were published in the following article: R. Mitchell Bush. "External Fixation to Repair Long Bone Fractures in Larger Birds." *Current Veterinary Therapy: Small Animal Practice* vol. 8, 1983, 630–633.

Physical Description

There are 10,000 silver gelatin radiographs, some measuring up to 14″ × 17″.

Subjects

The radiographs, which document NZP veterinary cases from 1972 to the present, are x-ray images of injured or sick amphibians, birds, mammals, and reptiles. Animal illnesses and injuries illustrated include a hock joint of a rat kangaroo with tuberculous arthritis caused by *Mycobacterium avium;* an inflamed tympanic bulla of a brush tail rat with pseudomonas otitis media; and a radius of a baby reindeer with an osteolytic lesion caused by phycomycosis.

Arranged: Chronologically.

Captioned: Some with date. Teaching slides also list accession number, age, animal group, diagnosis, infections, cross-referenced pathology number, sex, species, and x-ray number.

Finding Aid: An online database with the accession number, age, animal group, date, diagnosis, infections, cross-referenced pathology number, sex, species, teaching slide designation, and x-ray number.

Restrictions: Open to scholarly researchers by appointment.

ZP

Department of Conservation

Department of Conservation
Conservation and Research Center
National Zoological Park
Smithsonian Institution
Front Royal, Virginia 22630
Associate Director
(703) 635-4166
Hours: By appointment.

Scope of the Collections

There are three photographic collections with approximately 12,400 images.

Focus of the Collections

The photographs document the activities, animals, and facilities of the Zoo's 3,150-acre Conservation and Research Center (CRC) at Front Royal, Virginia, and comparable centers worldwide. The Department of Conservation breeds and manages endangered and rare wildlife species, conducts behavioral and reproductive research on rare mammals and birds, and provides education and training programs for scientists. Some photographs show the Front Royal facilities between 1915 and 1944, when they were maintained by the U.S. Army.

Photographic Processes and Formats Represented

There are color dye coupler photonegatives, photoprints, and slides and silver gelatin photonegatives, photoprints, and slides.

Other Materials Represented

The department also contains notebooks and scrapbooks.

Access and Usage Policies

The collections are open by appointment to scholarly researchers, who should write to the department and describe their research topic, the type of material that interests them, and their research aim. Portions of the collections are restricted due to their condition or copyright status.

Publication Policies

Researchers must obtain permission from the Smithsonian Institution to reproduce a photograph and may also have to obtain permission from the copyright holder, which is not necessarily the Smithsonian Institution. The preferred credit line is "Courtesy of the National Zoological Park, Smithsonian Institution."

ZP·2

Conservation and Research Center Bird Slide Collection

Dates of Photographs: 1974–Present

Collection Origins

The bird keepers at the NZP Conservation and Research Center (CRC) at Front Royal, Virginia, assembled the collection to document the breeding, care, and study of bird species at CRC and similar work at other centers worldwide for staff research and teaching purposes.

Physical Description

There are 2,100 color dye coupler slides.

Subjects

The photographs document bird species and their habitats in gardens, parks, and zoos in the United States and abroad. Birds shown at the CRC include cranes, emus, myna birds, ostriches, parrots, peafowls, rheas, thrashers, turkeys, and wood ducks. Birds and bird facilities are illustrated in collections, parks, and zoos worldwide including those in Australia (Melbourne and Sydney), Belgium (Antwerp), England (London), France (Cleres), India (Calcutta and New Delhi), Mexico (Mexico City), the Netherlands (Rotterdam), New Guinea (Baiyer River), Singapore (Jurong), Switzerland (Basel and Bern), Thailand (Bangkok), the United States (American Samoa, Honolulu, and San Diego), and West Germany (Frankfurt and West Berlin).

Arranged: In two series. 1) Birds of the National Zoological Park Conservation and Research Center, then by species or age. 2) Birds and bird habitats in other collections, then by zoo, collection name, or location.

Captioned: Some with age, location, and species.

Finding Aid: No.

Restrictions: Open to scholarly researchers by appointment.

ZP·3

Conservation and Research Slide Collection *A.K.A.* Christen M. Wemmer Slide Collection

Dates of Photographs: 1970s–1986

Collection Origins

Christen M. Wemmer, Associate Director, created the photographs for research purposes. Wemmer, who received a Ph.D. from the University of Maryland in 1972, worked at the Chicago Zoological Park's Brookfield Zoo from 1972 to 1974. His research specialties include comparative ethology (the study of animal behavior) with an emphasis on communication systems, conservation of large mammals in the Third World, and the reproductive ecology of ungulates (hoofed grazing animals).

Physical Description

There are 10,200 color dye coupler slides.

Subjects

The photographs document the activities, animals, and facilities of the NZP Conservation and Research Center (CRC) and comparable programs worldwide. Animals depicted include aardwolves, anoa, antelopes, apes, bantengs, basilisks, bats, bears, birds, bongos, bush dogs, camels, cats, deer, fish, foxes, horses, hyenas, insects, jackals, lesser pandas, marmosets, mongooses, mules, muntjacs, onagers, oryxes, rats, reptiles, rhinoceros, tigers, tree kangaroos, wisent, and wolves. Animal behavior (primarily of camels) illustrated includes animals feeding; giving birth; grooming including allo-grooming and calf auto-grooming; interacting including adults with calves, adults bucking and chasing, males fighting and sparring, and mothers nursing their young; molting; playing including play-fighting; posturing including moving, salivating/grinning, stretching, using threat-yawn sequences, and vocalizing; rearing including halter-training and hand-rearing; rutting including mounting and copulation; scenting including food-scenting; vocalizing including barking and bellowing; and wallowing. There are also photographs of injuries including fighting scars.

CRC facilities documented include the administration building, barns (Dilger and Meade), bird houses, commissary, cranes' yards, dump, holding yards, muntjacs' yards, residences, and the visitor center. Some photographs illustrate grazing pressure in the yards. Activities depicted around the facilities include construction, fence repair, hay storage, and maintenance. CRC events and people documented include an ice storm in March 1978, lectures, staff members, staff retirement ceremonies, and visitors' days in 1976 and 1977. Photographic reproductions of charts and graphs are also included. Other animal breeding centers, collections, parks, and zoos documented include Austria (Schönbrunn Zoo in Vienna), Czechoslovakia (Prague Zoo), East Germany (Belefeld and East Berlin Zoos), Indonesia (Jakarta Zoo and Sulawesi [forests, landscapes, people]), Italy (Venice Zoo), Nepal (Chitwan National Park and Katmandu Zoo), Norway (Oslo and Trondheim Zoos), Poland (Warsaw Zoo), Singapore (Jurong Bird Park), Switzerland (Achental, Altenfeld, Basel, Bern, and Zurich Zoos and Oberwil's Stamms Collection), the United States (Virginia's Busch Gardens and Florida's Ocala Zoo), and West Germany (Braunschweig, Duisburg, Hannover, West Berlin, and Wuppertal Zoos).

Arranged: In six series. 1) Large mammal slides, by animal name. 2) Camel slides, by behavior. 3) Travel slides, by zoo or locale, then by animal. 4) CRC slides, by animal, animal activity, or structure. 5) Slide lectures, by lecture title in subject order. 6) Unarranged slides, loosely grouped by creation date and occasionally by topic.

Captioned: Some with brief description or names.

Finding Aid: No.

Restrictions: Open to Smithsonian staff by appointment.

ZP·4

United States Army Scrapbook Collection

Dates of Photographs: 1915–1986

Collection Origins

The U.S. Army created the collection to document its facility at Front Royal, Virginia. The NZP acquired the collection when the Smithsonian Institution purchased the Front Royal facility in 1975.

Physical Description

There are 111 silver gelatin photoprints in an album that also contains handwritten notes.

Subjects

Most of the photographs show a U.S. Army facility near Front Royal, Virginia, between 1915 and 1944. The facility was purchased in 1975 by the Smithsonian Institution, which converted it into the Zoo's 3,150-acre Conservation and Research Center (CRC). The photographs are landscapes which depict Army barns, houses, and stables. The photographs also document German prisoners of war assisting U.S. Army staff at a World War I–era (1916) horse show at the Front Royal facility.

Arranged: In two series. 1) An album containing 101 silver gelatin photoprints, arranged by building number. 2) Ten unarranged silver gelatin photoprints of the horse show.

Captioned: Series 1 (on the album pages) with building name and number; capacity; construction cost; construction materials; date completed; dimensions of each room; fixture details such as heating, lighting, and plumbing; furniture installed; plan number; repairs and their costs; structural additions; and total building dimensions. Series 2 with dates, names, negative number, and subject information.

Finding Aid: No.

Restrictions: Researchers must obtain permission from the collection custodian and the U.S. Army before having photographic or xerographic copies produced.

ZP

Department of Pathology

Department of Pathology
National Zoological Park
Smithsonian Institution
Washington, D.C. 20008
Richard J. Montali, Head Pathologist
(202) 673-4869
Hours: By appointment.

Scope of the Collection

There is one photographic collection with approximately 12,500 images.

Focus of the Collection

The photographs document NZP animals' diseases, pathological conditions, and normal animal anatomy. The photographs also illustrate veterinary surgical procedures performed at the NZP.

Photographic Processes and Formats Represented

There are color dye coupler slides.

Other Materials Represented

The department maintains an online database on pathology.

Access and Usage Policies

The collection is open to Smithsonian Institution staff and scholarly researchers by appointment.

Publication Policies

Researchers must obtain permission from the Smithsonian Institution to reproduce a photograph and may also have to obtain permission from the copyright holder, which is not necessarily the Smithsonian Institution. The preferred credit line is "Courtesy of the National Zoological Park, Smithsonian Institution."

ZP·5

Pathology Slide Collection *A.K.A.* Pathological and Clinical Entities of Zoo Animals Slide Collection

Dates of Photographs: 1975–Present

Collection Origins

Richard J. Montali, Head Pathologist at NZP, created the photographs for use in diagnosing diseases of exotic animals and in teaching comparative pathology. Montali, who received a doctorate in veterinary medicine from Cornell University in 1964, completed post-doctoral work in comparative pathology at Johns Hopkins University School of Medicine (1967–1970), then became a member of its medical faculty (1971–1975). He joined the NZP Department of Pathology in 1975. The photographs appear in numerous publications, including the following articles: 1) R. Mitchell Bush and Richard J. Montali. "Principles of Zoological Animal Medicine." *Veterinary Scope* vol. 21, no. 1 (1977): 9–24. 2) Richard J. Montali, ed. *Mycobacterial Infections of Zoo Animals: Proceedings of a Symposium Held at the Conservation and Research Center, National Zoological Park, Smithsonian Institution, October 6–8, 1976.* Washington, D.C.: Smithsonian Institution Press, 1978.

Physical Description

There are 12,500 color dye coupler slides. Other materials include an online pathology database.

Subjects

Most of the photographs document pathological conditions in zoo animals including infectious and nutritional diseases, tumors, and veterinary surgical procedures. There are also photographs of normal zoo animals and their anatomy, as well as NZP equipment, exhibits, and facilities. Pathological entities documented include bacteria, fungi, gross lesions, parasites, tumors, and viruses. Some of the 108 subcategories of animal syndromes illustrated are hypogenesis, torsion, and anomalies including bumblefoot, conjunctivitis, diseased organs, downers, eggbound, fatty infiltration, gout, lumpy jaw, mange, overgrown foot, ring-tail, scaly leg disease, splayleg, and wry neck.

Veterinary procedures documented include amniocentesis, anesthesia, artificial insemination, bandaging, capture, casting, electroejaculation, examination, force feeding, grooming, hoof trimming, laparoscopy, radiology, radio-tracking, restraint, sex determination, surgery, therapy, tuberculosis testing, venipuncture, and worming.

Arranged: By assigned number (referred to as "ZNO number" or "Kodachrome number" in zoo file guide), then by subject categories such as anatomy, antibiotics, bacteria, blood vessels, equipment, exhibits, facility, fungi, hematology, histology, organ diseases, parasitism, presentation slides, procedures, protozoa, syndromes, taxonomic order (primarily class, family, and common name), toxicity, tumors, unusual structures, and viruses. Each category is further subdivided by subheadings.

Captioned: With assigned number.

Finding Aid: 1) Photographer's log books. 2) Key Word in Context (KWIC) computer index containing information from photographer's log books and diagnostic information. The KWIC index is organized by slide number and subject. Each section includes the animal's class, common name, and taxonomic name; autopsy or case number; a letter designating the image as micrograph, chart, or gross image; slide number; and a topical description. Each slide is cross-referenced up to five times.

Restrictions: Available to Smithsonian Institution staff and scholarly researchers by appointment.

ZP

Office of Design and Exhibit Planning

Office of Design and Exhibit Planning
National Zoological Park
Smithsonian Institution
Washington, D.C. 20008
Jessie Cohen, Photographer
(202) 673-4862
Hours: By appointment.

Scope of the Collections

There are four photographic collections with approximately 235,730 images.

Focus of the Collections

These collections document all aspects of the National Zoological Park, from the 1880s to the present, including activities, animals, animal enclosures and houses, collecting expeditions, exhibits, facilities, grounds, special events, staff, veterinary projects, and visitors. Some zoos in other countries are also documented.

Photographic Processes and Formats Represented

There are albumen photoprints; color dye coupler photonegatives, photoprints, and slides; a color screen plate phototransparency (Autochrome); cyanotypes; a platinum photoprint; silver gelatin dry plate lantern slides; and silver gelatin photonegatives, photoprints, and slides.

Other Materials Represented

None.

Access and Usage Policies

The collections are available to scholarly researchers by appointment. Some materials are restricted due to condition or copyright status.

Publication Policies

Researchers must obtain permission from the Smithsonian Institution to reproduce a photograph and may also have to obtain permission from the copyright holder, which is not necessarily the Smithsonian Institution. The preferred credit line is "Courtesy of the National Zoological Park, Smithsonian Institution."

ZP·6

Design and Exhibit Planning Photograph Collection

Dates of Photographs: 1973–Present

Collection Origins

NZP staff photographer Jessie Cohen (1952–) assembled the collection from her own work and that of other NZP staff and volunteer photographers to document NZP activities, animals, exhibits, scientific projects, and staff. Cohen, who received a B.A. from Beloit College in Beloit, Wisconsin, in 1974, worked at the National Archives and Records Administration (NARA) and at the National Gallery of Art before coming to the Zoo in 1979. She specializes in animal and nature photography.

Other photographers represented include Stan Barouh, Brenda Clymire, Max Hirshfeld, Ann Huzzy, Larry Jenkins, Pat Johnson, Theodore H. Reed, Jan Skrentry, Barbara Speckhart, Pat Vosburgh, and Raylene Wenzle. NZP staff use these images for animal stud records, exhibits, lectures, official documentation, research, and slide shows. The photographs have appeared in publications such as books, calendars, magazines, newspapers, posters, and scientific journals. Cohen's photographs appear in the following publications: 1) Bet Hennefrund. "A Day with the Panda." *Ranger Rick* (June 1988): 102–107. 2) Devra G. Kleiman. "Reintroduction of Captive Mammals for Conservation." *BioScience* 39 (March 1989): 152–161. 3) Stephen J. O'Brien. "The Ancestry of the Giant Panda." *Scientific American* 257 (November 1987): 102–107. 4) Edward Parks. *Treasures of the Smithsonian*. Washington, D.C.: Smithsonian Books, 1983.

Physical Description

There are 225,600 photographs including color dye coupler photonegatives and slides, and silver gelatin photonegatives and photoprints.

Subjects

Most of the photographs document the NZP's captive animals, some of which are pictured in naturalistic environments designed for the Zoo. There are also images of Zoo activities including the reintroduction of endangered captive species into the wild; facilities construction and renovation; research and veterinary projects; staff and visitors; as well as some photographic reproductions of NZP graphics and banners, traffic signs, and Zoo buttons.

Animals illustrated include amphibians (frogs); birds (bald eagles and cranes); carnivores (bears, cats, giant and lesser pandas, and wolves); invertebrates (coral, cuttlefish, and scorpions); primates (gorillas, monkeys, orangutans, and tamarins); reptiles (crocodiles, lizards, and snakes); rodents (mice); and ungulates (deer, gazelles, and zebras). Scientific projects shown include veterinary examinations and medical treatments of baby animals, giant pandas, and golden lion tamarins. Photographs also document the construction and renovation of Zoo animal houses, exhibits, and facilities including the Beaver Valley; the Bird House; the Elephant House; the Conservation and Research Center (CRC) at Front Royal, Virginia; North American Mammals; the Reptile House; and Smokey the Bear's honey tree. Four photographs from this collection are reproduced in this volume's illustrations.

Arranged: In five series by process and format. 1) Color dye coupler slides. 2) Silver gelatin photonegatives and contact photoprints, by subject. 3) Duplicate color dye coupler slides, by subject and type of material. 4) Silver gelatin copy photoprints, by subject; animal photographs then by taxonomic order. 5) Color dye coupler photonegatives.

Series 1 (color dye coupler slides) has four subseries: a) animals; b) veterinary medicine and research projects; c) activities, official functions, and staff; and d) animal houses, exhibits, facilities construction and renovation, and graphics and signs. Subseries 1a (color dye coupler slides of animals) has four subdivisions: *i)* mammals, *ii)* birds, *iii)* reptiles and amphibians, and *iv)* invertebrates. Mammals are arranged either by family or by their location at the Zoo or the CRC.

Captioned: No.

Finding Aid: No.

Restrictions: Available by appointment only.

ZP·7

Historical Photograph Collection

Dates of Photographs: 1889–1970s

Collection Origins

NZP staff photographer Jessie Cohen assembled the collection from diverse Smithsonian Institution sources including NZP staff, NZP volunteer photographers, and OPPS, as well as from outside sources such as local newspapers and amateur photographers who provided copy and duplicate photographs. For a biography of Cohen see the *Collection Origins* field of *ZP·6*. One group of 66 photographs documenting Zoo safety was taken in 1958 by OPPS staff after a child was killed by an NZP lion. The photographs were used in a Congressional presentation on NZP safety hazards and in a Zoo-public safety brochure. Former NZP Historian Sybil E. Hamlet, who later assembled the photographs for an unpublished book on Zoo history, gave the photographs to the Office of Design and Exhibit Planning in 1989. Photographers represented include Vernon O. Bailey, Frank Baker, Charles M. Bell, William H. Blackburne, H.F. Carl, H.A. Farnham, E. Hardy, Frances B. Johnston, A.J. Olmsted, Thomas W. Smillie, A.E. Sweeney, Ernest P. Walker, and John Woerner. Studios represented include Ludwig Photo Labs, Washington, D.C.; NZP staff photographers; OPPS; and the *Washington Star.*

Physical Description

The collection contains 10,000 photographs including albumen photoprints (some stereographs), color dye coupler photonegatives and photoprints, a color screen plate phototransparency (Autochrome), cyanotypes, a platinum photoprint, silver gelatin dry plate photonegatives, and silver gelatin photonegatives (some nitrate) and photoprints. Most photographs are vintage originals. Other materials include microforms and xerographic copies.

Subjects

The photographs document the history of the NZP from 1889 to the present. Subjects portrayed include animals; animal enclosures and houses; ceremonies and events; collecting expeditions; exhibits; facilities; landscapes and scenery including aerial shots; medical procedures performed on animals such as autopsies, capture gun use, surgical operations, and treatments; NZP staff; and visitors. Animals illustrated include alligators, bison, cavies, chimpanzees, deer, dingoes, eagles, elephants, gazelles, hippopotamuses, kangaroos, leopards, llamas, ostriches, otters, penguins, prairie dogs, pumas, pythons, tapirs, Tasmanian wolves, wart hogs, and zebras. Other zoos depicted include the Antwerp Zoo, the Cairo Zoo, the Cologne Zoo, and the London Zoo.

NZP animal houses and exhibitions shown include the Bear Cages, the Belvedere Carnivore House, the Bird House, the Eland House, the Elephant House, the Flight Cage, the Lion House, the Raccoon House, the Reptile House, the Small Duck Pond, the Small Mammal House, and the Zebra House. Other NZP facilities documented include the director's office, the first permanent building on the grounds (1891), the Harvard Street bridge, Holt House, paddocks, parking areas, shops, the stone feeding house, and Zoo restaurants. The Works Progress Administration (WPA) murals in the Bird, Elephant, and Reptile Houses are also illustrated. Landscapes represented include the bridle path, snow scenes in Rock Creek Park, and the woods above the sheep mound. NZP zoo keepers are shown reaching toward cages, fences, and walls to show animal accessibility and other safety hazards.

Staff portrayed include Zoo Superintendent Frank Baker; Head Keeper William H. Blackburne; Smithsonian Secretary Leonard Carmichael; Chief Taxidermist William Hornaday; Captain James; Keeper C.W. Lewis; NZP Directors William M. Mann, Theodore H. Reed, and Michael H. Robinson; and Policeman Ladislaus A. Tabinski. Other employees portrayed include Bert Barker, N.S. Cook, John Eisenberg, Caldwell Graham, Clinton Gray, R. Sebastian, and Arthur B. Wood. Group portraits of unidentified animal keepers, cleaning staff, and WPA workers (1939) are also included. Visitors and staff activities documented include children feeding bears (1949); keepers and veterinarians caring for animals; school children visiting the Zoo; staff planting new greenery in the Bird House (1968); and visitors and staff skating on the Swan Pond. Events documented include a Christmas party and awards (1967), Easter Monday (1939), and J. Lear Grimmer's retirement party. Sixteen historical photographs from this collection are reproduced in this volume's illustrations.

Arranged: In three series. 1) By date. 2) By subject. 3) Unarranged. Series 1, then arranged by format into four subseries: a) photonegatives, by assigned number; b) photoprints, by subject; c) microforms, by assigned number; and d) unarranged photoprints and photonegatives.

Captioned: Some with subject and negative number. Photonegatives (Series 1a) with negative number. Photonegative sleeves with date, negative number, and subject. Photoprints (Series 1b) with date, negative number, photographer, publications, remarks, size, and subject.

Finding Aid: 1) Photoprint and photonegative index titled "NZP Photo List," by number (001–3818). Includes date, frame number, location, negative number, personal names, photographer, species, and subject. 2) Photoprint and photonegative index, by date (1889–1978). Includes date, frame number, negative number, photographer, and species.

Restrictions: Some photographs are restricted due to their fragile condition or copyright status.

ZP·8

Lantern Slide Collection *A.K.A.* William M. Mann Lantern Slide Collection

Dates of Photographs: 1925–1959

Collection Origins

William M. Mann (1886–1960), Director of the National Zoological Park from 1925 to 1956, assembled the collection for public relations and public speaking purposes. The collection reflects his interest in historical and contemporary animals, menageries, and zoos, as well as his studies in entomology and zoology. Before he received an Sc.D. from Harvard University in 1915, Mann participated in entomological collecting trips in Brazil (Stanford Expedition, 1911), Haiti (1912), Cuba and Mexico (1913), and the Middle East (Philip Expedition, 1914), as well as visiting the Fiji and the Solomon Islands (1915–1916) as a Sheldon Traveling Fellow. While employed by the Bureau of Entomology of the U.S. Department of Agriculture (1916–1925), Mann also served as Assistant Director of the Mulford Biological Expedition to the Amazon Basin (1921–1922).

As NZP Director Mann's major accomplishments included a building program and a significant increase in the live animal population. His animal-collecting expeditions include the Smithsonian-Chrysler Fund Expedition to East Africa (1926–1935), the National Geographic Society-Smithsonian Institution East Indies Expedition (1937), and the Smithsonian-Firestone Expedition to Liberia (1940–1943). Upon his retirement in 1956, Mann was made an honorary Smithsonian research associate. Photographers represented include E.B. Thompson, Washington, D.C. Note: This collection complements the William M. Mann and Lucile Quarry Mann Papers, circa 1885–1981 (Record Unit 7293) at the Smithsonian Institution Archives, which is described in the following: *Guide to the Smithsonian Institution Archives 1983.* Archives and Special Collections of the Smithsonian Institution, Number 4. Washington, D.C.: Smithsonian Institution Press, 1983.

Physical Description

There are 50 silver gelatin dry plate lantern slides.

Subjects

The photographs document captive animals, Mann's collecting trips, his visits to European zoos, and some reproductions of drawings, engravings, mosaics, murals, and paintings of animals, menageries, and zoos. Collecting trips to British Guiana (now Guyana), Liberia, Mexico, and the Solomon Islands are illustrated, as are Mann's visits to zoos in Austria, Denmark (Copenhagen), Germany (Frankfurt, Hannover, Leipzig, Munich, and Nuremberg), and Great Britain. Captive animals shown include lions in Leipzig, monkeys in Copenhagen and Dresden, polar bears in Nuremberg, and sea lions in the Hannover Zoo. Informal portraits of men and women in African, German, and Mexican landscape settings are included. One image, titled "Snake Rites," shows an unidentified snake society ritual. Art works reproduced include an American painting titled *Peaceable Kingdom,* bird murals from Egyptian tombs, an engraving of a medieval hunt scene, an engraving of the Versailles menagerie, and a Roman mosaic of a lion hunt. An image from this collection is reproduced in this volume's illustrations section.

Arranged: By assigned number.

Captioned: Some with location.

Finding Aid: No.

Restrictions: Available by appointment.

ZP·9

Veterinary Photograph Collection *A.K.A.* James F. Wright Photograph Collection

Dates of Photographs: 1950s–1960s

Collection Origins

James F. Wright (1924–) created the collection to document his work in the NZP hospital and park. Wright received doctorates in veterinary medicine from the University of Pennsylvania in 1951 and in pathology from the University of California at Davis in 1969. A specialist in comparative pathology and toxicology, he was among the first veterinarians to use a tranquilizing capture gun. Wright worked at Plum Island Animal Laboratory (1954–1957); at NZP as Veterinarian (1957–1962); at the U.S. Air Force Radiology Laboratory (1962–1964) as a research scientist; at the Yerkes Regional Primate Research Center (1964–1965); at the Environmental Protection Agency's Twinbrook Research Laboratory (1969–1973); at the Health Effects Research Laboratory (1978–1982) as a chief of pathology studies; and currently at the North Carolina Zoological Park in Asheboro (1988–) as a veterinarian and pathologist. Photographers represented include NZP and OPPS staff. Note: After completion of this volume the collection was transferred to the Smithsonian Institution Archives, A & I 2135, 900 Jefferson Dr., SW, Washington, D.C. 20560. Telephone: (202) 357-1420.

Physical Description

There are 80 photographs including color dye coupler photonegatives, photoprints, and slides and silver gelatin photonegatives.

Subjects

The photographs document Wright's veterinary activities at the NZP during the 1950s and 1960s. Autopsies, general animal medical care, and operations are recorded, as well as animals, animal enclosures, and landscapes. NZP staff portrayed include Frank Baker, William Hornaday, and Arthur B. Wood.

Arranged: No.

Captioned: Some with subject.

Finding Aid: No.

Restrictions: Some photographs are restricted due to condition or copyright status.

ZP

Office of Education

Office of Education
National Zoological Park
Smithsonian Institution
Washington, D.C. 20008
Judith S. King, Writer-Editor
(202) 673-4735
Hours: By appointment.

Scope of the Collection

There is one photographic collection with approximately 58,000 images.

Focus of the Collection

The collection, used for teaching and outreach purposes, documents administrative activities, animal houses, animals, events, exhibits, facilities, staff, and visitors at the National Zoological Park from 1905 to the present.

Photographic Processes and Formats Represented

There are duplicate color dye coupler slides and silver gelatin photonegatives, photoprints, and slides.

Other Materials Represented

The office also contains correspondence, motion-picture film footage, and press releases.

Access and Usage Policies

Open to scholarly researchers by appointment.

Publication Policies

Researchers must obtain permission from the Smithsonian Institution to reproduce a photograph and may also have to obtain permission from the copyright holder, which is not necessarily the Smithsonian Institution. The preferred credit line is "Courtesy of the National Zoological Park, Smithsonian Institution."

ZP·10

Education Office Photograph Collection

Dates of Photographs: 1905–Present

Collection Origins

The NZP Education and Public Affairs office staff assembled the collection for outreach and teaching purposes including classes, lectures, pamphlets, press releases, public relations activities, seminars, and slide shows. Many of the photographs are duplicates of originals housed at OPPS or at the NZP Office of Design and Exhibit Planning. Photographers and studios represented include Ilene Berg-Akerman; the Berral-Jasper Company, Washington, D.C.; Jessie Cohen; the Commercial Photo Company, Washington, D.C.; the Harwood Nebel Construction Company, Inc.; Max Hirshfeld; Everett Johnson, Arlington, Virginia; Judith S. King; Robert Lawrence, Washington, D.C.; the Ludwig Photo Laboratories, Washington, D.C.; Ernest Meyers; OPPS; J. Perry; Reni Photographer, Washington, D.C.; the San Diego Zoo; Francie Schroeder; Jan Skrentry; the Society of Mammalogists; the U.S. Department of Agriculture; Constance Warner; and the *Washington Star.*

Physical Description

There are 58,000 duplicate photographs including color dye coupler photonegatives, photoprints, and slides and silver gelatin photonegatives (some nitrate) and photoprints. Other materials include motion-picture film footage.

Subjects

The photographs document the NZP from 1905 to the present, including animal houses, animals, events, exhibitions, facilities, staff, and visitors. Animals illustrated include anoles, baboons, bats, bears, condors, deer, eagles, emus, giraffes, gorillas, gulls, hippopotamuses, hyenas, Komodo dragons, lions, monkeys, pandas, penguins, snakes, terns, and weasels. NZP animal houses and facilities shown include the Bird House; Conservation and Research Center in Front Royal, Virginia; Holt House; Hospital and Research Building; Lion House in 1907; Lion House hill; Monkey House in 1929; Sea Lion Pool and waterfall in 1909; Tiger Yard; and the NZP restaurant in 1940.

Staff portrayed include R. Mitchell Bush, Leonard Carmichael, Jaren Horsley, Anthony Kadlubowski, Edward Kohn, Lucille Mann, William M. Mann, Theodore H. Reed, S. Dillon Ripley, and Zoo police during training. Visitors portrayed include Amy Carter, H.R.H. Ashi Choki, President Dwight D. Eisenhower, Girl Scout Troop 60, Prime Minister Keith Holyoake, Senator Claiborne Pell, Mrs. Charles Percy, Ambassador Jules Razafimbahing of Madagascar, and Ambassador J.K. Waller of Australia. Events documented include the birth of a black rhino in 1967; Leonard Carmichael's farewell party in 1964; the Easter egg roll in 1936 (an early integrated public event in Washington, D.C.); a fence survey in 1970; a Friends of the National Zoo art contest in 1968; and a Smokey the Bear ceremony in 1978.

Arranged: In three series, by process. 1) Duplicate slides, by assigned number, animal name, subject, or slide show name. 2) Photonegatives, in two subseries: a) color and b) black-and-white, then by animal name or assigned number. 3) Photoprints, in two subseries: a) historical photoprints, by process or subject and b) contemporary photoprints, by subject or assigned number. Many animal prints and slides are then arranged by taxonomic order.

Captioned: Many with subject and technical data. Some envelopes list date, location, negative number, project, species, and zoo name.

Finding Aid: 1) Photoprint and photonegative index titled "NZP Photo List," by number (001–3818); includes date, frame number, location, negative number, personal names, photographer, species, and subject. 2) Photoprint and photonegative index, by date (1889–1978); includes date, frame number, negative number, photographer, and species. 3) Motion-picture film footage index includes date, location, title, topic, and whether silent or with soundtrack.

Restrictions: Available to scholarly researchers by appointment.

SMITHSONIAN ASTROPHYSICAL OBSERVATORY

Irwin I. Shapiro, Director

The Smithsonian Astrophysical Observatory (SAO) pursues research into the physical processes that determine the nature and evolution of the universe. Established in 1890 by Smithsonian Secretary Samuel P. Langley, SAO was originally housed on the Mall behind the Smithsonian Institution Building. Early SAO research concentrated on the study of solar radiation. Under Charles G. Abbot, Langley's successor, solar observation stations were built in the western United States, as well as in Africa and South America, and the SAO became a center for research into the relationship between solar and geophysical phenomena.

In 1955 Fred L. Whipple of Harvard University was named director of SAO and its headquarters were moved to Cambridge, Massachusetts. In preparation for the International Geophysical Year of 1957–1958, Whipple established an optical network for tracking the first artificial satellites. With the development of the international space program, SAO's research grew to include geodesy (the study of the size and shape of the Earth), meteoritics (the study of meteors and meteorites), space sciences, and theoretical astrophysics (the study of the chemical and physical natures of the heavenly bodies and their origin and evolution).

Beginning in 1955, SAO staff conducted astronomical research in close cooperation with colleagues at the Harvard College Observatory (HCO). This close association between SAO and HCO was formalized on July 1, 1973, with the establishment of the Harvard-Smithsonian Center for Astrophysics (CfA), a joint enterprise designed to coordinate research activities under a single director. Today, some 150 scientists led by Irwin Shapiro are grouped programmatically into seven divisions: 1) Atomic and Molecular Physics, 2) High-Energy Astrophysics, 3) Optical and Infrared Astronomy, 4) Planetary Sciences, 5) Radio and Geoastronomy, 6) Solar and Stellar Physics, and 7) Theoretical Astrophysics.

Data-gathering facilities include the Whipple Observatory at Mount Hopkins, Arizona; the Oak Ridge Observatory in Harvard, Massachusetts; the George Agassiz radio astronomy facility in Fort Davis, Texas; and various satellite, balloon, or rocket-borne telescopes for observations above the atmosphere. In addition to the research in space sciences, ongoing SAO research activities include developing new instrumentation for both ground-based and space-borne experiments, identifying celestial phenomena, and mapping and measuring large-scale structures in the universe. SAO also conducts public and scholarly education, information, and publication programs, including the development of astronomy-based curriculum materials for secondary school teachers, monthly "observatory nights," public lecture series, and tours of the Whipple Observatory.

The 635,700 images in SAO's 16 photographic collections (including those at the Harvard College Observatory) document the history of astronomy from the late 1840s to the present. The photographs also show a variety of astronomical phenomena and celestial objects including comets, meteors, nebulae, planets, sky section images used in mapping, stars, and star clusters; and optical- and laser-tracking images of artificial earth satellites. Other photographs illustrate astronomical equipment, astronomers, support staff, and SAO and HCO activities, events, facilities, and visitors. In addition to these photographs, SAO's research resources include correspondence, library resources, notes, and other information bases. Note: SAO's Atomic and Molecular Physics Division and Theoretical Astrophysics Division do not contain any photographs, according to divisional sources.

SA

High-Energy Astrophysics Division

High-Energy Astrophysics Division
Smithsonian Astrophysical Observatory
Harvard-Smithsonian Center for Astrophysics
60 Garden Street
Cambridge, Massachusetts 02138
Polly Sullivan, Administrative Assistant
(617) 495-7208
Hours: By appointment.

Scope of the Collections

There are three photographic collections with approximately 8,100 images.

Focus of the Collections

The photographs in this division document celestial objects such as comets, galaxies, nebulae, pulsars, quasars, satellites, star clusters, the Sun, and supernovae. Many of the photographs are x-ray images taken from the *Einstein* satellite or the National Aeronautics and Space Administration's *Skylab* satellite.

Photographic Processes and Formats Represented

There are color dye coupler slides and silver gelatin photonegatives, photoprints, phototransparencies, slides, and x-ray photographs.

Other Materials Represented

The division also contains charts, drawings, graphs, and inventory sheets.

Access and Usage Policies

The collections are open to scholarly researchers by appointment only. Researchers should call or write two weeks in advance to arrange for an appointment. Certain materials may be restricted due to copyright status or preservation conditions. There is no charge for the creation of single copies of photographs to be used in news, feature, or educational contexts. In general, allow four weeks for routine processing. All orders are shipped via U.S. mail, unless the requestor is willing to pay for C.O.D. express shipments to their billing address. The SAO Publications Department Photography Laboratory requests the return of photographic materials after use, if possible, and appreciates receiving copies of any publications resulting from this use. Restrictions may apply on making copies of certain marked photographs in these collections. Please contact the collection custodians for further information.

Publication Policies

Most of the SAO images are copyright-free, and most restricted photographs are marked as such. However, researchers must obtain permission to publish a copyrighted image from the copyright holder, which is not necessarily the Smithsonian Institution. The preferred credit line is "Courtesy of the Center for Astrophysics, Smithsonian Astrophysical Observatory." The photographer's name, if known, should be added to the credit line.

SA·1

Einstein Satellite Photograph Collection

Dates of Photographs: 1978–1981

Collection Origins

Riccardo Giacconi (1931–), Associate Director for the High-Energy Astrophysics Division from 1973 until 1981, assembled the collection for research purposes from the 5,000 images taken by the *Einstein* satellite. Giacconi received a Ph.D. in physics in 1954 from the University of Milan where he served as assistant professor of Physics for the next two years. He also was a Fulbright fellow at Indiana University (1956–1958); a Research Associate at Princeton University (1958–1959); Executive Vice President of American Science and Engineering, Inc. (1959–1973); a Professor of Astronomy at Harvard University (1973–1981); and Director of the Space Telescope Science Institute in Baltimore (1981–).

Harvey Dale Tananbaum (1942–) later supplemented and expanded the collection. Tananbaum, Associate Director of the High Energy Astrophysics Division from 1981 to the present, received a Ph.D. in physics from Massachusetts Institute of Technology in 1968 and joined SAO in 1973. The collection also includes presentation, publication, and research visuals prepared by Giacconi and Tananbaum. Photographers and studios represented include American Science and Engineering, Inc.; Columbia University; Massachusetts Institute of Technology; and the National Aeronautics and Space Administration (NASA) Goddard Space Flight Center. A selected set of 56 images and accompanying study guide were published as "Visions of Einstein," which is available for purchase from OPPS, Smithsonian Institution, NMAH, CB054, Washington, D.C. 20560, or call (202) 357-1933.

Physical Description

There are 2,500 photographs including color dye coupler slides and silver gelatin photonegatives, photoprints, and slides. Most are x-ray images.

Subjects

The photographs, representing the first focused images of cosmic sources of x-rays, were obtained by the *Einstein* satellite between 1978 and 1981. The celestial objects photographed include galaxies, nebulae, pulsars, quasars, star clusters, and supernova remnants. There are also numerous photographic reproductions of charts, diagrams, and graphs. Specific celestial objects documented include Alpha Centauri, Canopus 1800, Carina Nebulae, Cas-A supernova remnant, Centaurus Cluster, Crab Nebula, Crab SNR x-ray spectrum, Draco, Eta Carinae, M84, M87 halo, M86, M33 nucleus, Small Magellanic Cloud, Orion Nebula, Perseus Cluster, starburst galaxy NGC 5885, Vela Pulsar, Vela SNR, and Virgo Cluster.

Arranged: In three series by type of material and date. 1) Slides, arranged chronologically. 2) Vugraphs, arranged chronologically. 3) Photoprints, arranged by assigned numbers that correspond to the slides in series 1.

Captioned: Some with subject.

Finding Aid: 1) An online keyword descriptive index inventory, organized chronologically. 2) A printout of the computer index, in three binders containing color slides.

Restrictions: No.

SA·2

Skylab Solar X-Ray Image Collection

Dates of Photographs: 1973–1974

Collection Origins

NASA astronauts used a solar x-ray telescope on *Skylab's* Apollo telescope mount to produce original photonegatives of the Sun between 1973 and 1974.

Phototransparencies produced from these photonegatives were given to SAO for research purposes. The images appear in the following article: R. Rosner, L. Golub, and G.S. Vaiana. "On Stellar X-Ray Emission." *Annual Review of Astronomy and Astrophysics* vol. 23. Palo Alto, California: Annual Reviews Inc., 1985.

Physical Description

There are 5,000 silver gelatin x-ray phototransparencies. These reduced-contrast copy images were produced from internegatives on Kodak copy film 4135. The originals were made with Kodak SO212 film.

Subjects

The photographs are x-ray images of the Sun taken by *Skylab* in 1973 and 1974. The images show different features of the Sun's corona and surface.

Arranged: Chronologically, subdivided by type of filter used.

Captioned: With code number or date.

Finding Aid: A computer printout catalog giving image date, exposure length, filter type, location on the Sun, and time.

Restrictions: No.

SA·3

Uhuru Satellite Photograph Collection

Dates of Photographs: 1970–1971

Collection Origins

The High-Energy Astrophysics Division staff assembled the collection for publication, public relations, and research purposes.

Physical Description

There are 600 photographs including color dye coupler slides and silver gelatin photoprints. Many of the images are x-ray photographs. Other materials include inventory sheets.

Subjects

The photographs, many of which are x-ray images, document various celestial objects including *Uhuru* (a small astronomy satellite launched in 1971) and its equipment (such as rocket heat shields and thermal blankets). Photographic reproductions of binary source tables, charts, drawings, graphs, and sky maps are also included.

Arranged: By assigned numbers that match inventory sheets dated "9/1/77."

Captioned: With assigned number, date, description, and subject identification code.

Finding Aid: Inventory sheets are used as a rough finding aid. Note: The images will be described online in a keyword database inventory, which will include the *Einstein* Satellite Photograph Collection.

Restrictions: No.

SA

Optical and Infrared Astronomy Division

Optical and Infrared Astronomy Division
Smithsonian Astrophysical Observatory
Harvard-Smithsonian Center for Astrophysics
60 Garden Street
Cambridge, Massachusetts 02138
Rudolph E. Schild, Astronomer
(617) 495-7426
Hours: By appointment.

Scope of the Collection

There is one photographic collection with approximately 4,500 images.

Focus of the Collection

The photographs document astronomical objects such as interstellar nebulae and spiral galaxies.

Photographic Processes and Formats Represented

There are color dye coupler photoprints and slides and silver gelatin photoprints.

Other Materials Represented

The division also contains charts, digitally-stored information, drawings, and notes.

Access and Usage Policies

The collections are open to scholarly researchers by appointment only. Researchers should call or write two weeks in advance to arrange for an appointment. Certain materials may be restricted due to copyright status or preservation conditions. There is no charge for the creation of single copies of photographs to be used in news, feature, or educational contexts. In general, allow four weeks for routine processing. All orders are shipped via U.S. mail, unless the requestor is willing to pay for C.O.D. express shipments to their billing address. The SAO Publications Department Photography Laboratory requests the return of photographic materials after use, if possible, and appreciates receiving copies of any publications resulting from this use. Restrictions may apply on making copies of certain marked photographs in these collections. Please contact the collection custodian for further information.

Publication Policies

Most of the SAO images are copyright-free, and most restricted photographs are marked as such. However, researchers must obtain permission to publish a copyrighted image from the copyright holder, which is not necessarily the Smithsonian Institution. The preferred credit line is "Courtesy of Rudolph E. Schild of the Center for Astrophysics, Smithsonian Astrophysical Observatory."

SA·4

Optical and Infrared Astronomy Collection *A.K.A.* Rudolph E. Schild Research Collection

Dates of Photographs: 1983–Present

Collection Origins

Rudolph E. Schild (1940–) created the collection for publication, public relations, and research purposes. Schild, who received a Ph.D. in astrophysics from the University of Chicago in 1966, has been employed by the SAO since 1969 and by the Harvard University Astronomy Department since 1973. Most of the images were created with "charge-coupled devices" (CCDs), which are light-sensitive arrays of silicone chips that convert photons of light gathered by a telescope into electrical signals. These electronic detectors are linked directly to online computers, where the data is stored digitally for later processing into images. The Center for Astrophysics' Wolbach Image Processing Laboratory (WIPL) converts the data into an analog format (television signals). The images can then be manipulated, enhanced, interpreted, and photographed. By contrast with standard photographic plates, CCDs are extremely light-efficient, thus allowing very faint and distant objects to be seen more easily with unusually short exposure times.

The images appear in several books and journals, including the following: *Sky and Telescope*. Cambridge, Massachusetts: Sky Publishing Corporation (August 1986 and February 1988). Images have also appeared in "Art in Astronomy," a traveling exhibit organized by Iowa State University's Brunnier Gallery in Ames, Iowa, for the 1985 Annual Meeting of the American Astronomical Society. A selected set of 43 images and accompanying booklet were published as "The Electronic Sky: Digital Images of the Cosmos." The slide set is for sale from OPPS, Smithsonian Institution, NMAH, CB054, Washington, D.C. 20560, or call (202) 357-1933.

Physical Description

There are 4,500 photographs including color dye coupler photoprints and slides and silver gelatin photoprints. Many were originally digitized images. Ninety-nine percent of the photographs are color slides. A photograph of a spiral galaxay from this collection is reproduced in this volume's illustrations.

Subjects

The collection consists of images of astronomical objects such as interstellar nebulae and spiral galaxies.

Arranged: By subject.

Captioned: With camera filters used, subject, and occasionally with date or subject location.

Finding Aid: No.

Restrictions: No.

SA

Planetary Sciences Division

Planetary Sciences Division
Smithsonian Astrophysical Observatory
Harvard-Smithsonian Center for Astrophysics
60 Garden Street
Cambridge, Massachusetts 02138
John A. Wood, Senior Geologist
(617) 495-7278
Hours: By appointment.

Scope of the Collections

There are three photographic collections with approximately 19,700 images.

Focus of the Collections

These photographs document the division's research activities and the study of planetary science, including astrogeology and planetology.

Photographic Processes and Formats Represented

There are color dye coupler phototransparencies and slides and silver gelatin photonegatives and photoprints.

Other Materials Represented

This division also contains correspondence, motion-picture film footage, notes, and other textual materials.

Access and Usage Policies

The collections are open by appointment only to educators and scholars with the prior consent of John A. Wood. Due to space and staffing constraints, researchers should notify Wood of a proposed visit at least two weeks in advance. Certain materials may be restricted due to copyright status or preservation conditions. Restrictions may apply on making copies of certain marked photographs in these collections. There is no charge for the creation of single copies of photographs to be used in news, feature, or educational contexts. In general, allow four weeks for routine processing. All orders are shipped via U.S. mail, unless the requestor is willing to pay for C.O.D. express shipments to their billing address. The SAO Publications Department Photography Laboratory requests the return of photographic materials after use, if possible, and appreciates receiving copies of any publications resulting from this use.

Publication Policies

Most of the SAO images are copyright-free, and most restricted photographs are marked as such. However, researchers must obtain permission to publish a copyrighted image from the copyright holder, which is not necessarily the Smithsonian Institution. The preferred credit line is "Courtesy of the Center for Astrophysics, Smithsonian Astrophysical Observatory." The photographer's name, if known, should be added to the credit line.

SA·5

Extraterrestrial Petrology Research Collection

Dates of Photographs: 1958–Present

Collection Origins

SAO geologists John A. Wood (1932–) and Ursula Marvin (1921–), and their colleagues and students created this collection to document SAO research activities between 1958 and the present. Wood, who received a Ph.D. in geology from Massachusetts Institute of Technology in 1958, joined SAO in 1959 and later became Associate Director. Wood also served as a research associate at the University of Chicago's Enrico Fermi Institute of Nuclear Studies (1962–1965). Marvin, who received a Ph.D. from Harvard University in 1969, taught at the University of Chicago, served as a mineralogist at Union Carbide Company, and taught at Tufts University before joining the SAO in 1961 and Harvard College Observatory (HCO) in 1965. Charles Hanson, SAO photographer, took most of the photographs. Other studios represented include the National Aeronautics and Space Administration (NASA). Researchers interested in the NASA photographs should contact the Audio-Visual Branch, Public Information Division, NASA, 400 Maryland Ave., SW, Room 6035, Washington, D.C. 20546; (202) 453-8375.

Physical Description

There are 3,000 photographs including color dye coupler phototransparencies and slides (many are copies). Other materials include motion-picture film footage. Note: The exact number of photographs changes constantly because photographs are added and removed almost daily.

Subjects

These photographs document the division's research activities, particularly microprobe analyses of lunar samples and meteorites, between 1958 and the present. There are photographs of lunar samples (such as soil samples in thin-sections) and meteorites (including both macro images and thin-sections of meteorites of approximately 30-micron thickness). There are also photographs of laboratory analysis and preparation of lunar samples and meteorites.

Arranged: In two major series by subject. 1) Meteorites, subdivided by name. 2) Lunar samples, subdivided by sample number.

Captioned: With name or number.

Finding Aid: No.

Restrictions: Private research collection available by appointment only.

SA·6

Planetary Science Research Collection *A.K.A.* John A. Wood Research Collection

Dates of Photographs: 1960s–Present

Collection Origins

SAO photographer Charles Hanson created the collection for John A. Wood, who uses the collection for lectures, publications, and research. For a biography of Wood see the *Collection Origins* field of *SA·5*. Some of the photographs have appeared in the following book: John A. Wood. *The Solar System*. Englewood Cliffs, New Jersey: Prentice Hall, 1979.

Physical Description

The are 5,400 photographs including color dye coupler slides and silver gelatin photonegatives and photoprints.

Subjects

The photographs document drawings, equipment, facilities, procedures, scientists, and tools involved in the study of planetary science including astrogeology and planetology. Specimens shown include lunar samples, meteorites, and meteorite thin-sections. There are also photographs of NASA's Houston, Texas, staff creating thin-sections of meteorites and of NASA astronaut Harrison H. Schmitt *(Apollo 17)* with dignitaries.

Arranged: In five series by subject and type of material. 1) Color dye coupler slides of astrogeology, lunar samples, meteorites, meteorite thin-sections, planetary materials, and planetology drawings, arranged by subject. 2) Miscellaneous photoprints, arranged by assigned negative number. 3) Photonegatives and photoprints of meteorites, arranged by meteorite name. 4) Color dye coupler slides of samples, arranged by assigned sample number. 5) Color dye coupler slides of meteorites used in lectures, arranged by lecture topic.

Captioned: With subject information and/or assigned negative number or lunar sample number.

Finding Aid: No.

Restrictions: Some images are copyrighted.

SA·7

Prairie Meteorite Recovery Network Collection

Dates of Photographs: 1965–1975

Collection Origins

SAO Prairie Meteorite Recovery Network staff members, including Richard E. McCrosky (1924–) and field operator Gunther Schwartz, created the collection. McCrosky, who received a Ph.D. in astronomy from Harvard University in 1956, began lecturing on astronomy at Harvard in the same year and became a research associate at SAO in 1957, before joining the Prairie Meteorite Recovery Network staff. Funded by NASA and the Smithsonian Institution, the network consisted of 16 unmanned camera stations in seven Midwestern states that operated between 1965 and 1975. At the stations, wide-angle reconnaissance cameras activated by bright light surveyed the night sky. The resulting time-exposure photographs provided information on bright meteors, such as their deceleration, position in space, and velocity. With several images made simultaneously from different locations, scientists could determine a meteorite's impact point, orbit, and size at the end of its visible trajectory.

The images and research results produced by the SAO Prairie Meteorite Recovery Network appear in the following publications: 1) Edward L. Fireman. "The Lost City Meteorite—A Deep-Space Probe for Cosmic Rays." *Sky and Telescope* no. 39 (March 1970). 2) Richard E. McCrosky. "The Lost City Meteorite Fall." *Sky and Telescope* no. 39 (March 1970). 3) Richard E. McCrosky, C.Y. Shao, and A. Posen. "Prairie Network Fireball Data: I—Summary and Orbits." *Meteoritika* no. 37 (1978): 44ff. 4) Idem. "Prairie Network Fireball Data: II—Trajectories and Light Curves." *Meteoritika* no. 38 (1979): 106ff. 5) Richard E. McCrosky, A. Posen, G. Schwartz, and C.Y. Shao. "Lost City Meteorite—Its Recovery and a Comparison With Other Fireballs." *Journal of Geophysical Research* no. 76 (June 10, 1971): 4090–4097.

Physical Description

There are 11,000 silver gelatin photonegatives. Other materials include a database, publications, and reprints.

Subjects

The photographs are long exposures of the night sky showing meteor paths and star trails as seen over Illinois, Iowa, Kansas, Missouri, Nebraska, Oklahoma, and South Dakota between 1965 and 1975.

Arranged: In three series. 1) Images with no visible meteors (on rolls for use by astronomers). 2) Single-station images of meteors. 3) Multi-station images of meteors (more than two images of a meteor from more than one station). Within series 1 and 3, all images made on the same night from each of the 16 stations are kept together, and are arranged by Julian date and assigned number.

Captioned: On envelopes with camera name and location, Julian date, station number, and technical notes (such as angle of sighting, estimated distance of the sighted meteor from the station, exposure length, magnitude, and range).

Finding Aid: No.

Restrictions: Available to experienced scholarly researchers by appointment.

SA

Solar and Stellar Physics Division

Solar and Stellar Physics Division
Smithsonian Astrophysical Observatory
Harvard-Smithsonian Center for Astrophysics
60 Garden Street
Cambridge, Massachusetts 02138
George L. Withbroe, Associate Director
(617) 495-7438
Hours: By appointment.

Scope of the Collection

There is one photographic collection with approximately 101,000 images.

Focus of the Collection

The photographs are spectroheliographs, or images of the Sun's ultraviolet emissions, made from *Skylab* satellites, showing bright points, coronal holes, and solar active regions. The collection also includes photographs of *Skylab* satellites and photographic reproductions of charts, diagrams, and graphics.

Photographic Processes and Formats Represented

There are color dye coupler photoprints and slides, silver gelatin photonegatives (72mm), photoprints, and phototransparencies (some 72mm).

Other Materials Represented

The collection also contains microphotographs mounted on microfiche.

Access and Usage Policies

The collection is open to educators and scholars by appointment. Researchers should call or write two weeks in advance to arrange for an appointment. Certain materials may be restricted due to copyright status or preservation conditions. There is no charge for the creation of single copies of photographs to be used in news, feature, or educational contexts. In general, allow four weeks for routine processing. All orders are shipped via U.S. mail, unless the requestor is willing to pay for C.O.D. express shipments to their billing address. The SAO Publications Department Photography Laboratory requests the return of photographic materials after use, if possible, and appreciates receiving copies of any publications resulting from this use. Restrictions may apply on making copies of certain marked photographs in these collections. Please contact the collection custodian for further information.

Publication Policies

Most of the SAO images are copyright-free, and most restricted photographs are marked as such. However, researchers must obtain permission to publish a copyrighted image from the copyright holder, which is not necessarily the Smithsonian Institution. The preferred credit line is "Courtesy of the Center for Astrophysics, Smithsonian Astrophysical Observatory." The photographer's name, if known, should be added to the credit line.

SA·8

Skylab Ultraviolet Solar Photograph Collection

Dates of Photographs: 1973–1974

Collection Origins

The National Aeronautics and Space Administration (NASA) and the Solar Satellite Project of the Harvard College Observatory (HCO) created the photographs from data obtained by an ultraviolet-sensitive instrument aboard the *Skylab* spacecraft. The data was first recorded digitally, then converted onto microfiche for research use. Finally, photoprints and slides were produced by the Wolbach Image Processing Laboratory (WIPL) of the Center for Astrophysics (CfA) for public relations purposes. For more information on this process see the *Collection Origins* field of *SA·4*. The photographs appeared in the following book: John A. Eddy, ed. *A New Sun: The Solar Results from Skylab, NASA SP-402*. Washington, D.C.: NASA, Scientific and Technical Information Office, 1979.

Physical Description

There are 101,000 photographs including color dye coupler photoprints and slides, silver gelatin photonegatives (72mm), photoprints, and phototransparencies (some are 72mm phototransparencies mounted on microfiche). Note: Some images were originally digitized images, others are three-wavelength composite images or x-ray images.

Subjects

The photographs are spectroheliographs, or pictures of the Sun's ultraviolet emissions. The images document the solar atmosphere and surface such as active regions, bright points, and coronal holes, as well as illustrating *Skylab*. There are also photographic reproductions of charts, diagrams, and graphs. A photograph of the sun from this collection is reproduced in this volume's illustrations.

Arranged: In two series. 1) Card-mounted photonegatives and photoprints, arranged by date and detector number. 2) Unarranged photonegatives, photoprints, and slides.

Captioned: Series 1 with date, detector number, and subject keywords.

Finding Aid: To series 1, a ten-volume computer-printout in catalog form lists keyword caption information.

Restrictions: No.

SA

Publications Department

Publications Department
Smithsonian Astrophysical Observatory
Harvard-Smithsonian Center for Astrophysics
60 Garden Street
Cambridge, Massachusetts 02138
James C. Cornell, Jr., Manager
(617) 495-7461
Hours: 8:45 a.m.–5:15 p.m.

Scope of the Collections:

There are seven photographic collections with approximately 103,000 images.

Focus of the Collections

These photographs depict the facilities, history, projects, research, and staff of the SAO from its founding in 1890 to the present, with a concentration on activities after 1957. The collection also includes photographs of the Baker-Nunn satellite-tracking stations, the F.L. Whipple Observatory (including the Multiple Mirror Telescope) on Arizona's Mount Hopkins, and the people and projects of the Harvard College Observatory (HCO). Most of the photographs show celestial objects, including comets, galaxies, meteors, and satellites. The division also collects photographs used in staff publications.

Photographic Processes and Formats Represented

There are color dye coupler photoprints and slides and silver gelatin photonegatives and photoprints.

Other Materials Represented

The department's collections also contain clippings, cutlines, databases, graphs, press releases, publications, record forms, reprints, and xerographic copies.

Access and Usage Policies

The collections are open to educators and scholars by appointment. The division staff provides limited reference assistance. Researchers should call or write James C. Cornell, Jr., SAO Publications Department Manager, at least two weeks in advance to arrange for an appointment. Certain materials may be restricted due to copyright status or preservation conditions. Restrictions may apply on making copies of certain marked photographs in these collections. There is no charge for the creation of single copies of photographs to be used in news, feature, or educational contexts. In general, allow four weeks for routine processing. All orders are shipped via U.S. mail, unless the requestor is willing to pay for C.O.D. express shipments to their billing address. The SAO Publications Department Photography Laboratory requests the return of photographic materials after use, if possible, and appreciates receiving copies of any publications resulting from this use. Please contact the collection custodians for further information.

Publication Policies

Most of the SAO images are copyright-free, and most restricted photographs are marked as such. However, researchers must obtain permission to publish a copyrighted image from the copyright holder, which is not necessarily the Smithsonian Institution. The preferred credit line is "Courtesy of the Center for Astrophysics, Smithsonian Astrophysical Observatory." The photographer's name, if known, should be added to the credit line.

SA·9

Baker-Nunn Satellite-Tracking Station Collection

Dates of Photographs: 1957–1970s

Collection Origins

SAO Publications Department Manager James C. Cornell, Jr., assembled the collection from various sources to document SAO's optical satellite-tracking program. Cornell, who received an M.S. from Boston University, is the author of several science books. After working for the Worcester, Massachusetts, *Telegram and Gazette* and Rustcraft Publishers in Dedham, Massachusetts, Cornell joined the SAO as Public Information Officer in 1963, becoming Publications Department Manager in 1971.

The optical satellite-tracking program was originally established in 1956 to support research during the International Geophysical Year of 1957–1958 and operated until the early 1980s under contract with NASA. The principal instrument, the Baker-Nunn camera, was a modified Super-Schmidt-type telescope with a tri-axial mount for precise satellite-tracking designed to the specifications of SAO scientists. The prototype Baker-Nunn camera was in operation by October 1957 and photographed *Sputnik I*, the first man-made satellite. Subsequently, an international network was established, with the first stations in Villa Dolores, Argentina; Woomera, Australia; Curaçao; Naini Tal, India; Shiraz, Iran; Tokyo, Japan; Arequipa, Peru; Olifantsfontein, South Africa; and in Jupiter, Florida; Maui, Hawaii; and Organ, New Mexico in the United States. Later movement of the camera sites led to the establishment of stations in Comodoro Rivadavia, Argentina; Whipple Observatory on Mount Hopkins, Arizona; Natal, Brazil; Debre Zeit, Ethiopia; and Athens, Greece.

In the mid-1970s, laser-ranging systems were added to several cameras. Data obtained from the stations was used to estimate the shape and size of the Earth's atmospheric density and continental drift. The camera station network also photographed comets, studied flare stars, tracked satellites, and participated in a unique global "patrol" allowing simultaneous and continuous surveys of newly discovered celestial objects such as asteroids and supernovae.

Physical Description

There are 4,200 photographs including color dye coupler photoprints and silver gelatin photonegatives and photoprints. Other materials include clippings, record forms, and xerographic copies.

Subjects

The photographs document the assembly and use of 12 Baker-Nunn satellite-tracking camera stations by SAO staff between 1957 and the 1970s, particularly the remote overseas stations. There are photographs of camera operators; camera-station interiors; construction work such as Baker-Nunn camera assembly and station building construction; and visitors to the stations, for example, Haile Selassie at the Ethiopian tracking station. Equipment documented includes Baker-Nunn cameras including engineering diagrams, internal assemblies, and plans; the camera parts and electronic controls; darkroom equipment; laser transmitters and receivers; power amplifiers; timing systems; and other equipment in and around the tracking stations.

Celestial bodies and phenomena documented include various comets, such as Ikeya-Seki and Kohoutek; flare stars; lunar eclipses; and meteors. Satellites and spacecraft documented include *Alpha A.K.A. Explorer 1* (1958); *Apollo 9 SIUB* Rocket (observed from Maui and Mount Hopkins); *Beta 2 A.K.A. Vanguard 1* Satellite (1958); *Cosmos 1* (1969—*Theta 1* and *Theta 2*); *Cosmos 191* reentry on January 8, 1968; *Delta A.K.A. Sputnik 3* Rocket Carrier (1958); *Delta 1* Satellite (1958); *Delta 1* (1959); *Project Echo 1; Epsilon 2 A.K.A. Discoverer 5* recovery capsule (1959); *Epsilon Explorer 4* (1958); *Eta Vanguard 3* (1959); *Gamma* (1958); *Lunik 3; Pageos* Geodetic Satellite; *Pegasus 1* Satellite; *Ranger 7; Satellite Beta* (third-stage rocket of *Vanguard*, 1958); and Satellite *Syncom 2*.

Arranged: First by geographic location, then chronologically by type of activity.

Captioned: With the dates, equipment or activity shown, location and occasionally with the names of individuals shown.

Finding Aid: No.

Restrictions: No.

SA·10

Harvard College Observatory Historical Photograph Collection

Dates of Photographs: 1970s

Collection Origins

The staff of the Harvard College Observatory (HCO) created this collection to document the observatory's activities, facilities, staff, and visitors. Some of the photographs of satellites and solar coronagraphs were made by solar orbiting observatories. Most images were taken by staff photographer Michael Kennedy.

Physical Description

There are 10,100 silver gelatin photoprints.

Subjects

Most of the photographs depict colleagues, equipment, facilities, research activities, and staff of the HCO during the 1970s. There are photographs of the observatory's facilities in Cambridge, Massachusetts, including the business office, the infrared laboratory, the Mars project, the Oak Ridge Observatory, the photography laboratory, the Plate Stacks (photographic storage area), and the radio observatory. A series of ultraviolet coronagraphs taken from orbiting solar observatories is also included. The solar spectra images illustrate the Sun in spectral wavelengths from several locations including the Apollo telescope mount aboard NASA's *Skylab.* A photograph of the moon from this collection is reproduced in this volume's illustrations.

Arranged: In three series by subject and/or requestor/creator. 1) HCO equipment, facilities, and staff, arranged by subject. 2) HCO staff-requested images, arranged alphabetically by requestor's last name. 3) Solar satellites, arranged by assigned solar-satellite number (from SS7701 to SS7203-17).

Captioned: With assigned negative number.

Finding Aid: Photographer's log book which lists the image's assigned number, requestor's name, type of photograph, and a brief description of the number of shots, film, or subject.

Restrictions: No.

SA·11

Multiple Mirror Telescope Collection

Dates of Photographs: 1970s–Present

Collection Origins

SAO Publications Department Manager James C. Cornell, Jr., assembled the collection to document the Multiple Mirror Telescope designed and built by the Smithsonian Institution and the University of Arizona. The telescope is located on the summit of Arizona's Mount Hopkins. For a biography of Cornell see the *Collection Origins* field of *SA·9*. Photographers represented include Daniel K. Brocious, James C. Cornell, Jr., and Joseph T. Williams of SAO; and R. Schiff of the University of Arizona.

Physical Description

There are 100 photographs including color dye coupler photoprints and silver gelatin photoprints.

Subjects

The photographs document the design and construction of the Multiple Mirror Telescope, located on the summit of Arizona's Mount Hopkins. There are photographs of the fabrication of the telescope's mount in Italy in 1974 and its later assembly, as well as associated instruments and equipment, drawings, plans, and models created for the multiple-mirror telescope assembly. There are photographs of other proposed sites and the summit of Mount Hopkins, as well as celebratory and commemorative activities, such as the burying of a time capsule in the foundation of the telescope site in March 1977.

Arranged: No.

Captioned: Some with subject.

Finding Aid: No.

Restrictions: No.

SA·12

Publications Department Photoprint Collection

Dates of Photographs: 1890–Present

Collection Origins

The Publications Department staff assembled the collection from OPPS images, outside donations, and SAO staff images to document SAO's colleagues, facilities, research interests, and staff. Photographers represented include D. Brocious, James C. Cornell, Jr., Charles Hanson, Steve Seron, Arlene Walsh, and OPPS staff.

Physical Description

There are 5,000 silver gelatin photoprints (some x-ray images). Other materials include cutlines, graphs, press releases, and xerographic copies.

Subjects

The photographs depict facilities, history, projects, and staff of the SAO, and the related activities of colleagues at the Harvard College Observatory (HCO) between 1890 and the present, with the largest concentration of photographs after 1957. There are also photographs of artificial satellites and celestial objects such as comets, galaxies, and meteors studied by the staff of these institutions.

Celestial objects illustrated include comets such as Arend-Rigaux, Halley's Comet, and Wilson-Harrington; constellations such as Centaurus and Pegasus; cosmic dust; galaxies; gamma rays; lunar soil; meteorites; meteor trails; nebulae such as Crab and Ring Nebulae; planets; quasars including multiple quasars and twin quasars; star fields; and the Sun including solar corona, solar disk, solar prominence, and solar x-rays. There are also photographs of aircraft, balloon flights, satellites, and spacecraft, including *Apollo 8, 9,* and *15*, *Cosmos 197* re-entry, *Delta* (1961), *Explorer 1*, *Gemini 6* and *7*, OAO rocket launch, orbiting solar satellite, *Project Echo 1*, *Ranger 7*, rocket launches, a *Saturn* rocket, *Sputnik*, *Starlette* satellite, *Surveyor* (1966), and *Uhuru A2* satellite.

Equipment illustrated includes astrolabes, multiple-mirror telescopes, radio astronomy receivers, reflector-telescopes, and telescopes on Mount Hopkins and on Mount Palomar. Facilities photographed include the George R. Agassiz Station in Fort Davis, Texas; Baker-Nunn tracking stations; the Harvard College Observatory including the Harvard Radio Meteor Project; Haystack Observatory; Mount Graham; Mount Hopkins; Mount Palomar; the Multiple Mirror Telescope; NASA installations; SAO buildings; the University of Arizona Lunar and Planetary Laboratory; and the Wise Observatory in Israel. Locations of Baker-Nunn camera stations documented include Villa Dolores, Argentina; Australia; Brazil; Cold Lake, Canada; Curaçao; Ethiopia; Greece; India; Iran; Israel; Japan; Peru; South Africa; Spain; and Florida, Hawaii, and New Mexico in the United States. Other SAO meteor research installations in Illinois and Virginia are documented. Nine photographs from this collection are reproduced in this volume's illustrations.

Arranged: In two series by subject. 1) Celestial objects or historical equipment, facilities, and figures alphabetically by subject. 2) Staff members, alphabetically by last name.

Captioned: With subject, including names.

Finding Aid: No.

Restrictions: No.

SA·13

SAO Photographic Laboratory Collection

Dates of Photographs: 1963–Present

Collection Origins

SAO staff photographers Charles Hanson, who worked at SAO between 1963 and 1985, and Steve Seron, who has worked at SAO from 1986 to the present, created the collection at the request of other SAO staff members. The collection documents SAO events and new electronic equipment on site; records staff appearances for passports and Smithsonian Institution identification badges; and illustrates funding and research proposals and professional presentations and publications.

Physical Description

There are 81,400 photographs including (a few) color dye coupler photoprints and slides and silver gelatin photonegatives and photoprints (some copies). About half of the photonegatives are on Ortho-type film; Kodak 4125 and Kodak 4127 films are also used for internegatives.

Subjects

The photographs depict SAO's equipment, facilities, public relations events, research activities, and staff including awards, activities, identification badge and passport portraits from 1963 to the present. There are also photographic reproductions of book pages and graphs.

Arranged: In three series by format, then chronologically by photographer's assigned job number. 1) 4″ × 5″ photonegatives. 2) 35mm photonegatives and 35mm contact photoprints. 3) Loose photoprints.

Captioned: With assigned job number.

Finding Aid: Photographic log books with assigned job number, date, subject description, and notes including film type, SAO internal account number, request date, date the work was done, number and type of images, and requestor's name.

Restrictions: No.

SA·14

SAO Publications Department Slide Collection

Dates of Photographs: 1950s–1980s

Collection Origins

SAO Publications Department Manager James C. Cornell, Jr., and his predecessors assembled the collection to document the facilities, research, and staff of SAO and other institutions engaged in astronomy, astrophysics, and space exploration, including the Harvard College Observatory (HCO) and the University of Arizona. For a biography of Cornell see the *Collection Origins* field of *SA·9*. Photographers represented include James C. Cornell, Jr., Charles Hanson, Dane A. Penland, Mark Saffir, Steve Seron, and A. Walsh, as well as other SAO and OPPS staff. Studios represented include the European Southern Observatory, the National Aeronautics and Space Administration (NASA), and Fred L. Whipple Observatory; and commercial vendors of studio photographs such as Tersch.

Physical Description

There are 1,800 color dye coupler slides (some digitized or x-ray images).

Subjects

The photographs document colleagues, educational activities, facilities, research, and staff of SAO between the 1950s and the 1980s. The photographs also document celestial objects including asteroids, comets, fireballs, meteorites, planets, and stars; and observatories and their instruments worldwide including Baker-Nunn cameras, satellites, satellite-tracking stations, and telescope construction.

The buildings and observatories photographed include Mount Hopkins Observatory in Arizona; SAO in Cambridge, Massachusetts; and observatories worldwide including Ethiopia, Peru, and South Africa. The collection also contains the original images of two slide sets published by the Smithsonian Institution: 1) "The Electronic Sky: Digital Images of the Cosmos." 43 images and 1 booklet, 1985. 2) "Visions of Einstein." 56 slides. The slide sets are available for purchase through OPPS at the Smithsonian Institution, NMAH, CB054, Washington, D.C. 20560, or call (202) 357-1933.

Astronomical objects and phenomena documented include asteroids—some in time exposures; comets; fireballs, including the Springfield, Massachusetts, fireball of April 1966; galaxy clusters; lunar eclipses; meteorites such as the Antarctic and Lost City meteorites; nebulae such as Orion; planets; satellites including the *Echo* satellite silhouetted over the Minute Man statue near Boston, Massachusetts; the solar corona in x-rays; and spacecraft including the *Apollo* afterburn and the Soviet lunar lander. Individuals portrayed include astronauts such as Frank Borman, James A. Lovell, and Edward White, Jr.; famous astronomers; and past and present SAO staff.

Arranged: By subject.

Captioned: With subject.

Finding Aid: No.

Restrictions: No.

SA·15

SAO Published Slide Collections

Dates of Photographs: 1978–1981

Collection Origins

SAO Publications Department Manager James C. Cornell, Jr., assembled the collection for use by educators, the general public, journalists, and scholars. For a biography of Cornell see the *Collection Origins* field of *SA·9*.

The collection consists of two duplicate Smithsonian Institution slide sets available for sale through OPPS at the Smithsonian Institution, NMAH, CB054, Washington, D.C. 20560, or call (202) 357-1933: 1) "The Electronic Sky: Digital Images of the Cosmos." 43 images and 1 booklet. 1985. 2) "Visions of Einstein." 56 slides.

Images in "The Electronic Sky" were taken with charge-coupled devices (CCDs). For information on this procedure see the *Collection Origins* field of *SA·4*. The slides in "Visions of Einstein" were selected from more than 5,000 images of celestial x-ray sources made by the satellite *HEAO 1* (Einstein Observatory and NASA). This Earth-orbiting observatory carried the first telescope capable of producing focused images of cosmic sources of x-rays. Researchers interested in the NASA photographs not in the slide sets should contact the Audio-Visual Branch, Public Information Division, NASA, 400 Maryland Ave., SW, Room 6035, Washington, D.C. 20546, or call (202) 453-8375.

Physical Description

There are 100 duplicate color dye coupler slides. Most are either x-ray images or color enhanced and/or digitally stored information later converted into photographic images.

Subjects

"The Electronic Sky" slide set includes photographic reproductions of color-enhanced images of celestial objects such as the elliptical galaxy M87 and spiral galaxies M51, NGC 3184, NGC 3992, and NGC 7479. The "Visions of Einstein" slide set includes x-ray images of celestial objects taken by the *Einstein* satellite and then rephotographed with standard photographic emulsions. Both sets include images obtained (and copyrighted) by other institutions, including NASA photographs of the *Einstein* satellite's construction and instrumentation.

Arranged: In two slide sets.

Captioned: With the subject and occasionally the date.

Finding Aid: Guides to the slide sets include subject descriptions.

Restrictions: No.

SA

Harvard College Observatory

Harvard College Observatory—Plate Stacks
Harvard-Smithsonian Center for Astrophysics
60 Garden Street
Cambridge, Massachusetts 02138
Martha Hazen, Curator
(617) 495-3362
Hours: Monday–Friday, 9 a.m.–5 p.m.

Scope of the Collection

There is one photographic collection with approximately 400,000 images. Note: The Harvard College Observatory (HCO) is not part of the Smithsonian Institution. However, HCO and the Smithsonian Astrophysical Observatory (SAO) comprise the Harvard-Smithsonian Center for Astrophysics (CfA). The Harvard Plate Collection is included in the *Guide* as a courtesy to researchers.

Focus of the Collection

The photographs document the sky over both the Northern and Southern hemispheres for more than a century, serving as a resource to verify astronomical change and variation over time. The photographs also document the early equipment, events, observations, and staff of the HCO's stations in Massachusetts, Peru (Arequipa), and South Africa.

Photographic Processes and Formats Represented

There are collodion wet plate lantern slides and photonegatives; color dye coupler slides; daguerreotypes; silver gelatin dry plate lantern slides and photonegatives; and silver gelatin photonegatives and slides. Some photographs are on blue-sensitive emulsions.

Other Materials Represented

This facility also has a card catalog.

Access and Usage Policies

The collections are open by appointment to qualified astronomers. Researchers should write to the facility and describe their topic, the type of material that interests them, and their research aim. Certain materials may be restricted due to copyright status or preservation conditions. Restrictions may apply on making copies of certain marked photographs in these collections. There is no charge for the creation of single copies of photographs to be used in news, feature, or educational contexts. In general, allow four weeks for routine processing. All orders are shipped via U.S. mail, unless the requestor is willing to pay for C.O.D. express shipments to their billing address. The HCO/SAO shared Photography Laboratory requests the return of photographic materials after use, if possible, and appreciates receiving copies of any publications resulting from this use.

Publication Policies

Researchers must obtain permission from the HCO to reproduce a photograph and may also have to obtain permission from the copyright holder, which is not necessarily the HCO. The preferred credit line is "Courtesy of the Center for Astrophysics, Harvard College Observatory." The photographer's name, if known, should be added to the credit line.

SA·16

Harvard Plate Collection

Dates of Photographs: 1840s–Present

Collection Origins

The Harvard College Observatory (HCO) was established in 1839 by William Cranch Bond (1789–1859) under the direction of Harvard President Josiah Quincy. Bond, an Astronomical Observer to the College, was involved in assembling the Observatory's initial equipment and facilities. During 1848 William Bond and his son George Phillips Bond (1825–1865) attempted producing daguerreotypes and Talbotypes of the Sun. In late 1849, with the assistance of Boston daguerreotypist J.A. Whipple, the Bonds made the first daguerreotype of the moon. In 1850 they made the first daguerreotype of a star (Vega) and in 1851 a daguerreotype of Jupiter. In 1857 the Bonds began experimenting with collodion wet plates, and obtained images of double stars, an occultation of Spica by the Moon, and planets.

George Phillips Bond, director of the HCO from 1859 to 1865, is credited with showing the relation between the size of a star's photographic image and its magnitude. Bond also suggested the use of color indexes to note the difference between photographic and visual magnitudes. During the 1860s and 1870s, experiments with collodion wet plates continued at HCO. Plates from this era include additional exposures of the moon, planets, and stars, and a long series of almost daily exposures of the Sun with a lens of 35-foot focal length.

In 1883, Edward C. Pickering (1846–1919), director of HCO from 1877 to 1919, and his brother, William H. Pickering (1858–1938), experimented with dry plates to determine the colors and magnitudes of brighter stars and to prepare a photographic map of the sky. This effort marked the beginning of the Harvard College Observatory Plate Collection, which subsequently undertook consistent photography of star spectra using objective prisms. The Pickerings' research was published in the following: Annie Jump Cannon and Edward C. Pickering. "The Henry Draper Catalog." *Annals of the Astronomical Observatory of Harvard College* vols. 91–99. Cambridge, Massachusetts: The Observatory, 1918–1924.

The Harvard Plate Collection includes images which date from 1849 to the present, with the majority acquired after 1883. Photographs from the collection have appeared in many publications, including the following: 1) Betty Zaban Jones and Lyle Gifford Boyd. *The Harvard College Observatory: The First Four Directorships, 1839–1919*. Cambridge: The Belknap Press of Harvard University Press, 1971. 2) Rick Gore. "The Once and Future Universe." *National Geographic* 163(6) (June 1983): 704–749. In addition, images from the collection have appeared in many popular books, professional astronomical journals, and texts on astronomy.

Physical Description

There are 400,000 photographs including collodion wet plate lantern slides and photonegatives, color dye coupler slides, daguerreotypes, silver gelatin dry plate lantern slides, and silver gelatin photonegatives, photoprints, and slides. Some photographs are on blue-sensitive emulsions.

Subjects

These photographs document and verify astronomical change and variation in the Northern and Southern hemispheres. The photographs also illustrate the early equipment, events, and staff of the Harvard College Observatory's stations in Massachusetts, Peru (Arequipa), and South Africa.

Most of the photographs are direct images on blue-sensitive emulsions of wide-angle fields covering the entire sky at focal scales of 40 to 1200 arcsec/mm. The deepest plates reach a blue magnitude of 17, and many plates have a limit of 15th magnitude. The collection also contains some yellow and red plates, which generally do not reach as deep as the blue plates. A small portion of the collection consists of objective-prism spectrum plates.

Photographs of celestial phenomena include the bright quasar 3C-273 (the earliest image); Eta Carinae during its outburst at the end of the 19th century (a spectrum of the eruptive variable); a Gamma Ray Burster (the optical counterpart); Halley's Comet during its 1910 appearance; and Saturn's ninth satellite (the discovery plate). A daguerreotype of the moon from this collection is reproduced in this volume's illustrations.

Arranged: In five series by type or subject. 1) Glass plate photonegatives of the sky. 2) Collodion wet plates and daguerreotypes, mainly of historical interest. 3) 200 historical images of equipment, people, and places. 4) Lantern slides. 5) Teaching slides. Series 1 is arranged into 20 subseries by telescope, then chronologically by plate number. The wide-angle plates are arranged by sky region, then chronologically.

Captioned: With date, exposure time, plate number, and sky position.

Finding Aid: Item-level card catalog lists the date, exposure time, plate number, and sky position.

Restrictions: The teaching slide collection is available only to members of the Harvard-Smithsonian Center for Astrophysics. The remainder of the collection is available by appointment to *bona fide* astronomers.

ST

SMITHSONIAN TROPICAL RESEARCH INSTITUTE

Ira J. Rubinoff, Director

The Smithsonian Tropical Research Institute (STRI) is an international center for the advancement of tropical biological research in animal and plant behavior, ecology, and evolution. Located in Panama, STRI is committed to the conservation of tropical ecosystems and environmental education, offering research opportunities to international scientists and students.

Since 1923 the National Research Council has sponsored a tropical field station on Barro Colorado Island (BCI) in the Panama Canal Zone. This field station became a separate government agency—the Canal Zone Biological Area—in 1940 and a bureau of the Smithsonian Institution in 1946. The bureau was renamed the Smithsonian Tropical Research Institute in 1966. In 1979 BCI was declared a Nature Monument under the 1940 Western Hemisphere Convention on Nature Protection and Wildlife Preservation. STRI is the custodian of this Nature Monument on behalf of the United States, Panama, and the other nations of the Americas.

The bureau's photographic holdings are largely documentary, illustrating the natural world of the tropics and the scientists who study it. The holdings include photographs of STRI environs, facilities, fieldwork, projects, special events, specimens, staff, and visitors. The 85,700 photographs in STRI's 16 collections form only part of the bureau's research resources. STRI provides graduate-level ecology courses at the University of Panama, a library of tropical ecology literature, nature trails, a publications program, and a variety of information bases documenting tropical ecology.

ST

Scientific Staff Collections

Scientific Staff Collections
Smithsonian Tropical Research Institute
Smithsonian Institution
P.O. Box 2072, Balboa, Republic of Panama
Elena Lombardo, Program Specialist
011-507-62-3227 (International Code-Country Code-Number)
Hours: Monday–Friday 10 a.m.–4 p.m.

Scope of the Collections

There are 13 photographic collections with approximately 68,700 images.

Focus of the Collections

These photographic collections document research by STRI staff scientists in Panama. Studies documented deal with the behavior, ecology, evolution, and habitats of tropical amphibians, birds, coral colonies, crustaceans, fish, insects, mammals, mollusks, and reptiles; conservation of the tropical forests; growth patterns of tropical trees; and intertidal ecosystems. There are also contemporary and historical images of STRI's activities such as animal sightings, and facilities, staff, and visitors. Panamanian landscapes and waterscapes are also illustrated.

Photographic Processes and Formats Represented

There are color dye coupler photoprints and slides; dye diffusion transfer photoprints (Polaroid); and silver gelatin photonegatives, photoprints, and slides.

Other Materials Represented

The department's collections also contain audiotapes, budgets, correspondence, data, log books, motion-picture film footage, notes, reports, timelines, and videotapes.

Access and Usage Policies

Most of these collections are open to scholarly researchers by appointment; some, however, are considered personal research collections and may not be viewed. Interested researchers should write to STRI and describe their research topic, the type of material they would like to view, and their research aim.

Publication Policies

Researchers must obtain permission from the Smithsonian Institution to reproduce a photograph and may also have to obtain permission from the copyright holder, which is not necessarily the Smithsonian Institution. The preferred credit line is "Courtesy of the Smithsonian Tropical Research Institute, Smithsonian Institution." The name of the specific collection and photographer may also be required.

ST·1

Biological Field Work Photograph Collection *A.K.A.* John H. Christy Photograph Collection

Dates of Photographs: 1970–Present

Collection Origins

STRI biologist John H. Christy created the collection to document his research interests, including his early zoological field work in Costa Rica, Panama, and in Florida and South Carolina in the United States. Christy received a Ph.D. in 1980 from Cornell University. He has conducted fieldwork on the behavior and ecology of crabs on the Pacific Coast of Panama.

Physical Description

There are 800 color dye coupler slides.

Subjects

The photographs document John Christy's biological fieldwork in the Americas between 1970 and the present, with particular emphasis on the behavior and ecology of marine invertebrates, especially crabs. Christy's field trips and studies documented include howler monkeys in a lowland deciduous dry forest in northwest Costa Rica (1970); amphibians, habitats, insects, and mammals in Costa Rica (1972); crabs, particularly fiddler crabs, in many locales including Charlotte Harbor, Florida (1973–1976); crab larvae and plankton in a salt marsh estuary (1978–1980); crabs in a mangrove habitat on the Pacific coast of Panama (1983–present); and crab habitats in South Carolina (1972–1986). There are also images of mangrove swamps and islands. Tropical organisms shown include amphibians, anteaters, birds, fiddler crabs, howler monkeys, insects, raccoons, and tortoises.

Arranged: In five series by field trip.

Captioned: Some with date.

Finding Aid: No.

Restrictions: No.

ST·2

Caribbean Bryozoans SEM Research Collection *A.K.A.* Jeremy B.C. Jackson SEM Collection

Dates of Photographs: 1983–1986

Collection Origins

STRI staff biologist Jeremy B.C. Jackson (1942–) created the collection as part of his primary research material for a 1983 to 1986 study of Caribbean bryozoan taxonomy. Jackson, who received a Ph.D. in geology from Yale University in 1971, was an Assistant Professor (1971–1977), Associate Professor of marine ecology (1977–1981), and Professor of ecology at Johns Hopkins University. He was a member of the Biological Oceanographic Panel of the National Science Foundation (1975–1976) and a Visiting Professor at both the University of the West Indies (1976–1982) and at Woods Hole Oceanographic Institute (1979–1981). Jackson is a Research Associate at the NMNH (1976–) and at the American Museum of Natural History (1981–).

Jackson researches the evolution of marine clonal invertebrates, the adaptive significance of form in sessile (fixed) organisms, and competitive theory. Portions of this collection have been published in professional journals, including the following article: Jeremy B.C. Jackson and Terence P. Hughes. "Adaptive Strategies of Coral-Reef Invertebrates." *American Scientist* 73(3) (May/June 1985): 265–274.

Physical Description

There are 1,000 photographs including 500 dye diffusion transfer photoprints and 500 silver gelatin photonegatives. Many images are scanning electron microscope (SEM) photographs.

Subjects

The photographs document Caribbean bryozoans (small aquatic moss-like animals) and bryozoan taxonomy, in particular their distribution and morphology. Bryozoans are shown individually and in branching colonies.

Arranged: By species.

Captioned: Most with date and taxonomic position.

Finding Aid: No.

Restrictions: Restricted private research collection.

ST·3

Cephalopod Photograph Collection *A.K.A.* Arcadio F. Rodaniche Photograph Collection

Dates of Photographs: 1972–1986

Collection Origins

STRI biologist and scientific illustrator Arcadio F. Rodaniche created the private research collection to document his research on the behavior and ecology of cephalopods. Rodaniche used many of the images as studies for his illustrations or for his publications on cephalopods including the following: 1) Martin Moynihan and Arcadio F. Rodaniche. "Behavior and Natural History of the Caribbean Reef Squid, Sepioteuthis sepioidea: With Consideration of Social, Signal, and Defensive Patterns for Difficult and Dangerous Environments." *Advances in Ethology* 25. Berlin: Verlag Paul Parey, 1982. 2) Martin Moynihan and Arcadio Rodaniche. "Communication, Crypsis, and Mimicry Among Cephalopods." *How Animals Communicate,* edited by Thomas A. Sebeok. Bloomington: Indiana University Press, 1977, 293–302. 3) Arcadio F. Rodaniche. "Iteroparity in the Lesser Pacific Striped Octopus, Octopus Chierchiae." *Bulletin of Marine Science* (Jatta, 1889) 35(1) (July 1984): 99–104. 4) Arcadio F. Rodaniche. *Courtship, Copulation and Spawning of the Australian Giant Cuttlefish, Sepia Spama.* (Gray 1849) (Cephalopoda: Sepiidae). 5) Arcadio F. Rodaniche. *Notes on the Behavior of the Larger Pacific Striped Octopus: Octopus Spilotus.* Voss, 1985.

Physical Description

There are 2,300 photographs including color dye coupler slides and silver gelatin photonegatives and photoprints. Other materials include super-8mm motion-picture film footage.

Subjects

The photographs document the behavior, ecology, and habitats of marine mollusks of the class Cephalopoda including cuttlefish, octopus, and squid. Other animals illustrated include birds, fish, and lizards and their land and sea habitats in Australia, Micronesia, Panama's San Blas Islands, and the Philippines.

Arranged: No.

Captioned: Most with date, subject or species, and occasionally location.

Finding Aid: No.

Restrictions: Restricted private research collection.

ST·4

Coral Reef Research Collection *A.K.A.* Jeremy Jackson Research Collection

Dates of Photographs: 1983–1986

Collection Origins

STRI biologist Jeremy B.C. Jackson created the collection to further his research on the evolution of marine clonal invertebrates, the adaptive significance of form in sessile (fixed) organisms, and competitive theory. The photographs in this collection, taken by George Bruno, are part of Jackson's primary research material on cryptic reef ecology. For a biography of Jackson see the *Collection Origins* field of *ST*·2.

Portions of this collection have been published in professional journals, including the following: 1) Jeremy B.C. Jackson and Terence P. Hughes. "Adaptive Strategies of Coral-Reef Invertebrates." *American Scientist* 73(3) (May/June 1985): 265–274. 2)

Jeremy B.C. Jackson and Karl W. Kaufmann. "*Diadema antillarum* Was Not a Keystone Predator in Cryptic Reef Environments." *Science* 235 (February 6, 1987): 687–689.

Physical Description

There are 17,500 photographs including color dye coupler photonegatives and slides; dye diffusion transfer photoprints (Polaroids and SEMs) and contact sheets; and silver gelatin photonegatives. Other materials include a log book.

Subjects

Most of the photographs document tropical coral and bryozoans (aquatic moss-like animals) including bryozoan colonies of the species Trematooecia in Jamaica; bryozoans releasing larvae; coral plates; coral plate tops (for a study of growth and mortality of two species of coral); cryptofauna of Los Roques, Venezuela, including a census of cryptofauna cover; and fish feeding on exposed rubble.

Arranged: In five series by subject. 1) Coral plates. 2) Larvae release photographs. 3) Tops of coral plates. 4) Bryozoan colonies of the species Trematooecia in Jamaica. 5) Cryptofauna of Los Roques Islands in Venezuela.

Captioned: Most with the date, site, and occasionally taxonomic order.

Finding Aid: 1) Log for series 5 with amount of regeneration, colony size, comments for each image, date, rubble ceiling, site, and species. 2) Notes on the depth and size of the coral punch taken for study. 3) Census of sites.

Restrictions: Restricted private research collection.

ST·5

Crustacea and Coral Reef Photograph Collection *A.K.A.* Nancy Knowlton Photograph Collection

Dates of Photographs: 1974–Present

Collection Origins

STRI biologist Nancy Knowlton (1949–) created the collection for use in lectures, research, and teaching. Knowlton, who received a Ph.D. from the University of California at Berkeley in 1978, has been a fellow at the University of Liverpool and Cambridge University (1978–1979) and an assistant and associate professor of biology at Yale University (1979–1984). Her research specialities include anemone commensals, coral population biology, the evolution of aggression, and sexual selection. Some of the photographs have been published in the following articles: 1) Nancy Knowlton and Brian D. Keller. "Two More Sibling Species of Alpheid Shrimps Associated with the Caribbean Sea Anemones *Bartholomea Annulata* and *Heteractis Lucida.*" *Bulletin of Marine Science* 37(3) (November 1985): 893–904. 2) Nancy Knowlton and Brian D. Keller. "Larvae Which Fall Far Short of Their Potential: Highly Localized Recruitment in an Alpheid Shrimp with Extended Larval Development." *Bulletin of Marine Science* 39(2) (1986): 213–223.

Physical Description

There are 800 photographs including color dye coupler slides and silver gelatin photonegatives.

Subjects

The slides document the behavior, biology, ecology, ecosystems, and natural history of coral reef populations and symbiotic marine crustaceans such as shrimp. The photonegatives reproduce electrophoretic data. Electophoresis is the migration of charged particles within a stationary liquid under the influence of an electric field.

Arranged: By subject such as taxonomic order.

Captioned: With date, location, and subject.

Finding Aid: An index to some of the slides.

Restrictions: No.

ST·6

Evolutionary Biology and Ornithology Photograph Collection *A.K.A.* Neal G. Smith Photograph Collection

Dates of Photographs: 1958–Present

Collection Origins

STRI biologist Neal G. Smith (1937–) created this private collection as part of his ongoing research in evolutionary biology. In 1963 Smith received a Ph.D. from Cornell University, where he later served as assistant botanist (1958–1959) and teaching assistant (1959–1963). He joined STRI in 1963, and became the STRI Assistant Director of Academic Planning in 1974. Smith's fieldwork involves experimental studies in the evolution of behavioral, morphological, and physiological adaptations of birds and butterflies with emphasis on species competition, migration, parasitism, recognition, and butterfly-plant interaction. Many of these photographs have been duplicated by VIREO at the Philadelphia Academy of Sciences, where they are available. See the *Restrictions* field for information.

Physical Description

There are 16,400 photographs including color dye coupler slides and silver gelatin photonegatives and photoprints (many are contact prints). Other materials include audiotape (60 reels), super-8mm, 8mm, and 16mm motion-picture film footage, and 3/4″ British format and cassette videotape (the moving image materials include raw footage, working versions with annotations, and edited footage).

Subjects

Most of the photographs document the behavior, evolutionary biology, and physical characteristics of birds and butterflies. There are also photographs of landscapes, fieldwork sites, natural and hybrid orchids, Cape Dorset and Guatemalan Indians, and Uraniidae moths. Many photographs show neotropical birds including colonial nesting blackbirds, frigate birds, hawks in migration, petrels, terns, and vultures. Note: There are also edited videotapes and films of hawk migrations.

Places shown include Canada (Cape Dorset); Colombia; Costa Rica; Egypt; Greece; Greenland; Guatemala (Lake Atitlán); India; Israel; Mexico; Panama; Tobago; Turkey; and the United States (Acadia National Park, Bryce Canyon National Park, Grand Canyon National Park, and Yellowstone National Park). The Greenland photographs, dating from 1958, show flowers, gulls, landscapes, and polar bears. Culture groups documented include the Cape Dorset Eskimos and the Huehuetenango (Huehuetengo) Indians of Lake Atitlán, Guatemala.

Arranged: First by type of material, then by subject, lecture title, or project.

Captioned: Many with activity or subject, date, and locale; occasionally with taxonomic information.

Finding Aid: No.

Restrictions: Restricted private research collection. For copy images of birds contact Visual Resources for Ornithology (VIREO), Academy of Natural Sciences of Philadelphia, 19th and Parkway, Philadelphia, Pennsylvania 19103. Attention: Doug Wechsler. Telephone: (215) 299-1069.

ST·7

Fishes and Coral Reef Photograph Collection *A.K.A.* D. Ross Robertson Photograph Collection

Dates of Photographs: 1970–Present

Collection Origins

D. Ross Robertson (1946–) created this private research collection for his studies of the behavior, ecology, and evolution of coral reef fish and evolutionary sequential hermaphroditism in fish. Robertson, who received a Ph.D. from the University of Queensland in 1974, is an STRI staff biologist (1974–). Concurrently, Ross was a scholar of the Australian Commonwealth Science and Research Organization (1974) and a member of the Great Barrier Reef Conference of Australia.

Physical Description

There are 4,000 photographs including color dye coupler slides and silver gelatin photonegatives.

Subjects

The photographs document the behavior, ecology, and evolution of coral reef fish. Animals and plants illustrated include algae, birds, corals (hard and soft), echinoderms (sea cucumbers, sea urchins, and starfish), fish, sea lions, sponges, and giant tortoises. Island habitats documented include Aldabra of the Seychelles (Indian Ocean), Hawaii (Pacific Ocean), Heron Island (Australian Great Barrier Reef), Lizard Island (Australian Great Barrier Reef), Palau Island (Pacific Ocean), San Blas Islands in Panama (Caribbean Sea), and Tahiti (Pacific Ocean).

Arranged: By subject.

Captioned: With the date and subject.

Finding Aid: No.

Restrictions: Restricted private research collection.

ST·8

Iguana Photograph Collection *A.K.A.* Dagmar Werner Photograph Collection

Dates of Photographs: 1983–Present

Collection Origins

The collection was created by STRI biologist Dagmar Werner to document her iguana management project, which re-establishes iguana populations in Central and South American wilderness areas both to create a food source for indigenous populations and to conserve iguanas and their habitat, the tropical forest. Since leaving STRI in 1989, Werner has continued this work with the National University of Costa Rica's wildlife management program in Heredia, Costa Rica. Photographers represented include Eldridge Adams, Richard Brosnahan, Carl C. Hansen, Richard K. Hofmeister, and Willi Mueller. These images have appeared in books, journals, and Panamanian newspapers including the following: 1) *Enciclopedia de la Cultura Panamena para Niños y Jovenes*. Vol. 5, Fauna, 9–19. 2) *La Prensa,* Año 5 (Numero 1479), Panama: 1 and 5b. 3) "Green Cuisine: Iguanas Studied as Important Food Source," *Smithsonian News Service* (August 1984). Washington, D.C.: Smithsonian Institution.

Physical Description

There are 5,000 color dye coupler slides.

Subjects

The photographs show captive and wild iguanas, iguana experiments, and iguana habitats. Habitats shown are tropical landscapes in Central and South

America, including artificial iguana nests. Experiments shown include incubation of iguanas and reintroduction of iguanas to the wild.

Arranged: By subject.

Captioned: With date.

Finding Aid: No.

Restrictions: No. Contact Dagmar Werner, Universidad Nacional de Costa Rica, Apdo. 86-3000, Heredia, Costa Rica.

ST·9

Insect Field Research Photograph Collection *A.K.A.* Hendrik Wolda Photograph Collection

Dates of Photographs: 1971–Present

Collection Origins

STRI biologist Hendrik Wolda (1931–) created the collection for use in teaching and lecturing. Wolda, who received a Ph.D. from the State University of Groningen (Rijksuniversiteit Groningen) in the Netherlands in 1963, specializes in research on diapause in tropical beetles, the systematics of leafhoppers, and temporal and special variations in the abundance of tropical insect species. Wolda is the author of "Insect Seasonality: Why?" *Annual Review of Ecology and Systematics* 19 (1988): 1–18. Photographers and studios represented include Richard Brosnahan, Kerrie Dressler, Carl C. Hansen, OPPS, and the Panama Canal Commission.

Physical Description

There are 1,000 photographs including color dye coupler slides and silver gelatin slides.

Subjects

The photographs document field research sites; insects such as tropical beetles and leafhoppers; and insect habitats, particularly Panamanian landscapes.

Arranged: Chronologically by subject.

Captioned: With subject and location.

Finding Aid: No.

Restrictions: Restricted private research collection.

ST·10

Panamanian Natural History Collection *A.K.A.* Nicholas Smythe Photograph Collection

Dates of Photographs: 1964–1980

Collection Origins

STRI biologist and photographer Nicholas D. Smythe created the collection for his personal scientific research. Smythe, who received a Ph.D. from the University of Maryland in 1970, is interested in the behavior and ecology of mammals and has done extensive photographic work in Panama. Note: This descriptive information is courtesy of Smythe. The collection was not available for viewing. A series of photographs from this collection was published in the following: 1) Nicholas D. Smythe. "Ecology and Behavior of the Agouti (Dasyprocta punctata) and Related Species on Barro Colorado Island, Panama." Ph.D. dissertation, University of Maryland, 1970. 2) Nicholas D. Smythe. *The Natural History of the Central American Agouti (Dasyprocta punctata).* Smithsonian Contributions to Zoology, no. 257. Washington, D.C.: Smithsonian Institution Press, 1978. 3) Nicholas D. Smythe. "The Paca (Cuniculus paca) as a Domestic Source of Protein for the Neotropical, Humid Low Lands." *Applied Animal Behavior Science* 17 (1987): 156–170.

Physical Description

There are 10,000 color dye coupler slides (Ektachrome and Kodachrome).

Subjects

The photographs document South American peoples such as the Chocho Indians and the natural history of Argentina, Ecuador, Panama, and Venezuela between 1964 and 1980. There are also photographs of South American fruits, cryptic insects, and mammals, as well as Panamanian animal habitats and landscapes.

Arranged: By subject, some in taxonomic order.

Captioned: Some with date, genus, and species.

Finding Aid: No.

Restrictions: Restricted private research collection.

ST·11

Panamanian Reforestation Slide Collection *A.K.A.* Gilberto Ocaña Slide Collection

Dates of Photographs: 1981–Present

Collection Origins

The Conservation Resource Manager of Barro Colorado Nature Monument (BCNM), Gilberto Ocaña, created the photographs for use in teaching. Ocaña, who received a Ph.D. from the University of California at Riverside in 1967, is a specialist in the development of conservation areas and phytopathology (the study of plant diseases). Ocaña has taken photographs of his STRI field experiments since 1984 for public lectures at meetings and seminars of IDIAP (Instituto de Investigaciones Agropecuarias de Panama), RENARE (a Panamanian national directorate of renewable resources), and the University of Panama. Ocaña brought tropical trees and plants to Panama to renew areas destroyed by slash-and-burn agriculture. He has also introduced experimental agricultural techniques including alley farming, raising penned goats, growing imported root crops and leguminous plants, and tree cropping.

Physical Description

There are 400 color dye coupler slides.

Subjects

The photographs illustrate the destruction of tropical forests by man and techniques developed to reverse or retard future damage. The images document deforestation due to slash-and-burn agriculture on Panamanian tropical forest areas since 1979, including the development of desert-like areas, erosion, and the loss of soil fertility since 1984. Experimental techniques to reverse ecological damage illustrated include new farming methods and the raising of imported animals, crops, plants, seeds, and trees. Non-native plant species documented include acacias, evergreens, grasses, leguminous plants imported from Belize and other tropical areas, and tropical trees brought to Panama as seeds from New Guinea and North Australia. Experimental procedures illustrated include alley farming and tree cropping; planting leguminous vines, shrubs, and trees in over-farmed soil to enhance fertility; and raising caged goats for their milk. There are also photographic reproductions of charts and graphs.

Arranged: By subject.

Captioned: With date and subject.

Finding Aid: No.

Restrictions: No.

ST·12

Tree Architecture Photograph Collection *A.K.A.* Egbert Giles Leigh, Jr., Photograph Collection

Dates of Photographs: 1975–1985

Collection Origins

STRI biologist Egbert Giles Leigh, Jr., assembled the collection to illustrate growth patterns of tropical trees. Leigh, who received a Ph.D. from Yale University in 1966, has been an instructor of biology at Stanford University (1966); assistant professor at Princeton University (1966–1972); and a STRI biologist since 1969. Leigh's research specialities include communication ecology and the mathematical theory of evolution. The photographs have appeared in the following publications: 1) Egbert G. Leigh, Jr. "Why are Elfin Forests Stunted?" *Federation Museums Journal* 6 (Part 1) (1981). 2) Egbert G. Leigh, Jr., A. Stanley Rand, and Donald M. Windsor. *The Ecology of a Tropical Forest: Seasonal Rhythms and Long Term Changes*. Washington, D.C.: Smithsonian Institution Press, 1982.

Physical Description

There are 80 silver gelatin photoprints.

Subjects

The photographs reproduce drawings of tropical trees, trophic organization or groupings of trees and their structural characteristics, and tropical rain forests primarily on Barro Colorado Island, Costa Rica, Madagascar, and Malaysia. There are also a few photographic reproductions of illustrations of rocky intertidal scenes at Tatoosh near the Olympic Peninsula in Washington, as well as several photographs of living trees and tree groupings. Illustrators whose work is reproduced in this collection are George Angher, Daniel Glanz, Judith Gradwohl, Marshall Hasbrouck, Lynn Siri Kimsey, and Alex Murawski.

Arranged: No.

Captioned: No.

Finding Aid: No.

Restrictions: No.

ST·13

Tropical Amphibians and Reptiles Photograph Collection *A.K.A.* A. Stanley Rand Photograph Collection

Dates of Photographs: 1955–Present

Collection Origins

A. Stanley Rand (1932–) created this personal research collection to document the behavior and ecology of tropical amphibians and reptiles, particularly frog and lizard social behavior and communications as an adaptation to resource partitioning. Rand, who received a Ph.D. from Harvard University in 1961, served as Assistant Curator of mammals at the Field Museum of Natural History in Chicago (1957); Research Assistant in herpetology at the Museum of Comparative Zoology at Cambridge University (1961–1962); Zoologist for the Secretary of Agriculture in São Paulo, Brazil (1962–1964); and Biologist and Herpetologist at STRI (1964–). Rand is also an Adjunct Associate Professor at the University of Panama.

Physical Description

There are 9,400 photographs including color dye coupler photoprints and slides and silver gelatin photonegatives, photoprints, and slides. Other materials include super-8mm motion-picture film footage.

Subjects

The photographs document tropical amphibians and reptiles and their habitats including general landscape and waterscape settings. Many of the slides were taken on field trips in Panama and the West Indies between 1955 and the present. Most images are of animals including frogs, lizards, and snakes; landscapes including animal habitats and landslides; and waterscapes including lakes, oceans, and shorelines. There are numerous animal-behavior photographs of iguana nesting and anolis display.

Arranged: By taxonomic category and geographic location.

Captioned: With date and location.

Finding Aid: No.

Restrictions: Private research collection. Researchers must write for an appointment. Some materials are copyrighted.

ST

Office of Facilities Management

Facilities Management, Barro Colorado Island
Smithsonian Tropical Research Institute
Smithsonian Institution
P.O. Box 2072, Balboa, Republic of Panama
Barro Colorado Island Scientific Coordinator
011-507-52-1022 (International Code-Country Code-Number)
Hours: By appointment.

Scope of the Collection

There is one photographic collection with approximately 400 images.

Focus of the Collection

The collection documents the facilities, flora and fauna, natural history, and staff of Barro Colorado Island (BCI), Barro Colorado Nature Monument (BCNM), and the Panama Canal between 1926 and the present. There are several aerial views of these areas.

Photographic Processes and Formats Represented

There are color dye coupler photoprints and slides and silver gelatin photoprints.

Other Materials Represented

The collection also contains handwritten notes.

Access and Usage Policies

The collection is housed on BCI, where it is open to scholarly researchers by appointment. Researchers should write to STRI and describe their research topic, the type of material that interests them, and their research aim.

Publication Policies

Researchers must obtain permission from the Smithsonian Institution to reproduce a photograph and may also have to obtain permission from the copyright holder, which is not necessarily the Smithsonian Institution. The preferred credit line is "Courtesy of the Smithsonian Tropical Research Institute, Smithsonian Institution."

ST·14

Barro Colorado Nature Monument Photograph Collection

Dates of Photographs: 1927–1983

Collection Origins

STRI staff members working on Barro Colorado Island (BCI) assembled the collection to document their life on BCI and BCI natural history for exhibits and publications. Some images were displayed in the BCI lounge and dining hall. The collection consists of several series which STRI staff created or assembled independently: STRI biologist Robert Silberglied took aerial photographs of BCI in 1979; Stanley Rand and Leo J. Fleishman created a notebook, dated January 1984, of color photographs of snakes and lizards on the island, titled "Common Snakes of BCI & BCNM"; and STRI biologist Brian Bock assembled aerial views of the Panama Canal, BCI, BCNM, and STRI facilities.

Photographers represented include Brian Bock, Frank Chapman, Leo J. Fleishman, J.G. Fuller, Charles O'Handley, Katharine Milton, A. Stanley Rand, Michael Robinson, Robert Silberglied, Nicholas D. Smythe, and Richard W. Thorington. Studios represented include the Defense Mapping Agency, the National Air and Space Museum, and the U.S. Navy Archives. Kodak Tropical Research Laboratory, formerly on BCI, printed many of these photographs.

Physical Description

There are 400 photographs including color dye coupler photoprints and slides and silver gelatin photoprints. Other materials include handwritten notes.

Subjects

The photographs document the Panama Canal area and the facilities, fauna, natural history, and staff of BCI and BCNM from 1927 to 1983. Animals illustrated include agoutis, bats, coati mundis, lizards, monkeys (including black howler monkeys, red spider monkeys, and white-faced monkeys), pacas, peccaries, pumas, sloths, and snakes (including coral snakes and boa constrictors). BCI facilities shown include the boat landing, the dining hall, housing, and laboratories. People portrayed include BCI staff, such as Frank Chapman, and male and female visitors in safari-type clothing. There are also aerial views of the BCNM forests including the Advent Islands, Aqua Clara, Bohio, Las Brujas, Cat Islands, Cerro Balboa, Cerro Gigante, Chagres River, Gatun, Lion Hill, Peña Blanca, and Zora.

Arranged: In five series by creator and subject. 1) Fauna of BCI and BCNM, created by various staff members, particularly Nicholas D. Smythe. 2) Aerial photographs of BCI, created by Bob Silberglied. 3) Aerial photographs of BCNM, assembled by Brian Bock, then by assigned number. 4) Images of common snakes and lizards of BCI, created by Leo J. Fleishman, J.G. Fuller, and Stanley Rand (with notes and text), then by taxonomic order. 5) Miscellaneous photoprints of BCI staff, visitors, and facilities. Series 1, 2, and 5 are unarranged beneath the series level.

Captioned: Series 4 photoprints are extensively captioned with the snake or lizard's common name, habits, and taxonomic order.

Finding Aid: An index to Series 3 titled "Barro Colorado Nature Monument Photo Index" (compiled by Brian Bock) lists date, negative numbers, project code (image source), and subject location.

Restrictions: No.

ST

Office of Photographic Services

Office of Photographic Services
Smithsonian Tropical Research Institute
Smithsonian Institution
P.O. Box 2072, Balboa, Republic of Panama
Carl Hansen, Photographer
011-507-62-2008 (International Code-Country Code-Number)
Hours: By appointment.

Scope of the Collection

There is one photographic collection with approximately 11,600 images.

Focus of the Collection

The collection documents Panamanian architecture; Panamanian natural landscapes including parks; Panamanian fauna and flora; STRI programs including the Office of Conservation (1979–1983) and the Office of Education and Conservation (1983–present); STRI research projects; and STRI staff members. Panamanian fauna illustrated includes amphibians, arachnids, birds, fish, insects, mammals, and reptiles.

Photographic Processes and Formats Represented

There are color dye coupler slides and silver gelatin photonegatives and photoprints.

Other Materials Represented

None.

Access and Usage Policies

The collection is open to scholarly researchers by appointment. Interested researchers should write to STRI and describe their research topic, the type of material that interests them, and their research aim.

Publication Policies

Researchers must obtain permission from the Smithsonian Institution to reproduce a photograph and may also have to obtain permission from the copyright holder, which is not necessarily the Smithsonian Institution. The preferred credit line is "Courtesy of the Smithsonian Tropical Research Institute, Smithsonian Institution."

ST·15

STRI Photographic Services Collection

Dates of Photographs: 1979–Present

Collection Origins

OPPS staff photographer Carl C. Hansen and other STRI staff created the collection to document STRI conservation, educational activities, and research, especially the STRI Office of Conservation (1979–1983), later renamed the Office of Education and Conservation (1983–). Photographers represented include Richard Brosnahan, Marcos A. Guerra, Carl C. Hansen, Richard K. Hofmeister, Julio Jean, Neal G. Smith, Nicholas D. Smythe, and Jorge Z. Ventocilla. Images have been published in Panamanian newspapers, including *La Prensa* (Monday, December 16, 1985, 1c).

Physical Description

There are 11,600 photographs including color dye coupler slides and silver gelatin photonegatives and photoprints. Many are copies of original photographs.

Subjects

Most of the photographs document Central American landscapes, natural history, and STRI history. Central American images represented include Colombian parks, Costa Rican parks, and Panamanian animals, architecture, deforested landscapes, natural history, and parks. There are also landscape photographs of the Galápagos Islands, New Guinea (Nuevo Guinea), and Washington, D.C., including the National Zoological Park and the Smithsonian Institution Building (Castle). Creatures illustrated include amphibians (such as poison arrow frogs), arachnids, birds, fish, insects, mammals (including agouti and paca), and reptiles (including iguanas and sea snakes).

Photographs of STRI show conservation projects, educational activities, facilities, research projects, staff, and visitors from the 1950s to the present. STRI research projects documented include archeology, army ant studies, and an El Niño coral study. Panamanian landscapes illustrated include Barro Colorado Island, the Barro Colorado Nature Monument, the Panama Canal, Parques Nacionales del Extranjero, Parque Nacional Soberanía, and the San Blas Islands. Note: Fourteen photographs from this collection are reproduced in this volume's illustrations.

Arranged: In four series by subject, then by photographer's file number. 1) Projects. 2) People. 3) Animals or vegetation. 4) Facilities.

Captioned: With negative numbers; many also with date, location, or subject (specimen).

Finding Aid: In two parts. 1) A computer database listing the subject heading, the photographer's file number, and date. 2) A typed list of subject headings with rack numbers for locating slides in the cabinet.

Restrictions: No.

Library

Library
Smithsonian Tropical Research Institute
Smithsonian Institution
P.O Box 2072, Balboa, Republic of Panama
Tina Lesnik, Acting Librarian
011-507-62-3215 (International Code-Country Code-Number)
Hours: By appointment.

Scope of the Collection

There is one collection with approximately 4,800 images.

Focus of the Collection

The collection was created to illustrate the early history of STRI in Panama. STRI conservation and educational activities, events, research, staff members, and visitors are shown. The collection documents STRI's Ancon Office, the Barro Colorado Nature Monument, the Naos Marine Laboratory, and the Tivoli Office. Other images show animals and vegetation in Panama, Central America, South America, and other tropical regions.

Photographic Processes and Formats Represented

There are albumen photoprints, collodion wet plate lantern slides, color dye coupler photoprints and slides, and silver gelatin photonegatives (some nitrate) and photoprints.

Other Materials Represented

The office also contains budgets, a brief chronology of STRI's history, correspondence, notes, timelines, and oral history interviews on audiotape cassettes.

Access and Usage Policies

The collection is open by appointment to scholarly researchers. Interested researchers should write to STRI and describe their research topic, the type of material that interests them, and their research aim.

Publication Policies

Researchers must obtain permission from the Smithsonian Institution to reproduce a photograph and may also have to obtain permission from the copyright holder, which is not necessarily the Smithsonian Institution. The preferred credit line is "Courtesy of the Smithsonian Tropical Research Institute, Smithsonian Institution."

ST·16

STRI Library Historical Collection

Dates of Photographs: 1923–Present

Collection Origins

STRI interns, staff members, visitors, and volunteers first assembled the collection in 1923 to provide ongoing documentation of STRI conservation work, educational activities, and research. In the 1980s OPPS photographers and STRI staff created a significant portion of the collection to document staff activities. STRI staff, including Assistant Director of Academic Planning Neal G. Smith (1937–) and Director Ira Rubinoff (1938–), assembled the collection while preparing a historical introduction to STRI for incoming Smithsonian Institution Secretary Robert McCormick Adams. Copies of some of these photographs have been incorporated into a historical display in the library room of the Barro Colorado Nature Monument (BCNM).

Photographers represented include Richard Brosnahan, Carl C. Hansen, Martin H. Moynihan, Arcadio Rodaniche, Ira Rubinoff, Nicholas D. Smythe, and James Zetek. Many images were originally processed by Kodak Tropical Laboratory, which was once housed on Barro Colorado Island (BCI).

Physical Description

There are 4,800 photographs including albumen photoprints, collodion wet plate lantern slides, color dye coupler photoprints and slides, and silver gelatin photonegatives (some nitrate) and photoprints. Other materials include budgets, a brief chronology of STRI's history, correspondence, notes, timelines, and six oral history interviews on audiotape cassettes.

Subjects

The photographs illustrate animals and landscapes in the Galápagos Islands, New Guinea, and in Central and South America, with emphasis on STRI's environment, events, facilities, research projects, and staff from the 1920s to the present. There are photographs of animals such as coati mundis, crabs, octopus, and peccaries; birds such as bayono birds and blue footed boobies; and lepidoptera such as butterflies and moths. There are also images of marine and terrestrial vegetation, waterscapes such as the Miraflores Locks, and landscapes such as Cali, Colombia and Turrialba, Costa Rica. Most locations documented show either STRI Panamanian facilities or STRI research sites in or around Colombia, Costa Rica, the Galápagos Islands, or New Guinea.

STRI's early history and facilities in and around Panama City between the 1960s and the 1980s are well documented including the Ancon Administration Office and library, BCI laboratories and houses, BCNM, Galeta Island, and Naos Island marine laboratory. STRI events shown include awards ceremonies, retirement parties, seminars, and visits by SI regents. STRI staff and visitors portrayed include SI Secretary Robert McCormick Adams, former SI Assistant Secretary David A. Challinor, Frank Chapman, evolutionary biologist Martin H. Moynihan, evolutionary biologist and STRI Director Ira Rubinoff, evolutionary biologist Neal G. Smith, and behavioral biologist Nicholas D. Smythe. Also shown are Francisco (Chichi) Vitola, Dr. Wigglesworth, and James Zetek.

Arranged: In seven series by subject. 1) Vegetation. 2) Animals. 3) Portraits. 4) STRI events and group shots. 5) Barro Colorado Island. 6) STRI facilities and equipment. 7) STRI research-in-progress.

Captioned: Many with date; some with subject identification or OPPS negative number.

Finding Aid: Partial inventory to several folders of images, including subject identification for individual images.

Restrictions: No.

Creators Index

The Creators Index is a list of photographers, studios, distributors, manufacturers, researchers, scientists, and collectors who produced or assembled the images in the Smithsonian Institution photographic collections. Photographers are listed alphabetically by surname. Photographers associated with a studio may be listed under both the studio name and their personal name. Corporate creators are listed in strict alphabetical order, for example "J.E. Purdy and Company" is listed under "J" rather than under "P."

All creators' names appearing in this volume are listed in this index. Due to space requirements, not all creators' names appearing in the collections were listed in this volume. Several exceptionally large collections with more than 100 creators' names were sampled to provide a representative overview of their contents. Photographers or studios who are substantially represented either in the Smithsonian collections or in the photographic literature are listed.

Information in brackets following a name is generally a fuller form of the same name. The abbreviation *A.K.A.*, or "also known as," indicates an alternate name of an individual or organization. Cross-references, indicated by *See* indicate alternative forms of the same name, which are used for indexing instead of the name initially cited. *See also* references indicate additional authorized names under which related information may be found. Collection names or titles are also listed in this index, as they sometimes provide the only existing clues to the collection's origins.

Most of the photographers listed are Smithsonian staff scientists and their colleagues who created the images to document their ongoing research. Scientists are unlikely to appear in other photographic union lists. The spelling of the scientists' names was checked against the Smithsonian staff telephone directories and the Smithsonian Archives 1983 publication *Guide to the Smithsonian Archives*, as well as against standard biographical dictionaries, such as the following:

Clark A. Elliott. *Biographical Directory of American Science: the Seventeenth through the Nineteenth Centuries.* Westport, Connecticut: Greenwood Press, 1979.

Charles Coulston Gillispie, editor. *Dictionary of Scientific Biography.* New York: Charles Scribner's Sons, 1975.

Jaques Cattell Press, editor. *American Men and Women of Science.* New York: R.R. Bowker Company, 1982.

The final authorities on photographers' names were the following:

William L. Broecker, editor. *International Center of Photography Encyclopedia of Photography.* New York: Crown Publishers, Inc., 1984.

Turner Browne and Elaine Partnow. *Macmillan Biographical Encyclopedia of Photographic Artists and Innovators.* New York: Macmillan Publishers, 1983.

Gary Edwards. *International Guide to Nineteenth-Century Photographers and Their Works.* Boston: G.K. Hall & Co., 1988.

George Eastman House. *George Eastman House Photographers Biography File.* Rochester, New York: George Eastman House, 1986–1990.

Ross J. Kelbaugh. *Directory of Maryland Photographers 1839–1900*. Baltimore: Historic Graphics, 1988.

Carl Mautz. *Checklist of Western Photographers: A Reference Workbook*. Brownsville, California: Folk Image Publishing, 1986.

Oregon Historical Society. *Union Guide to Photograph Collections in the Pacific Northwest*. Portland: Oregon Historical Society, 1978.

George Walsh II, Michael Held II, and Colin Naylor. *Contemporary Photographers*. New York: St. Martin's Press, 1982.

Researchers unable to find a creator's name should first check the cross-references to pseudonyms or alternative spellings. Next, check the names of related studios, employers, or organizations. Individuals shown in a photograph are listed in the subject index. The collection codes indicate the location of the collection entry within the volume, for example, *NH·22* indicates that the reader should check the 22nd collection report within the section on the National Museum of Natural History (NH). Other collection codes are ZP for the National Zoological Park; SA for the Smithsonian Astrophysical Observatory; and ST for the Smithsonian Tropical Research Institute.

Forms and Processes Index

This index lists examples of physically distinct types of photographic formats (size, shape, and configuration of an image); processes (final image material, binder, base, and production process); techniques (specific manipulative procedures for obtaining visual effects in a variety of processes); and process modifiers (a group of terms which provide additional information on a process, format, or genre). The index also mentions other document types including audio-visual formats such as audiotapes, microfilm, motion-picture film, videodiscs, and videotapes when they form part of Smithsonian photographic collections.

The index is heavily cross-referenced to assist researchers with minimal knowledge of photographic processes and formats, for example, all photoprint processes and formats discovered in Smithsonian science bureaus are listed under their individual process and format names and also under "photoprints." Major headings are off-set to the left, with subheadings placed alphabetically beneath them in outline format.

Describing photographic processes is a challenge, since thousands of process variants exist. In this volume processes are described with as much of the following information as possible: 1) final image material; 2) binder; 3) image format or configuration; 4) base (Note: the base is not noted if a photoprint is on paper, or if a photonegative or phototransparency is on film.); 5) DOP or POP; 6) chemical process variant; 7) trade name; and 8) other descriptive or technical details. Descriptive elements (4) through (8) are enclosed within parentheses, for example, "silver gelatin photoprint (DOP chloride Velox gaslight paper)." Abbreviations are explained in the introduction.

On occasion, vernacular or generic descriptive process terms found throughout the photographic literature were used (such as tintypes and ambrotypes) when the terms adequately described a process or group of processes. Use of the phrases "photoprints," "photonegatives," and "phototransparencies" is based on the descriptive standards found in the following publication: Elisabeth Betz Parker and Helena Zinkham. *Descriptive Terms for Graphic Materials: Genre and Physical Characteristic Headings*. Washington, D.C.: Library of Congress, 1986. Other terminology was selected from 28 publications which served as source documents for the production on an inhouse glossary of photographic terminology. Limited quantities of this glossary are available to researchers who write the Smithsonian Institution Archives, Photographic Survey Project, A & I 2135, 900 Jefferson Drive, S.W., Washington, D.C. 20560.

Researchers unable to find a process, format, or other physical description term should check the cross-references. Variant terms including broader and narrower terms and alternative spellings should also be checked.

Subject Index

The subject index provides topical access to the Smithsonian photographic collections, which include formal and informal portraits of individuals and organizations of various culture groups, occupations, and associations; landscapes and waterscapes including animal habitats and fieldwork research sites; studies of activities including archeological digs, interplanetary space launches, and analyses of animal chromosomes; and illustrations of objects, from musical instruments to distant galaxies.

Broad terms used for index entries and cross-references were taken from the publication by Elisabeth Betz Parker and Helena Zinkham, *LC Thesaurus for Graphic Materials: Topical Terms for Subject Access.* Washington, D.C.: Library of Congress, 1987. Specific or technical language was standardized using the following sources:

Michael Allaby, editor. *The Oxford Dictionary of Natural History.* Oxford: Oxford University Press, 1985.

George Peter Murdock. *Outline of Cultural Materials.* New Haven, Connecticut: Human Relations Area Files, 1971.

George Peter Murdock. *Outline of World Cultures.* New Haven, Connecticut: Human Relations Area Files, 1975.

Sybil P. Parker. *McGraw-Hill Encyclopedia of Astronomy.* New York: McGraw-Hill, 1983.

Index entries followed by *See* refer the reader from an indexing term which is not used to a term that is used, for example, "Oceans. *See* specific ocean name." Index entries followed by *See also* refer the reader to another indexing term which is used, such as a synonym, antonym, related term, or narrower term, for example, "Scientists. *See also* Dipterists; Entomologists."

Information in parentheses after an index entry modifies or clarifies highly technical or ambiguous terms, for example, Compositae (flowering plants); "Our Mount St. Helens Story" (NMNH slide set); "Our Changing Land" (NMNH exhibit); Jekyll Island (Georgia); bantengs (oxen); metates (tools); or Datong (China). Authors' names; exhibit sponsors; geographical locations of culture groups, cities, parks, and islands; types of spacecraft or celestial phonomena; common names of taxonomic nomenclature; and other types of explanatory information appear in parentheses following the index entry term. Publication titles are in italics. Titles of exhibits and slide sets are in quotes.

Researchers unable to find a particular term should check the cross-references. Variant terms, including broader and narrower terms, technical and popular terminology, and alternative spellings, should also be checked.